Mission to Mach 2

Mission to Mach 2

A Fighter Pilot's Memoir of Supersonic Flight

ROBERT EARL HANEY
with LEE COURTNAGE

McFarland & Company, Inc., Publishers
Jefferson, North Carolina, and London

Library of Congress Cataloguing-in-Publication Data

Haney, Robert Earl, 1932–
Mission to mach 2 : a fighter pilot's memoir of supersonic flight / Robert Earl Haney, with Lee Courtnage.
p. cm.
Includes and index.

ISBN 978-0-7864-6316-9
softcover : 50# alkaline paper ♾

1. Fighter pilots — United States — Biography. 2. Test pilots — United States — Biography. 3. Supersonic fighter planes — History. 4. United States. Air Force — Officers — Biography. 5. Vietnam War, 1961–1975 — Aerial operations, American. I. Courtnage, Lee. II. Title.
UG626.2.H34A3 2011
358.40092 — dc22 2011011075
[B]

British Library cataloguing data are available

On the cover: Colonel Haney preparing for a mission over the White Sands Test Range, New Mexico, in March of 1982

Manufactured in the United States of America

McFarland & Company, Inc., Publishers
Box 611, Jefferson, North Carolina 28640
www.mcfarlandpub.com

Contents

Acknowledgments

This account of the evolution of supersonic fighters, as I, Robert Earl Haney, experienced the phenomenon over a 30-year career in the United States Air Force, began with my introduction to Lee Courtnage. At the time we met, Lee was in the process of personally compiling memories of more than one hundred veterans as a contribution to the national Veterans History Project to be housed at the Library of Congress. I was happy to be one of those Lee interviewed.

At Lee's invitation I later made a presentation to members of the Albuquerque OASIS chapter, an adult learning center that is one of the New Mexico local partners of the national Veterans History project. At that point Lee suggested that we continue to work together to expand the scope of his initial interviews to encompass in depth the era in which supersonic fighter aviation came of age. We continued to meet at intervals over the next year, sometimes at my home in Cedar Crest, New Mexico, and sometimes at his home in Albuquerque, where I met Lee's vivacious wife, Henri.

As the tapes rolled and the numbers of interviews grew, a third person joined our group. Ann Paden was then serving as a trainer in oral-history technique for OASIS volunteer interviewers for the Veterans History Project as well as for similar groups throughout the Southwestern states. At this point, Ann Paden, a professional writer and editor, joined the project. Ann has a special interest in all things military. Her father was an officer in the Air Force, and Ann accompanied the family as an "Army brat" throughout her childhood. Ann and Lee had worked together for some time and had become good friends. Seeing the sheer number of tapes that Lee and I had compiled, Ann volunteered to transcribe the tapes, which was no small task. We became a team.

The team of three used the transcripts to synthesize the interview material into a more coherent story. Lee and I undertook the task of doing the first rough draft. Ann offered to do a final edit in a form that eliminated redundancy among the many tapes and to work with me to refine for print some of the more technical aspects of my career in flight test.

I leave this page with heartfelt thanks to "The Team" who persuaded me that my experience, as both a witness to and a participant in, the evolution of the supersonic fighter could be of interest and, I hope, value to aviation enthusiasts and chroniclers of military history.

This story is not just the story of my aviation experience through this very unusual era. It is also the story of many individuals who found themselves in this explosive supersonic aviation arena and gave everything they had, their own life in many cases, to develop this supersonic capability that has been of great benefit to mankind. Many sacrifices were made by many in developing this combat strength for war, as well as shrinking the world with high-speed transportation. Many lost their lives in the war engagements that transpired during this supersonic aviation evolution. This story is about all of those who participated in this most unusual era in our history.—R.E.H.

Preface

Mission to Mach 2 is a first-person account of a very significant time in aviation history: the thirty-year period that marked the advent and coming of age of the supersonic jet fighter. I was one of the earliest and best of the high-performance jet fighter pilots. My Air Force career encompassed the era of supersonic flight and offered a window of opportunity to be on the cutting edge of jet fighters and tactical weapons development.

This story actually begins during the difficult days of the Great Depression. I was born in Champaign, Illinois, when times were difficult for most people. It was no different for the Haney family, except it did not seem so difficult to me because of the strength and love of my mother.

My childhood work ethic would serve me well. I got my first job at the age of six, selling the early edition of the Chicago Sunday newspaper on a street corner. At the age of ten, I worked after school shoveling coal to stoke neighborhood furnaces. At age 14, I talked a boss at the Illinois Central Railroad into hiring me to drive rail spikes on track being laid to accommodate the new diesel engines. Throughout my high school years, I worked summers on the railroad and every weekend at the Twin City Ice Plant. I learned hard work paid off from my football coach, Fred Major. My senior year in high school, we won the Illinois State Big 12 football championship under the leadership of Coach Major.

The Korean War began when I graduated from high school. The patriotic spirit from World War II was still well intact in our country. I felt this spirit and joined the Air Force, having no idea what was in my future. Still interested in football, I was active in this sport during my early Air Force enlistment. One day while I was recovering from a collision with a 235-pound tackle, still somewhat stunned, four F-86 supersonic fighters flew close over my head. This flyover was the beginning of my future with the evolution of the supersonic fighter. I received encouragement to enter pilot training. Two years to the day later, I checked out in the F-86, the supersonic fighter that had entered my life while practicing football. I had found my niche!

I found myself on a fast track to becoming one of the first, one of the youngest, of the elite band of high-performance jet fighter pilots who pioneered the era of the development of supersonic flight.

As the Korean War ended, the Cold War was just beginning. I was assigned to the Far East and the first fighter unit responsible to perform a worldwide nuclear weapons mission in fighter aircraft. As the Cold War expanded, so did the need for faster, more versatile and much safer fighter aircraft. Mach 1 was here, and Mach 2 and beyond was on the horizon.

As the development of the supersonic fighter accelerated, I moved into the world of flight test. I then joined the USAF Thunderbirds, demonstrating the capability and flexibility of supersonic fighter aircraft throughout the world. I served an extended three year tour with the Thunderbirds. The Thunderbird team demonstrates publicly what every fighter pilot does every day. The Thunderbirds also demonstrate to the public the aviation advancements made during the evolution of the supersonic fighter.

During my Thunderbird tour, the Vietnam War broke out. I had not lost my belief in duty and honor to country, and it was now time for me to put all I had learned in the evolution of the supersonic fighter to test. I volunteered to go to war. I flew more than two hundred combat missions, primarily over Vietnam and Laos. At the time I flew both night and day missions, at the same time continuing to do flight-test missions.

After the combat tour, I was assigned to the USAF fighter weapons school at Nellis Air Force Base (AFB) in Nevada to work with training combat pilots and testing new fighter tactics and weapons. In 1971, I was selected to attend Air War College. From there I was assigned to the Pentagon to fight from behind the "Mahogany Monster" desk. It was difficult for me not to fight from the cockpit of a fighter, as it was all I had ever known. I learned how important it was at the Pentagon to acquire appropriate funding and evaluation to advance aircraft requirements for the future.

After the Pentagon assignment, I returned to the field and assisted with the evaluation of the latest fighter weapons systems, the F-15, F-16, A-10, and required combat munitions for these new aircraft.

My final USAF assignment was in the Air Force Systems Command, where we were just breaking ground in Stealth technology and global positioning navigational systems and many other new technical avenues.

My 30-year career in the United States Air Force was one of historic proportions, spanning the earliest of the jet airplanes to go into service in Korea, the F-86 jet fighter, and coming full circle with pioneering and testing the ultimate generation of supersonic tactical weapons systems.

The range and breadth of my operational experience is extraordinary among 30-year career officers, experiencing flight test, combat and command during the supersonic fighter evolution.

During my 30 years of service to our great country, I was awarded two Legions of Merit, two Distinguished Flying Crosses, the Bronze Star, two Air Force Meritorious Service Medals, eleven Air Medals, three Air Force Commendation Medals, the Far East Air Force Flight Safety Award, the USAF "Well Done Safety Award," the Freedom Foundation Award, the Tactical Air Command "Pilot of Distinction" Award, plus other campaign and achievement awards.

During the development of the supersonic jet, much was learned about structure, engine performance and pilot capability. The physiology of the pilot, in how much he was able to withstand in terms of accelerations and speed, was a major factor to be considered. We became better in the development of the jet fighter. We began to build an airplane inside the knowledge that we had gained from the losses up to this point. As test flying continued, it become much safer because we had more technical knowledge on how to design the airplane to avoid structural, engine or pilot failure. We worked to decrease the pilot workload. This effort from the early 1960s through the 1970s became a major thrust to develop high-performance aircraft and also much safer aircraft. The F-4 Phantom was a good example of progress in fighter aviation.

By the time the development of the F-15 in the mid–1970s came, we knew how the airplane would fly and the stress loads it would take. We also had the pilots' control capabilities and control effectiveness honed down to make the mission a whole lot safer and more effective: the losses in the F-15 were minimal. In fact, an F-15 has never been lost in a combat situation. The F-15 has had accidents, and some structural failures, but these were very few in number.

The F-16 Falcon also increased fighter capability with increased technology. The "Fly by Wire" computer-controlled flight control system was a good example.

The day when a pilot was an optimist if he took his lunch for work in the fighter environment is pretty much over. Today, the pilot can expect to spend his whole career in fighter aviation with a fairly safe life, factoring in the modern-day fighter aircraft, and all the associated technology advancements of the evolution of the supersonic fighter.

Loss of pilots and airplanes was substantial over the course of jet history as the refinement of the supersonic jet continued in the 1970s and early 1980s.

This is not the story of an individual but one of a monumental evolution in aviation technology that not only greatly enhanced our defense capability but also provided increased air travel capability and set the stage for space travel. This is the story of the many people who dedicated themselves and the many that died in this evolution of the supersonic fighter. To them I want to dedicate this story so all will know of the many who sacrificed so much for our freedom during the supersonic jet aviation development.

I had the good fortune to be involved in the evolution of the jet fighter. I experienced this from the time I went into the Air Force in 1952 and retired 30 years later. My story is told in the ensuing chapters. As I said in the beginning, I had no idea what was in store for me, but what a ride it has been.—R.E.H.

Introduction
by Lee Courtnage

In May 2004 I got a phone call from Gil Martinez, retired Air Force colonel and the first Hispanic to fly supersonic in the SR-71 Blackbird during the Vietnam War era. Gil referred the name of a retired fighter pilot with a long career in the Air Force. With only the name of Col. Earl Haney and a phone number, I called to get more information in the hope that Earl would be interested in being interviewed for the Veterans History Project (VHP).

Armed with more details and Earl's willingness for an interview, we scheduled a meeting on June 25, 2004. The audio-taped interview went the full one hour and a half, the maximum time allowed by the guidelines of the VHP. The brief oral military history dictated during the interview gave a broad overview of Earl's Air Force career, but was barely adequate to his part in the development of supersonic jet aircraft. Here was an exciting story to be told. I had a nagging feeling compelling me to do more about Earl's love of the U.S. Air Force and the contributions made to his country. The two of us decided to meet further and expand the project into a full description of Earl's Air Force career with emphasis on the action of a flight test and fighter pilot flying at mach speed for 30 years.

At this point, Ann Paden, a professional writer and editor, joined the project. I met Ann while she was coordinating the local OASIS partnership with the Veterans History Project. It was through Ann's leadership and encouragement that I joined the OASIS project as an interviewer. If the opportunity to interview veterans had not come my way, I would not have met Earl, and the life story of this remarkable individual probably would not have come to pass. We were glad to have Ann join the team and accepted her insistence on working pro bono in recognition of her appreciation of thc USAF.

Earl was playing "Rhapsody in Blue" on his piano when I entered his Sandia Mountain home east of Albuquerque to begin his extended life story. We started the interviews with Earl's early life and proceeded on with the bigger task of his military career. It was this first interview and many more to follow that reinforced my belief that this was an exceptional story. All I had to do was turn on the tape recorder, and the stories would just roll out one after the other. I thought fighter pilots flew like crazy fighting the enemy, and when off-duty drank, stayed up late, and danced with the ladies, as in many of the war movies. Not Colonel Haney; he typified the more quiet, strong American. Earl did not make a lot of loud noise, take unnecessary chances, or do anything just for the sake of advancing his career. Earl believed in absolute safety for all military aircraft. Equally important was to test every new fighter jet in combat-like conditions before it went into production. If an airplane won't pass simulated combat situations, it will fail in real combat. He got into trouble believing that, but he never backed down if lives might be endangered.

In all the time we spent together as Earl dictated his memoirs, not once did he promote his oneness in the evolution of the supersonic jet. He believed he was not exceptional in his participation in the jet age era. All fighter pilots faced the same dangers, he said, put untold energy into the transition into the jet age, and displayed the same pride and loyalty for their country. Earl is a model for the best of the best of these pilots. His story is their story.

This is a story of a man who never deviated from his beliefs in hard work, honesty always, and the preciousness of human life. Colonel Haney was a test pilot during the most dangerous time of supersonic jet development. He survived three decades of flying fighters while many pilot friends died along the way. Now, later in life, many of those who also made it through their Air Force careers are getting older. Earl attended the funerals of four of his most respected flying buddies in just the past three years.

Earl and I have little in common career-wise. Earl's 30-year career in the Air Force was one of frenetic activity and the uncertainty about making it to the next day. My 35-year career in education was calm and serene by comparison. The only danger for me was driving down the street and getting hit by a drunken driver. I found myself absorbed vicariously with Earl as he told his story. It was like reading a book that you can't put down.

Earl was always relaxed and composed as he narrated each phase of his life as a fighter pilot.

Colonel Haney packed a far-reaching range of experience and achievements into his long career: Air Force cadet, flight test pilot, the Thunderbirds, fighter pilot in the Vietnam War, Fighter Weapons School, Air War College, the Pentagon, and Field Commander. Along the way, he was awarded many medals including two Legions of Merit, two Distinguished Flying Crosses, and a Bronze Star.

The many close calls Earl faced not withstanding, he always was able to get back to the ground safely. He survived by practicing what he believed in: utmost safety, diligence, and at all times striving to be at his best. Mixed in with these qualities was a little bit of luck. God bless Earl Haney and all of the USAF crews who starred in the development of the supersonic jet.

Chapter 1

Breaking the Sound Barrier

"Sabre One, ready to roll."

I had completed nearly two years of stringent military discipline and aviation training. By Air Force standards I was trained and ready to fly any aircraft. I was not yet sure. I was scheduled to fly my first unsupervised flight as a qualified Air Force pilot on a day in early October 1954.

It was still dark as I arrived at the USAF 96 Squadron operations building on Nellis Air Force Base to prepare for this monumental flight. Yes, I was a little nervous, but anxious to get in the air. I checked the weather, mission requirements, and navigational aids. It was time to go. I went to the personal equipment room to pick up my parachute, helmet, and "G" suit. The G suit is a pair of inflatable chaps that keep the blood from pooling in the lower extremities of your body and so prevent blackout under high-G forces.

As I left the personal equipment area and made my way to the flight line and my F-86 fighter jet, it was starting to get light enough to see. I found the row of aircraft where my jet was parked. As I walked by the line of aircraft, I saw the tail number of the new, gleaming F-86 "Sabre" that would be mine for this most important day. The Sabre crew chief met me with a sharp salute. I checked the aircraft Form 1 record to insure all the pre-flight preparations were in order. I made a walk-around inspection with the crew chief to insure final aircraft readiness.

Still a little nervous, as I had usually felt just before the opening kick-off of a football game, I strapped into the Sabre cockpit and prepared for engine start. Engine start for the J-47 engine was meticulous and careful, as it was very easy to overtemp the engine until you reached idle RPM (about 40 percent on the RPM indicator) and sufficient air flow through the multi-stage axial-flow engine compressor. All control checks complete; all instruments in the green. It was time to signal the crew chief to pull the chocks. As he pulled the wheel chocks and reappeared in front of the Sabre to signal Clear for Taxi, I wondered if the crew chief was as nervous as I was — probably not.

As I received the taxi instruction from the control tower, I released the brakes, and the aircraft immediately began to roll. I just had to make sure it rolled in the right direction. At 40 percent RPM the powerful engine moves the F-86 along at a rapid rate. It was not long before it was time to receive take-off clearance from the control tower.

I quickly went through the final pre-takeoff configuration — flight control trim set, speed brakes in, flaps 20 percent, don't forget to close the canopy — and I pressed the mike button and said, "Sabre One, ready to roll," followed by the tower response, "Sabre One, you are cleared for take off." As I aligned with the take-off runway to make the final power check, the sun was just beginning to peek over Sunrise Mountain southeast of Nellis.

I released the brakes, and it seemed the Sabre literally jumped into motion, like a thoroughbred running his first Kentucky Derby. The jet accelerated rapidly in the cool of the early morning. It seemed only a second and the airspeed indicator read 120 knots, time to bring the aircraft nose wheel off the runway. Just as quickly, we were off the ground. Gear up, flaps up, as we quickly accelerated to 320 knots and a 10,000-foot-per-minute rate of climb.

I could then see the sun glistening across Lake Mead just east of Nellis. It was a beautiful sight! I remember it seemed the whole world was still. The only motion was the Sabre and me as we rapidly accelerated up and away from the world below. All was well, both in the cockpit and outside, as I leveled off at 35,000 feet over the Nellis AFB Training Range, a free-air area north of Nellis where you could do about anything you and your fighter were big enough to do.

I rolled over, pulled the nose through to a 45-degree dive angle, and rolled upright as the Sabre exceeded the sound barrier at Mach 1. Not much happens as you go supersonic, other than a little roll induced as the shock wave accelerates off the swept wing, creating the "sonic boom."

I pulled the nose up sharply and climbed to over 45,000 feet. At this altitude you can see forever — the Rocky Mountains 200 miles north, the Colorado River as it snakes through Nevada, Arizona, and south. The Grand Canyon looks like a furrow in the ground from near ten miles up.

You can see the curvature of the earth, and the sky begins to darken some. It is a picture no artist could paint.

In the next 30 minutes I attempted to complete every maneuver John Frederick Howard, my T-6 instructor, taught me in my early days learning to fly. I could hear him say, if I made a mistake, "Earl, I can make you look so natural"—a reference to the fact that he was a licensed mortician as well as fighter pilot personified.

Now totally alone in the first supersonic fighter, I was well aware I would have to correct any errors myself, for there would be no one to bail me out from then on. Although my early nervousness was beginning to wear off, I was very aware the arena I was in was not forgiving of bad judgment or foolish error. I was very careful and methodical.

Time had been moving as fast as the supersonic Sabre. The fuel gauge said it was time to look for the landing runway at home plate. I really did not want this flight to end, so I slowed to 250 knots and began a long, slow let down as I turned toward Nellis. In the 1950s Las Vegas, Nevada, was a small town of about 25,000 people and few buildings of any size. From 40,000 feet and a distance of 100 miles, it looked like a postage stamp in the middle of the desert. As I slowly descended it looked as if Las Vegas was coming up at me rather than me descending toward the small city.

As I reached 1,500 feet altitude north of Las Vegas and Nellis AFB, I called the Nellis control tower and informed them I was approaching the initial point for traffic pattern entry and landing. The tower gave me the winds and clearance to enter landing traffic and to report landing break point, beginning the 360-degree tactical fighter traffic pattern. (The 360-degree tactical fighter pattern enters at 1,500 altitude on the runway heading at approximately 350 knots. At the approach end of the runway breaking left 180 degrees to a downwind leg, gear down, flaps down, descending to base leg and continuing to final approach.) I wanted to make a perfect landing. I knew there would be an instructor in mobile control on the landing end of the runway.

On base leg I reported "gear down" and began slowing to final speed, 145 knots. The F-86 was very easy to land, with excellent low-speed controllability. I did make a good landing, but I think it was more great aircraft design than brand-new pilot ability. Maybe some of both.

As I turned off the runway and began the two-mile taxi to the ramp, my nervousness had completely worn off, almost like walking off the football field after winning the final game in Champaign, Illinois, my hometown. I was now winding down from the greatest sense of accomplishment I had ever experienced.

Images of my life in aviation up to this moment passed through my mind like a fast-moving film as I taxied in and the crew chief brought his arms to a cross signaling me to bring the aircraft to a stop. It was the end of this memorable flight. I realized then that I could never have dreamed of anything like what I had just experienced. I thought, "Heaven can't top this."

It was only the beginning.

* * *

Some 50 years later, my memorable ride in the F-86 seems like only yesterday. Here I am in my home in the Sandia Mountains in Central New Mexico wondering where to begin my life story and how to represent the life of many fighter pilots who lived and died in the evolution of supersonic fighter aviation. I am now in my seventies, happy in retirement and still enjoying a good life. It is nice to see the sunrise in the morning, to watch the hummingbirds in summer, to romp with my granddaughter, and play the piano at every opportunity.

It is at this stage of life when one is more prone to reminisce about the past. How did I get to where I am? Who were the most important people to influence me through life's hard choices? How is it that I survived a career so dangerous that no private insurer would touch a fighter pilot with a ten foot pole? If I died on the job, only the government provided the beneficiary with a standard dollar amount, plus a folded flag, a gun salute, and possibly, if you did really, really well, honor you with a flyover of F-16s roaring above the grave site.

As I look outside from the patio door watching the wind blow the boughs of pine trees, it occurs to me that my 30 years in the Air Force would not have been possible without the influences made available to me during my early childhood. If it had not been for a few important people in my childhood, I probably would not have had the necessary requirements to get admitted to pilot training and go on to complete 30 years of flying supersonic. My mother, like most mothers, loved me, cared for me, and provided guidance through the difficulties of childhood, but more than that, she was my very first mentor.

My actual story began 20 years before the start of my Air Force career in 1952. It was my early years that provided a belief foundation that continued to follow me the rest of my life. I grew up during the Great Depression, and in that austere environment, delivered newspapers from age six to help meet the basic needs of life. The meager family income pushed me to work weekends and summers during my school years. Although I had a loving mother to guide me and a devoted dog as my companion, my father was a heavy drinker, and domestic abuse occurred in our household. In spite of these obstacles, I managed to adopt a firm conviction that hard work, honesty, and fair play would lead to success. I was not disappointed in my faith that if I persevered in these principles, my life as it was in my childhood would extend on throughout my lifetime.

So that's the way it was for Robert Earl Haney: I became a pilot in my childhood and didn't even know it. I now realize my first pilot trainer was Mother and her crew. My story began the day I was born.

CHAPTER 2

My First Mentors

"My mother was the one who kept everything together."

I was born in a small house on Healy Street in Champaign, Illinois, on the 17th of July, 1932. It was just my mother, me, and a friend of my mother's who helped in the delivery.

My mother, Mae Smith, grew up in a farming community near a small town called Comargo, about 50 miles from Lexington, Kentucky. Families there were tenant sharecroppers who worked in the tobacco fields and raised small crops and some livestock for their own use. What they ate, they had to grow. Winters were cold, with virtually no heat for warming a house. Summers were hot and humid. A good harvest of tobacco depended on rainfall throughout the growing season. Workhorses were essential to the planting and cultivation of tobacco and also were the primary means of transportation. One of Mother's responsibilities on the farm was care of the animals. She was as at home on horseback as a kid is on a bicycle today.

Mother, who was born in 1900, never talked much about her childhood, and I never learned much about her parents. She had three brothers — Carl, Roy, and Earl — and despite their early circumstances, the four remained close throughout their lives. Mother was raised by a neighbor, Mrs. Sarah Carter, who owned a small tobacco farm and who, I believe, informally adopted my mother. I know life was very difficult for her, but I don't remember Mother ever complaining. She never saw the bad in people or circumstances. She always saw the good side. She was a young girl among three big, strapping brothers in an impoverished rural community where farming was the only way of life. Success or failure, survival even, required hard work by everyone. It was a hard life, yet she never expressed any regrets.

Few children in that area went beyond grade school because they had to work to help support the family. Going on to high school was not part of the mindset. My father, I was told, left school in the early elementary years. Mother was very bright and was able to complete the eighth grade. When she graduated she received an award recognizing her academic achievements. She carried that pin all her life. Had she been able to go on to high school and college, she would have done very well. She read well, she wrote well, and she excelled in whatever she did.

My father, Dillard McKinley Haney, was born in 1898, one of three children. The Haneys also lived and farmed in the tobacco country near Comargo. My mother and father met in childhood and married young.

My father's parents had left Kentucky around 1917 or 1918 and settled in Bushton, Illinois, where they continued to farm. My parents followed them and later relocated to Champaign, Illinois, about 40 miles from the Haney grandparents. They hoped to escape the rural poverty and better their circumstances by trading farm life for the city.

Five children were born within a four-year period: two boys in 1917 and 1918 (their names are unknown to me), twin girls Jean and Joanne in 1919, and then my sister Elizabeth. My mother and father were young parents in impoverished conditions with few resources and five babies to care for through cold winters.

Shortly after my parents moved to Bushton, tragedy struck. In the aftermath of the great flu epidemic of 1918–1919, the first four children died within a short time of one another. The boys died first. The twin girls, not yet a year old, soon died on the same night. My mother did the best she could to save them. She had already lost two and knew that the prognosis was not good. Any medical care was miles away, and my mother had no means of transportation or communication. There was little she could do. Elizabeth was the only child to survive. The babies were buried together in a little cemetery near Hindsboro, Illinois, which I have often visited in later years. Their headstone reads simply "The Haney Children."

Mother never talked much about the deaths of her four children. Occasionally she would make a comment when something reminded her of the heartbreak. It was just a tragic thing, something I have never totally been able to understand. The Haney family was not the only one to suffer a great catastrophe. Put in the context of the time when the flu epidemic struck, the conditions of life, and the lack of medical help, great losses were not unusual. The disease killed millions worldwide.

My brother, Stanley, was born in Champaign in 1930, and I came along two years later. The three of us often visited my paternal grandparents' farm near Bushton. Stanley, Elizabeth, and I were the recipients of our grandparents' love and admiration. As young children, we would play out in the fields. We were attracted to the horses and wanted to intermingle with them. One time I almost got my brains kicked out by a horse. I guess the horse got tired of me messing around with him.

My grandfather Haney was a big, strong man with a very quiet demeanor. Grandfather was always very entertaining. I have similar feelings about my grandmother Haney. She was very kind to her grandchildren and loved having us visit whenever we could. I have such fond memories of my grandparents. I always look back on my visits with my grandparents as a happy experience. Entertainment was cheap on the farm. This was significant, as money was scarce for us.

We also visited Mrs. Carter's farm back in Kentucky. Mother held Mrs. Carter close to her heart — the only mother she really ever knew. Our visits there were more infrequent than those to grandparent Haneys' farm. In either case there was lots of open farmland space for three restless kids. We didn't have toys, so we just horsed around with the horses or chased each other around the cornfield.

My father became a driver for Greyhound buses shortly after the move to Champaign. He had been interested in automobiles from an early age, and after losing his job with Greyhound he was able to find work as an auto mechanic. With self-acquired skills and time on the job, he developed into a very good automobile mechanic. He did well with what he did but had a drinking problem that overpowered everything else in his life. His longer-term employment was with Eichhurst-Bloom DeSoto Plymouth, a car dealer in Champaign located on Neil Street just six blocks from where we lived. He worked there when he was sober. When he was drinking he sometimes would not show up for work for days. Lloyd Eichhorst, who owned the business, would say, "He's as good a mechanic as there is. Whenever he can work, his job will be waiting." He was still working at Eichhurst when I graduated from high school.

I do not have any early childhood memories until I was about four years old. What I do remember after this age is very much etched in my mind. In the 1930s we probably were no better off or worse off than the majority of families. Shelter, food, and clothing were hard to come by. The only source of heat in the wintertime was one coal stove, which was not adequate to heat the entire house. We used the stove in the daytime, but the fire would die at night. On winter mornings there would be ice on the inside of the window panes. We did not have a telephone until I was in high school. As a young kid, I thought our living conditions were adequate. As far as I was concerned, every kid on the block lived as I did. The contrast for my parents must have been greater. In their rural life they had no running water, no indoor plumbing, and no electricity.

Foremost among my earliest memories is my mother's care for me, her youngest and last child. Mother was always concerned about my childhood illnesses. When I contracted whooping cough, she was especially fearful. The child mortality rate for whooping cough then was greater than 50 percent. She was fearful of losing another child. Nothing stood in her way when it came to keeping me alive and well. I am sure she felt the same when Elizabeth and Stanley became ill. We had no medical insurance, which was not unusual at the time. Family income barely paid for food and other basic expenses. I don't remember any family member ever going to see a doctor. Mother was not only our mother but our family doctor as well.

I became very dependent on Mother, and perhaps she became overprotective of me. I do know that we built a very close bond during my first six years. The time we had for each other decreased when I started first grade. It was difficult for me to make the transition to a new and different environment. The teacher was not my mother. My classmates were not my brothers and sisters. I gradually made the adjustment. Mother taught me that education was important. She was my first teacher. Her encouragement followed me throughout my life.

Champaign, where we lived, and Urbana are twin cities that had a combined population of about 30,000 at the time. One street separated the two. The University of Illinois in Urbana and Champaign was the focal point of business and employment in the area. When I was six years old I began delivering newspapers on a route for the *Champaign-Urbana Courier*. Most people then got their news from radio and the newspaper, so newspaper delivery was a big thing. I also sold Chicago newspapers on Saturday night in downtown Urbana. The Sunday Chicago papers came to Champaign on the Saturday nine o'clock evening train. I would pick up the papers from my boss, Louie Mays, and sell the papers on the corner of Main and Vine in Urbana. I would finish selling papers around midnight, and Louie would drive me from Urbana to Neil and Church streets in Champaign. I walked home from there. My income averaged somewhere around $1.50 for selling papers on Saturday nights and $2.00 a week for my weekly route. This doesn't sound like much in terms of the dollar's value today, but during the Depression that was a lot of money for a six-year-old kid.

I don't think my parents worried that their young son worked late. They grew up in a time and place where they had to be independent and know how to take care of themselves. They just assumed that because I had a job I could find my way home. Conditions, however, were harsh for such a young boy. I remember wearing down in the bitter cold of winter, with temperatures sometimes below zero in the darkness of night. The Methodist church on the corner of State and Church streets in Champaign, several blocks from Bradley Street where we were then living became my refuge. I first sought shelter in the church on a particularly cold and windy evening. I went up to the church porch to get out of the cold and opened the entry door. The church was a beautiful building, a lovely place with red carpeting and wood pews. I would go in and sit there until I got warm, then walk the rest of the way home. Sometimes I didn't get home until two or three o'clock in the morning. I fell asleep in a pew once, and Dr. Northcott, the minister, had to wake me when he arrived for Sunday service. He was a kind man and welcomed me to the church anytime. I returned often. My mother gave me a leather-bound Bible at this early age, which I value to this day.

I held other jobs besides delivering papers. Coal was the main source of fuel for heating homes. Many homes had a stoker system with a bin container for slowly moving the coal into the furnace. I would go into the basement of scheduled homes in the afternoons and shovel coal into the stoker bin, providing enough fuel to last through the night. At the age of ten, I went to work for the Pioneer Seed Corn Company. This was a summer job and fit in well with the school vacation break. I worked for Pioneer during the summers until I was 13 years old. When I was 12 we moved to 412 W. Columbia Avenue, just a few blocks from Bradley Street. The railroads were booming, and jobs there were available. The summer I turned 14 I went to the Illinois Central office and asked for a job. The employment office official said I wasn't old enough. I said, "I'm old enough to work." I was told, "You have to be 15 to work here." Somehow I convinced the section chief that this 14-year-old could do a day's work. Reluctantly, he said, "I'll give you one week."

I admit that first week was difficult. I was working with guys much older who had been on the railroad for a number of years. New rails were then being installed to accommodate diesel trains with faster engines and carrying heavier loads. Rail spikes were driven with three sizes of hammers:

eight-pound, twelve-pound, and sixteen-pound. The heaviest I could handle was the eight-pound hammer. Some of the older, more experienced men could swing a sixteen-pound spike maul with ease. They could put a railroad spike in with two hits. It would take half-dozen swings for this 14-year-old kid. I survived the first week. I stayed on until school started in the fall. The railroad boss told me that a job would be waiting for me next summer. I was proud to have made the cut.

Employment was easier to come by when World War II started and the country marshaled its resources to win the war. I was growing pretty fast in my teenage years and able to do more hard labor. I needed a job during the school year to support myself. During the weekdays I was engaged in classes and sports, but weekends were free. I applied for a job at the Twin City Ice Plant. The owner, Mr. Pic Dodds, and Mr. Carroll, supervisor of the company, gave me a try. Mr. Carroll told me I probably wouldn't stay in the job because I would have to work all day Saturday and all day Sunday. He said, "Normally people who take this job don't last very long because the hours are long, the work is hard, and the pay is not very good." My starting wage was 50 cents an hour, which for 12 hours each Saturday and Sunday amounted to a total of $12 a week. I would go to work at seven in the morning and get off at seven at night. My assignment was to work in the ice house making ice, storing it, readying blocks of ice for delivery, and direct sales at the plant. Most people had iceboxes made of oak, with a compartment to hold ice. Perishable foods were placed in other sections of the icebox, so hot summers meant lots of ice. I didn't have many idle moments working in the ice plant while at the same time meeting academic and athletic requirements during the week at school.

At the ice plant I met Ike Sayles, a huge black fellow. He looked like Jim Brown, the pro football player. He was about six-two and weighed over 200 pounds. I've never known anyone as strong as he was. He could pick up a 400-pound block of ice as easily as he would an ice cube. Ike was responsible for making the ice, and I would help him whenever extra help was needed. We became friends. He apparently had little or no education. While he possessed mammoth strength and physical capabilities, he thought I had great strength because I could read and write. Ours grew into an unusual relationship. I would read things to him and help him interpret content while he helped me with physical loads. I even signed his paychecks.

I worked at the ice plant every Saturday, every Sunday, the entire year around, until I graduated from high school. Even when I worked summers at the railroad, I came home to work weekends for Mr. Carroll. He kept me on because I was a reliable employee. He was impressed that I stayed with both the ice plant and the railroad, working seven days a week. He paid me for the weekend's work at the end of my shift on Sunday night. One Sunday in my second year on the job I was paid not the usual $12 but $24. I said, "You gave me too much money." Mr. Carroll said, "No, I'm going to give you what you're worth. You're worth more than 50 cents an hour." He had upped me from 50 cents an hour to a dollar an hour, and I was in hog heaven. I thought, "I'm a rich man!" I felt a little guilty about my pay raise. I was being paid more than Ike Sayles even though Ike could do more work in a day than I could do in a week. Mr. Carroll's rationale was twofold: It was difficult to get good workers for the hard labor required and even more difficult to get someone to work weekends. I stayed at the ice plant, year round, for a buck an hour until I graduated from high school and joined the Air Force.

I found a little lost dog one day while I was working on my paper route. I didn't have any pets at the time. I was six years old, and this lonely puppy was probably six to eight weeks old. I adopted him immediately. Skippy was a small dog with a dachshund body and a Scottie head. He had a dark brown and black body with a perfect white star on his neck and chin. The bottoms of Skippy's feet were white. He looked like he was wearing four white sweat socks. I named him Skippy because he didn't run; he just sort of skipped along. That little dog became my partner and best friend. Wherever I went, Skippy went with me. He became my alarm clock for both school and work. Skippy went to school with me every day. He would go back home, but when the school day ended he would be in front of the school waiting for me. Skippy and I were constant companions. When I played football, he would go to the athletic field. He would lie around and watch us practice. Then we would go home together. He went with me to the ice plant on Saturdays and Sundays and would be there waiting when my work day was done. Skippy even shared lunch hour with me. Whatever I had to eat, he got half.

Skippy communicated in many ways. At night he would lie on the floor at the end of the bed. When everything was quiet in the house, he would jump up on that bed so softly I could hardly feel it. In the morning he would nudge me a couple of times or lick me on the nose until I woke up. Then we'd go off to school. Sleep didn't come easily the night my front teeth were knocked out in a football game, but I had to go to work in the morning. At six A.M. Skippy began licking my face to wake me up. When I didn't stir, he barked at me, low at first and then louder and louder until I had no choice but to get up. If he wanted something he would sit up and push on my leg with his paws to let me know that he wanted to go out or he wanted to eat. If I ate something, he would sit up and make an audible sound like "Hey, it's time for you to give me something, too." It was a subtle thing, but it became just a matter of fact: we could communicate. He knew what I needed, and I knew what he needed.

Sometimes I would play a game with him. I would fold the papers for the paper route and put them in the bicycle basket. I purposely ignored him, as if he wouldn't be going along this time. When it came time for me to get on the bicycle and start the route, Skippy would stubbornly sit in front of the bicycle, as if to say, "You're forgetting me, I'm going too!" The joke was over. I would joyfully place him in the bike basket, where he always got a free ride around the paper route.

Skippy and I occasionally stopped at a Diamond DX gas station on Washington Street, where I would buy a bottle of RC Cola for a nickel and listen to the older men who went there to talk and gossip. One day at the station, a slovenly, ill-mannered man was sounding off, annoying those who had no choice but to listen. Skippy apparently felt the same way as the others in the store. On this particular day, Skippy went forth, right in front of the man, and peed all over his white socks. The startled man let out a big war whoop, laced with a few swear words. Skippy and I wasted no time getting out of the place. After that before I entered the station, I checked to see if that obnoxious fellow was there. If he was, Skippy and I moved on to other adventures. As I think back on that event, I realize my little dog had great insight into human character.

He never had a collar on his neck. Everybody in town knew that dog. He could move about and do whatever he wanted to do during the day when I was in school. My junior high school was about eight blocks from home. The school had a large student enrollment, some four hundred kids. We got out of school at nine minutes after three, and the kids would pour out of the building. There were several doors. Fifteen or twenty minutes before school was out, Skippy would wander up and sit at the regular place to wait for me. I sometimes tried to spook him by attempting to sneak out a different door. Within an instant of my coming out that other door, Skippy would be right by my heels. He darted through the hurrying students like a bullet, happy, as I was, to be side-by-side.

My mother was the pillar and the foundation for our family. No matter how difficult the circumstances, she was the one who kept everything together and was the stabilizing force as we grew up. She always worked and provided a steady income. When I was about three years old Mother took a job as seamstress for the Jane Howell Dress Shop, an exclusive custom clothing establishment in Champaign. The neighbor who had assisted in my birth became our daytime babysitter. Mother worked there six days a week for 20 years, until her death in 1955. She could do absolutely anything with a needle and thread. She became known for the elaborate and beautiful wedding gowns fashioned single-handedly for Jane Howell's clientele. People asked for her to do their work. A dress or gown by Mae Haney contributed to the growing reputation and prestige of the shop. Although it was not part of her job, she generously gave her own time training other employees in the fine points of dress design and construction. Mrs. Howell always realized how valuable Mother was to the business, and her skills were recognized by bonuses and regular increases in her wages. By the time I was in high school her income, about $35 a week, had become a main source of support for the family.

She had an extraordinary kindness about her. We lived near the railroad tracks, and the hobos riding the freight trains came to our door in the evenings looking for something to eat. I don't remember Mother ever turning anyone down. I used to say, "You're giving them your dinner, your meal." She would reply, "I'll have something tomorrow, and they probably won't." Missing a meal did not bother her at all. She seemed more satisfied seeing that someone else would have something to eat. The hobos must have known of her kind heart. I believe our house was marked, as was the custom during the Depression, because we had a steady flow of men coming to the door looking for food.

Haney's mother, the pillar of his life.

Our family holidays were

Thanksgiving and Christmas. My mother was an unbelievable cook, and we always looked forward to having chicken or turkey. The celebration centered on having the biggest feast possible. Beyond that, Christmas never was an extravagant affair. I don't remember getting toys as a boy. We just didn't do much gift exchange. There wasn't enough money to provide for presents. The gifts were what people shared at the dinner table and a day of family togetherness.

Skippy had a great sense of humor, and was a loyal companion, a faithful buddy, and Haney's dependable alarm clock (drawing by Hank Henry).

We didn't have a lot of family time together, but, no matter what the conditions, Mother always found enough time to sit down and talk to us. I don't remember ever hearing her raise her voice to anyone. If I made mistakes or there was something that she saw that was not beneficial, she would explain a better way in very understandable terms. I didn't have much association with other kids and didn't run around with the more mischievous ones. I didn't have time for play in the neighborhood, but, more importantly, I didn't want to do anything that would hurt her. I felt Mother had enough problems and didn't need any more from me. Mother was good to all of us, but I think I was closer to her than my brother and sister because I was the youngest, although I wouldn't be surprised to know that Elizabeth and Stanley each felt that they were equally special. My brother got along better with our father than I did. My sister was like me: She tried to stay away from him as much as possible. He did not treat her well.

I don't think my mother ever went to a movie while I was growing up. She worked six days a week. On Sunday she would wash the clothes and do all the things the family needed. I don't remember going to movies myself during my childhood. I did see *Bambi*, one of the first Walt Disney films. It cost a dime for a ticket. That was a lot of money. My recreation was work and skating. There was a small pond across from our house that provided a place in the winter for ice hockey and playful skating. I skated a lot and became very interested in speed skating. The University of Illinois campus, only a few blocks from where I lived, had a huge ice rink where college and professional figure and speed skaters trained. I skated there often.

High school brought about a major change in my life. I enrolled in the tenth grade at Champaign High School in the fall of 1946. Coincidentally, the summer of 1946 was the summer that I went to work for the railroad. I added the weekend job at the ice plant that fall. I don't know why or how I became interested in sports. Perhaps my enjoyment for ice skating played a part in my decision to try out for other sports. I went out for football my sophomore year. Rumors were that football practice was tough. Practice was twice a day. After working five days a week all summer on the railroad and two days a week at the ice plant, going to football practice was actually a vacation. It was easy, and it was fun. The competitiveness and camaraderie with teammates was something I had not experienced before.

Fred Major, the football coach, was very instrumental in my life from the very first day we met. He became the third influence to make a difference in my life, following my mother and my dog, Skippy. Mr. Major was very disciplined but equally honest and fair. I don't remember him preach about winning. He stressed hard work, emphasizing that being a good football player required one to always give one's maximum effort. Good sportsmanship, conditioning, and doing one's very best were the keys to having winning teams. His attitude was very much like that of my mother: Do the right thing, do the best you can do, and you will win in the end. I liked football. I found a new mentor in Mr. Major. I also developed some very good friendships. Teammates Kenny Stahl and Chuck Flora and I had a lot in common, and we became friends for life.

I played left guard on offense. I was not very big, but I was pretty fast. On defense I would either play in the line or in a backup line position. By my junior year, I was good enough to play on a regular basis. There was not a player on our team who was a super athlete. Our forte was attitude, hard work, and superior coaches. By the time we became seniors, we were really solid. Most of the players had been together since the sophomore year. Quickness and mobility were the secret to our success. The coach instilled discipline and conditioning in all of us, and he developed formations and strategy for what was to become a championship team.

In addition to Coach Fred Major, we had assistant coaches Harold Jester and Roy Swindell. Mr. Swindell was the wrestling coach during the winter. Mr. Jester was the track coach in the spring. I participated in all three sports. These men pretty much controlled our lives during the school year. We all had tremendous respect for them and for the example of strong moral character that they instilled in a bunch of young eager kids. The team faced strict discipline. I was afraid to step out of line because no matter what, win or lose, you followed the rules or you did not play. One of our best running backs was a kid named Bobby Mason. One night he was caught out after curfew hours. He got a one-game suspension and did not play the following Friday night. If you did something wrong, Coach Major was sure to find out. He had some kind of intuition or instinct.

He knew that I worked at the ice plant on Saturdays and Sundays and probably was aware that I was too tired or too busy to get into much trouble, but because he was concerned about the players maintaining good grades, Mr. Major interceded at times to assure my academic success. He would talk with teachers and make sure that I did my schoolwork before coming to practice. On one occasion I wasn't caught up in my geometry class and had to stay after school to complete an assignment. As a result I was late for football practice. Mr. Major rewarded my tardiness by making me run extra wind sprints after team practice. The lesson was that it was necessary to keep up with academic work, and I was to get to practice on time and avoid the consequences of showing up late. I learned that following the rules was easier than ignoring them.

I played better defense than offense. I could move and shed blockers quicker than the average guy, and I did make the sports page a few times. But seldom did one player alone win a game. Coach Major never belittled or embarrassed players in team meetings. Accordingly, he never put anyone on a pedestal either. He would stop and say, "OK, here's why we were successful here: The defense played a good game, and everybody did his part to allow that to happen."

In 1949, my senior year, Champaign won the Big 12 State Championship. The Big 12 Conference was then made up of the largest twelve schools in the state of Illinois. All of the major cities were included: Chicago, Champaign, Springfield, Danville, Mattoon, and others. Winning the conference was significant. High school football and basketball in the Midwest was a big thing. Everybody lived for it. When we won the state title a winners' banquet was held at a very nice restaurant on the east side of Urbana. I had never been to a restaurant in my life, let alone for the purpose of receiving praise and congratulations. The business people of the town gave us a little gold football that had a maroon "C" and the inscription "1949 Big 12 Champs." I still have it. The coaches pointed out important plays or circumstances that culminated in a win. The news media took pictures and wrote articles about the Big 12 Conference champions, the supermen of Champaign High. The recognition and publicity was new to me. I had never experienced anything quite like that before. I didn't really understand at that time what leadership was, but I think it was leadership, including moral leadership, that took us to the championship.

I graduated from high school in the spring of 1950. At the graduation ceremony Bob Richards, who became a two-time Olympic gold medalist in the pole vault, was the main speaker. Bobby grew up in Champaign and graduated from high school about five years before I did. He was a very popular homegrown citizen of Champaign and in 1950 was already a nationally recognized decathlete and pole vaulter. My mother attended the graduation ceremony. I was pleased for her sake that Coach Major made some specific comments about me and about my accomplishments under difficult circumstances. He said, "Earl will be successful in his life." She was very happy that night.

Mother always supported me in whatever I did, but she wasn't able

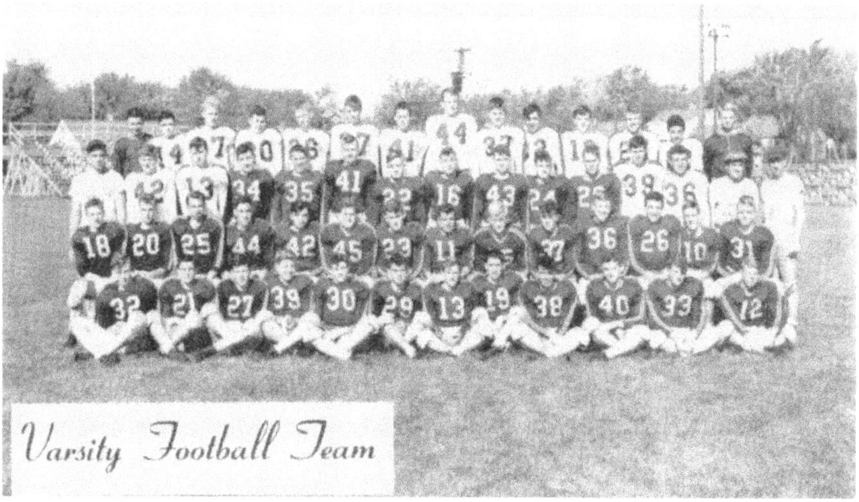

Big twelve State Football Championship Team, Champaign, Illinois, 1949. Earl is Number 37. His playing position was left guard in the starting lineup.

to go to my football games because she didn't get home until six o'clock at night and did not drive a car. My father never attended a football game or an athletic event and did not go to my graduation. His drinking was especially heavy on weekends. The more he drank, the more belligerent he became. He would take his belligerence out on my mother even though she would not argue or fight with him. He would pick on her, belittle her, and from time to time strike her or push her around. As a little boy, it scared me.

Robert Earl Haney, graduation day, May 1950, a proud moment for him and his mother. The suit is Haney's, but the tie was borrowed from the father of his friend, Dick Barham.

I don't remember my father and me ever doing anything alone together. As a family we visited our grandparents in Bushton. Occasionally in the summer we went to Kentucky where my mother and father lived before moving to Champaign. But even then I sat in the back of the car fearful of being too close to him. My father was not physically abusive to me until later in life. It was more that he just didn't want me around, so I stayed away from him. As I grew older and went on to high school, I would not get home from practice until six or seven o'clock in the evening. I worked 12-hour days at the ice plant on the weekends, so it became easier to avoid him.

I didn't really understand the extent of what was going on or why it was going on, but I learned to live with it. I grew up with that, and I grew away from him. But I had a very close relationship with Mother. We had a hard life, but I was not unhappy with anything. I only wished it could be different. I wish I could have made it easier for Mother.

There was yet another tragedy to come. My sister, Elizabeth, worked as a waitress while she was in high school. She was married the year that she graduated and moved out of the house to set up her own home but continued to work. In 1943 she was a waitress at a place called the Club 45, a restaurant and bar located between Champaign and Chanute Air Force Base. On an extremely cold Saturday night in February, the weather was too bad for her to get home. There were five or six little cabins on the property, and Elizabeth was allowed to stay in one that night. She turned on the gas to warm the place up but did not realize that the gas fumes from the defective heater were exhausting into the room. She woke up at some time during the night and tried to get out but couldn't get the door open. Elizabeth was found dead the next day in reach of the door.

I was then 12 years old and in junior high school. I remember the moment the coroner came to our house on that Sunday morning and told my mother. She just turned ghost white. It was such a blow. She had had a lot of tragedy in her life, but the loss of yet another daughter was terribly hard for her to accept. As always, she went on. Elizabeth had two children, Betty and Dean, who at that time were about two and four years old. Mother took in the children. It was up to us to continue to raise them, and we did. My mother, my brother, and I took care of them the best we could until they graduated from high school and went on with their own lives.

My brother, Stanley, went to work when he was about 12 years old at a place called Dave and Harry Locksmiths. He worked after school and on Saturdays until he graduated from high school and became a full-time employee. Eventually Stanley was able to buy the shop from Dave Percy, who was then the sole owner. The lock-and-key business was my brother's livelihood until health problems forced his retirement when he was in his mid–50s. Although Stanley had been with the shop for nearly 40 years, the name was never changed. It was always known as Dave and Harry Locksmiths, even when Stanley Haney owned it.

After high school my life changed again. I joined the Air Force. When I graduated from pilot training and came home for a visit, Mother asked me to go see my father at the gas station where he worked. I knew it was going to be a mistake. He had been drinking at the time. He was closing the station as I went in. When my back was turned, he attacked me with an 18-inch extension handle. I saw his reflection in the window and realized that he was going to hit me. He swung the extension handle, and I just stepped back from it. He missed and fell on the floor. I left. From the time I went into the service I wondered if his treatment of Mother got better or became worse. She would never have said.

There were much happier visits. Whenever I came home in the early period of my pilot training, Skippy and I would reunite and spend every minute together. I came home for what would be a last visit before I went to the Far East in 1955. By that time Skippy's whole head had turned gray, just like any older person. He was a puppy when I got him. I had him for 17 years. Mother wrote me about a week after I left for Japan to tell me that Skippy had crawled under the house and died there. It was as if he knew he wasn't going to see me again. I didn't realize until I was older how very important Skippy was in my early life. He taught me the meaning and value of faith and loyalty. His was the kind of total loyalty that is irreplaceable. My little dog Skippy was my partner until the day he died, and he is always in my memory.

While it may seem that I faced unusual hardships in my growing-up years, in fact the opposite is the case. These were the years when enduring values were given to me by the most significant figures in my young life—including the lesson of loyalty I learned from Skippy—values that governed much of my later life as an Air Force officer and beyond.

I learned by my mother's example as well as her words the value of honesty and the value of endurance. She would say, "Always be honest, and you will always be happy." By her intelligence and encouragement she impressed on me the value of education. My high school coach Fred Major believed and lived the same way. He exemplified courtesy, character, and fairness in the way he related not only to his young athletes but also to the world around him. He did not teach us to win by any means. He taught us that if we did the right things and did our absolute best at whatever we did, the "win" would follow. As time went on I came to understand with ever greater certainty that if you are satisfied that you played by the rules, win or lose, you will be happy with yourself and what you did with your best effort.

I don't believe that anyone spoke to me then of leadership. That came later when I realized that these values, learned early—loyalty, honesty, character—formed the foundation of the qualities of leadership that I would see and come to deeply admire in many mentors who would come into my life as my 30-year career in the U.S. Air Force moved forward.

Chapter 3

Aviation Cadet: Jet Age Training

"You're a dumb fighter pilot; that's all you are ever going to be."

The Korean War started shortly after I graduated from high school in the spring of 1950. Although there was a draft in effect, I grew up with the understanding that when it was necessary to fight for one's country, one had a patriotic duty to volunteer. Two high school buddies, Kenny Stahl and Bill Ducsey, and I went together to the post office where all four recruiting offices were located. My intention was to join the Marines, but the Marine recruiting officer, who was about to retire, convinced me that the Marines were not the place to go. "All you'll learn to do is crunch gravel and get shot at," he said. He suggested that the three of us see the Navy recruiter, telling us that there we would have more educational opportunities that could be of advantage when we got out.

As it turned out, I went to the Air Force recruiting office, Kenny chose the Navy, and Bill went into the Army. I don't know exactly why I decided on the Air Force, other than that Air Force recruiter was right next door to the Marine recruiting office. I didn't have any great ideas about flying or ideas about any career direction at that young age. Little did I know, at the time, I would become a fighter pilot and spend the next 30 years of my life as a participant in one of the most dynamic eras in the history of aviation — the evolution of supersonic flight.

During the next few weeks I took a series of tests — physical, mental, and academic — to evaluate my qualifications for the Air Force. When I learned it would be several months before the results would return, I went to work for the Jackson Plastering Company, which was doing some large construction projects at the University of Illinois. It would be hard to forget the company's motto, emblazoned on the side of Mr. Jackson's truck: "Get Plastered with Jackson."

With some of my savings from the ice plant I had been able to buy a 1949 Harley Davidson from a friend, Johnny Webb, whose father had given him the motorcycle on the condition that he graduate from high school with good grades. Johnny didn't live up to his father's expectations and was forced to sell the bike. It was the latest Hydra-Glide design and a beautiful turquoise color. Johnny said his dad had paid $1,100 for it. I told him, "I've got about $400; that's the best I can do." That was not enough. A week went by. Johnny was told that if he didn't have the motorcycle sold in seven days his dad was going to take it to Abe Silkovitch's junk yard and throw it in the junk pile. The following Saturday Johnny rode the bike over to the ice plant and said, "Earl, $400 will take it." I said, "OK."

At the end of the summer I had not yet heard from the Air Force, so I decided that this might be a good time to take my first solo trip out of Champaign. Mother suggested I visit her brother Carl who was living in Miami. It was beginning to get cold in Champaign, and Florida seemed like a good idea. I got on my motorcycle clad in an old jacket with almost no money in my pocket and rode all the way to Miami. I said, I'm going to ride until it gets warm. It didn't take very long to get hungry. When I reached Miami I found out that banana boats from the Bahamas came into the Florida bay: If the bananas were overripe they were put out for people to take. I lived on bananas and coconuts until I found work.

I got job a with a construction company working on a housing development in the northeastern part of Miami. I was hired as a truck driver, charged with picking up and dumping gravel at the construction site. When I signed on, I claimed I could "drive anything." It turned out on my first run that mastering the complex mechanics of a dump truck did not come as easily as I expected, but I learned. I was transferred to the roofing crew later because of the work demand. The job involved carrying tar, tar paper, and other materials from the ground to the top of the building where the tar was heated and where we then mopped it over the roof.

I worked twelve hours a day, seven days a week spreading tar on the roofs of a complex of four-story buildings with eight to ten apartments in each one. The boss was onto us all the time because the work was always behind schedule. We were working like gangbusters.

I learned a lesson on that job that has stayed with me until the present day and influenced my approach to many situations I would experience in the future. I saw a man walking backward while mopping roof tar walk right off the edge of the roof, falling four floors to his death. I was 19 years old and had never seen a man killed before my eyes. From that time on, instead of mopping by backing up the way it was being done, I mopped backward halfway and turned around and mopped the other half toward me. In the short time I worked on the roofing project four more guys were killed by walking off the end of the roof in the haste to get the job done. I learned then, and later, that you can find a safer way to do anything if you just think a little bit. Safety should always be paramount, and training for any hazardous job was essential.

I left that roofing job in November when my mother wrote that I was probably going to be inducted in February. I had a terrible time getting home because of a big snow storm. I was stranded on the highway and walked to a gas station, where I stayed overnight with other stranded travelers. I finally made it back home to Champaign in December, in time for Christmas. I had some spare time to kill. Ice-skating again became my recreation. I spent $19.95 for a pair of Johnson CCM speed skates and went to the ice rink every day. On the day I went into the Air Force, February 6, 1952, I had 37 cents in my pocket. I remember that because 37 was my football number when I was on the high school football team.

I was inducted into the Air Force in February and went to Lackland Air Force Base in San Antonio, Texas, to begin 12 weeks of very strict military training, discipline, and academics. Everyone took a series of academic and physical tests during that period of time. I did very well on the electronics test and was selected to go to an electronics school at Scott Air Force Base, Illinois. I arrived at Scott the first of May in 1952 to start the radio-maintenance electronics program.

The base had a football team made up of guys with enough talent to play competitive football. I liked to play football and was pretty good. I made the team and started practicing in August of 1952. Scott AFB sports teams lived in special barracks, were given a special diet for athletes, and were exempt from the one day a week others spent on kitchen police duty.

We played a number of games that fall. The team had plenty of talent. Many had played football in college. Several even had pro experience. This was not unusual. Gifted athletes called into service often were directed into the Special Services. So a lot of really good athletes from colleges and pro teams played for two years for the Air Force to complete their military commitment. I felt lucky to make the team, but the challenge was enormous competing against the best football players assigned to Scott AFB.

About midway through the season, while practicing punt returns, I received the football as a 235-pound tackle mowed me down. I was knocked unconscious. While I was coming to and trying to figure out who I was and where I was, four F-86 supersonic fighters approached and landed. The football practice field was right off the end of the runway. I remember seeing those four airplanes pitch out and land right over my head. I could almost have reached out and touched them.

Later that day in the training facility the coach asked me how I was doing after being wiped out on the punt return. I told him everything was fine. I said, "Did you see those airplanes that came in and landed?" He said, "Yes, those are the first four supersonic fighters the Air Force has. They're touring the country to show the new aircraft to be used in the Korean War." He then said, "You know, I think you could do that." I asked, "Do what?" He said, "I think you could fly those Air Force fighters." I told him I didn't even know how to spell airplane, much less fly one. He gave me encouragement to apply for the cadet flying program. Fortunately, I followed that advice.

I don't know why the coach encouraged me to apply for the cadet flying program. He probably thought that if I continued to play football, my fellow players were going to kill me. I was only about 165 pounds, a fairly good sized, strong kid. But I was the smallest guy on that football team. I have to admit I did take a beating that season. Maybe he saw that flying was something I could do. Before that, flying had never crossed my mind. I had never flown, I had no thoughts of aviation, and I had no aspirations to fly. I had no belief that I could go through pilot training. I just thought it was too far away from me.

I took all of the pilot training tests at Scott Air Force Base. This was a battery of very difficult academic and physical tests to determine the full extent of an applicant's capabilities and potential. The academic testing was a tiring day, eight hours of timed test batteries. You get 30 minutes to do a set number of problems or actions, and then you move on to the next. I was amazed that there was no way a test could be finished within the given time limit. You were to do what you could do within the time frame allowed. There were tests for mathematics, electronics, English — all on a much higher level than I ever faced in high school.

The physical and medical exams took an additional couple of days. Motor skill tests tested eye-to-hand coordination. They tested physical capability to assess a situation, come to a conclusion, and react to it. Reaction times to a variety of demanding situations were recorded. Perfect eyesight and color recognition were required. No test, physical or mental, was easy. When I finished the battery of tests, I thought there is no way I could have passed. I had never been exposed to anything so difficult before. As it turned out, I got very high scores across the board, in both the psychomotor tests and the academic tests. The highest you could get was nine points in a battery of tests, and I got a nine on quite a number of them. I really thought a mistake had been made, that my name had been mixed up with somebody else. The big 235-pound tackle did me a huge favor. I was selected to begin pilot training in March of 1953.

I returned to Lackland Air Force Base for the initial cadet training, 12 weeks of very intense military training and extreme discipline. Cadets had to stand at attention for hours. Demerits were given for the slightest infraction in appearance or demeanor. Even a movement of the eyeballs, called "gazing," earned a demerit. The punishment after an accumulation of a few demerits was to walk tours on weekends, one hour for each demerit. The curriculum included training in aviation weather, aviation history, aviation dynamics, and other academics to prepare a cadet for flight activity as a pilot.

I was 20 years old at the time and found myself thrust into a leadership role. I was chosen to become a cadet squadron commander. The cadets actually ran the organization with supervision from superior, already commissioned, officers. The commanders were placed in a leadership role to control, manage, and lead the cadets.

I didn't think the program was hard. I had a much more difficult time growing up and working at the railroad. I had been used to 12-hour days from childhood. I never really thought much about it. All I knew was you have something to do, you put the pieces together, get organized, and do it. Cadet training seemed like playing football. I knew how to compete. I'd been doing that in several athletic endeavors in high school. I knew it was better to win than to lose, but that's about all I knew. From childhood my mother taught me discipline. When I went into the Air Force I liked discipline. I liked seeing things accomplished, and I valued safety. I hate to see people hurt when it is so unnecessary. Those attitudes somehow were reflected to my superiors, so I was given responsibilities.

Every Saturday we had a parade with all the other cadet squadrons. The purpose was to determine which squadron performed the best military parade, demonstrating superior discipline and military organization. When I became a squadron commander in my last month of initial aviation cadet training, we won all the remaining parades, four parades in a row. We won because we went out and practiced. I learned that from Fred Major, my football coach. You practice and you will win, he would say. I just told the guys, "Let's win, so let's practice." One of the exercises we did was "jailhouse marching." In a hypothetical jailhouse you don't have a lot of room, but you still have to practice military discipline: You only do half-steps and quarter steps. It was fun to do this, just for show.

I was responsible for making sure that members of my squadron met cadet corps standards. The cadet washout rate was high, over 50 percent. The discipline was very stringent and the punishment severe. It was a fast-moving program for young kids who really didn't know at this point in their lives that the consequence of poor performance was failure. One day you are in, and the next day you are out because you didn't pass an academic test or meet a military standard. Washouts didn't get a second or third chance to prove themselves.

Ned Replogle, the cadet wing commander, was one of those guys who you knew within 30 minutes was a leader. He was six-foot-two, a tremendous athlete, and academics were a piece of cake for him. I don't think Ned Replogle ever thought he would fail at anything. He never had failed at anything. Everything was so easy for him. I was struggling to get through from day to day, and he had time to spare. The administrators of the cadet program saw right away that Ned Replogle was a natural. Everything he touched turned to gold. We would see a lot of each other in the future.

I finished the initial cadet indoctrination program at Lackland in June of 1953. With other cadet graduates I went to Spence Air Base, Moultrie, Georgia, to begin actual flight training. First, the pilot trainees received indoctrination into the PA-18 airplane. The PA-18 was small, much like a J-3 Cub, a one-engine prop aircraft. The purpose of the PA-18 orientation was to acclimate the pilot trainees to the flying environment. I soloed that airplane in about seven hours, flew it for three more hours, and then began training in the T-6. The T-6 was a propeller-driven, fairly large airplane. My instructor at that time was named Strutz and was as mean as a rattlesnake. It was the first aerobatic airplane that I had ever been in. He took each of his assigned four students, one at a time, in the T-6. The first hour he did continuous aerobatics. You are upside down and right side up, straight up, straight down, for the whole flight. His feeling was that if you could survive that first hour without getting sick and falling apart at the seams, you'd be a pilot.

I checked out in the T-6, in about seven hours and thirty minutes.

I'll never forget the day Strutz took me to a little field at Tifton, Georgia, to shoot landings. He was all over me, hollering at me, Do this, Do that! Just beating up on me all the time. While at Tifton, I shot three landings. He told me to pull off to the side of the taxiway and stop. So I did. He got out of the airplane, and came up on the wing and started hollering at me in the cockpit with the big, noisy engine on the T-6 running. Telling me he was tired of sitting back there watching me screw things up; I'd have to go do it by myself. He got off the wing, and I sat there and wondered, what does he really want me to do? I finally decided, "Well, I guess he wants me to fly it." So I pushed the throttle up, got back onto the runway, and shot three landings. After the third landing, I taxied over to the side where he was standing. It was the first time I ever saw him smile. I was now solo in the T-6.

There were a number of washouts in the first week, guys who just could not accept the pressure on them. I look back on it sometimes. I had been told how rigorous and rigid pilot training was. It was not easy, but I had worked harder, longer hours, with more stringent discipline from the section leader at the Illinois Central Railroad than I was getting in the Air Force. I had three meals a day, a good place to stay, and I was flying! I thought, "This is the best it's ever been for me."

I endured early training with Strutz. He was very difficult to get along with. When he was moved to another flight, I was assigned another instructor, John Frederick Howard. He was a World War II, P-40, combat pilot with thousands of hours of flight experience. He was an absolutely impeccable aviator. Better yet, he was the nicest guy in the world, a truly amazing man. In the spring and fall John Frederick Howard crop-dusted around Moultrie, Georgia. He also was a licensed mortician and was developing a funeral home in downtown Moultrie. Two of the four of us who started our training with Mr. Strutz washed out; Al Vollmer and I remained. With only two students to worry about, John Frederick Howard was able to devote much more time to really working with us. He did a magnificent job.

If I did well during the required part of the training, John Frederick would branch off and teach me aerobatics, double Immelmans, snap rolls, and other things that really were not in the curriculum, and he would expand the instrument flight requirements. It was extremely beneficial to be able to fly the airplane in all conditions, that is, to be able to fly in the highest performance levels the airplane could reach, both in visual and instrument conditions. He was very smooth and effective with any given directions. If I made a significant error in flight, he would say, "Earl, I can make you look so natural." I could see myself laid out in his mortician's coffin and would immediately straighten up and do my level best. His instruction and commitment were extremely valuable to me throughout my Air Force career. I was very fortunate at this early time to have had him as an instructor.

Near the end of the training, pilot trainees were selected to go either to bombers or fighters. You could make your personal desires known, but your flying scores decided whether you went to fighters or bombers. John Frederick never asked me what my preference would be. He just put me on the fighter list. I had very high scores and was selected to go to fighter training. Before I left Moultrie I asked him why he never asked me about my choice. He just looked at me in a very stern manner and said, "You're a dumb fighter pilot; that's all you are ever going to be." I wasn't sure whether that was a compliment or not. But because he was such an extraordinary fighter pilot, I took it as a compliment. By far, fighters would have been my choice. I think he knew that a 20-year-old kid really wasn't able to make that sort of decision himself. He was right. He knew more about my capabilities than I did. He made a decision for me that was life lasting, and I will always be grateful to him for sending me to fighters. I think that is where I belonged.

I left Spence Air Base and went to Laredo Air Force Base, Texas, for advanced training in October of 1953. It was the beginning of the supersonic jet fighter age and a turning point in aviation history. I was a member of one of the first classes to undergo jet training. In the pre-jet age, trainees went from a prop T-6 into other propeller-driven fighters, the P-51, the P-40, or other vintage props. The Air Force was concentrating very heavily on instrument techniques and capabilities — being able to fly the airplane in severe weather conditions — and formation flight. Now that jets were coming on board, pilots went from the T-6 and a short indoctrination in instruments and formation in the T-28, to then transitioning into jets. I flew about 40 hours in a T-28, which was still a prop-driven airplane but had a lot more power and instrument capability than the T- 6. I survived the T-28 training and moved into the T-33.

The T-33, a new Lockheed airplane, was the same airplane as the F-80 but with the cockpit modified from a one-seat to a two seat, allowing the instructor and the trainee to fly the same plane for training purposes. The T-33 was the first jet trainer, and my initiation into jet aircraft. When I moved into jets at Laredo many of the flight instructors had minimal

The T-33, an advanced jet training aircraft aviation cadet Haney flew at Laredo AFB, Texas.

experience in the new jet aircraft. My instructor, Lawrence Eppley, wasn't nearly as experienced an aviator as John Frederick Howard and had virtually no experience in jet training. We sort of learned together.

I was a little bit nervous about going into jets. I thought this was going to be difficult because they were so fast and so different from prop aircraft. In fact, the jets were much easier to fly than the prop airplanes. There is no torque effect on the jet. The dynamics by this time with fighter jet airplanes had become pretty sophisticated. While the jet aircraft was easier to fly, a mistake could be very, very critical. You could not afford to stall the airplane in a traffic pattern at low altitudes because recovering from a stall took altitude and power to recover. We spun the prop airplanes, T-6s and the T-28s, regularly, but to spin the jet airplanes was difficult. The dynamics for high-speed airplanes are not conducive to out-of-control — or out of the controlled flight envelope — maneuvering. At first it looked as if it would be difficult to fly at high speeds very close to another airplane with four airplanes in a formation. As it turned out that was pretty easy, too. You make a sight picture on the airplane you are to fly with and keep it there. The speed is not difficult to master.

But the jet fighters did move fast, and for that reason you had to be able to think fast. Again, I was fortunate to have had really good instruction from John Frederick Howard. He was just a magnificent instructor in teaching the kind of mindset needed to think in the air. I never had any fear or apprehension of flying. I never was airsick in my life. I was actually too busy to have much time to think about fear. I had a great desire to learn, to become a top-notch pilot.

The ability to fly a fast-moving machine on instruments and shoot instrument approaches at higher speeds is critical in jet training. In the jets you start an instrument approach at 20,000 feet at somewhere near 300 to 400 miles an hour and do a descending 180-degree turn down to approach altitude of somewhere around a thousand feet. You lose the 20,000 feet in a matter of minutes and then decrease the air speed to about 200 miles an hour to begin the final approach. The speeds and the process move very rapidly. You have to be ahead of the airplane all the time.

Instrument approach at high speed, together with formation training, were factors that took out a lot of pilots, that is, those who just could not move fast enough to develop the requirements to fly the airplane in formation and accurately on instruments. The washout rate in this area was very high for the flyers who failed to blend formation and instrumentation into a smooth, safe operation. The sad part about it is that I think many of those guys would have been able to go on if given a little more time. The training program moved too fast and did not allow for catch-up. You moved from phase to phase at a very rapid rate and either kept up to speed or went out the door. Training was rigid, not forgiving of errors or lack of physical and mental quickness.

The tower and ground control instrument facilities to guide jet airplanes, in the air and landing, were far from adequate. The ground control instrument facilities were designed for slow-moving prop airplanes. The high-speed jet airplanes moved into the same environment used by the older, slower-moving, propeller-driven airplanes typical of the World War II era. Jet pilots had to think way ahead in order to get the airplane to its destination and back safely under all kinds of flying conditions. Landings required accurate instrument facilities from ground control synchronized with the pilot's instrumentation in the cockpit. Coordination between out-of-date ground facilities and the pilot was an ongoing challenge, as were all phases of jet pilot training in the early years.

I graduated from pilot training, received my wings, and was commissioned a second lieutenant on the 17th of August 1954 at Laredo Air Force Base, Texas. I was now a commissioned officer and a qualified pilot. My initial pilot training ended as the era of supersonic fighter aviation began.

I had gained a significant amount of flying experience. Still, I didn't anticipate the extent of what I was going to be expected to do in the next years. I had no intention or thought at that the time of making the Air Force a life-long career. I was up to my ears in what I was doing every day just learning to fly, meeting the requirements, passing the tests, and doing all the things required. I really didn't give a lot of thought about anything outside that, or about what I was going to do, or what I was going to do in the future.

A significant turning point in 2nd Lt. Haney's young life was graduation from the cadet training program, Laredo AFB, Texas, August 17, 1954.

I never talked to Mother much about flying. When I graduated from the cadet training program, an article in the local Champaign, Illinois, newspaper appeared, stating I had graduated from USAF training and was a commissioned officer. Mother was elated, but I don't think she realized how big a project her son had taken on. She knew I was flying high-performance fighter airplanes with implications of going to war. She was very proud that I had accomplished these goals but equally worried about my future. She did not even know where Korea was or that Korea was where eventually I would be headed. For Mother it was bittersweet, a worrisome time but also a happy time to celebrate our achievements.

The Air Force didn't give

much leave time during the cadet program for fear of losing the continuity during the important training process. I had been home once when I was at Moultrie and later had a couple of weeks' leave at Christmastime. My primary reason for going home was to see my mother and my little friend Skippy. Skippy was getting old. Not only did he look old, but also I could tell he was not up to his normal speed. But as always he was elated to see me. My leave days at home with my mother and my dog were very happy occasions. We were happy to see each other and content to talk about our experiences. I know that life was just as difficult for Mother as it always had been, but she never complained. The subject of abuse or mistreatment by my father, if it occurred, never surfaced. She always focused on my happiness and future progress.

The F-86s I had watched fly over the football field at Scott Air Force Base nearly two years earlier were the front-runner for combat training. My life had changed dramatically in the two years since I saw those four F-86s fly over the football field. I had graduated third in my pilot-training class and was one of only three pilots from our class to receive assignments to the F-86 at Nellis Air Force Base in Las Vegas, Nevada, the fighter center of the world.

CHAPTER 4

Supersonic Flight: The F-86

"When I went to Nellis I thought I had gone to heaven."

Assignment to the F-86 program at Nellis Air Force Base in Nevada was a choice prize for graduating cadets. Three of us from our pilot training class made the cut. Ned Replogle, Al Vollmer, and I had become good friends while we were together in the cadet program. Ned became the cadet wing commander in the last phase of the program. Al and I were selected to be group commanders. We were three lucky guys. We would be flying the F-86, an advanced airplane with tremendous potential over earlier fighter aircraft.

Our F-86 training started in September 1954. There were twenty-one young lieutenants in the 54-P3 class. The commander of the fighter group was a man named Clay Tice, known as "Tiger" because he created what was known as the Tiger Program whose motto was "Every Man a Tiger." He stood before us the first day and explained the harsh reality of the program. At one point he said, "Look to the man on your left and look to the man on your right. When you leave here, one of those guys won't be here." It was a shocker for a 22-year-old kid to realize that one of the guys on my left or right, or me, was not going to leave the Tiger program alive. We understood at that moment that flying jets was a serious business.

The F-86 was a new development in the jet-age fighter world. The lessons learned from the older jet fighters used in the Korean War were now being phased in the F-86 Tiger Program along with new technology and capability. Many of the instructors, in fact almost all of them, were veterans of combat in Korea. Major Fred "Boots" Blesse, the commander of the 96th Squadron, to which I was assigned, was himself a famed ace

The F-86, the first supersonic fighter built in the United States. The F-86 was a front-line fighter during the Korean War. Second Lt. Haney flew the F-86 at Nellis AFB, Nevada, in 1954, his first experience flying supersonic.

from the Korean War. He was a master pilot and a great guy. He taught me a number of invaluable lessons.

The F-86 was a one-seat airplane. The instructors would give you the manual and some briefing on the known idiosyncrasies of the aircraft, but you had to fly the airplane by yourself. Not a lot was known about the aircraft. It was the first swept-wing, supersonic fighter, and pilots experienced in the F-86 were practically non-existent. A few of the instructors from Korea had flown it some. Training was sort of an earn-while-you-learn program, including very intense fighter flying activity.

My first flight was with Sam Johnson, a veteran from Korea. The instructors flew on your wing on the first flight in order to guide you along if things didn't go well. In the first flight he directed me through some basic stall maneuvers to get the feel of the airplane. The next step was to go supersonic to get that out of the way and to get the feel of the airplane moving out from subsonic through transonic into supersonic flight. I flew one solo flight. It was the experience of a lifetime. Then it was time to move to tactical formation. The idea was to learn to use the airplane for purposes beyond just getting from point A to point B. The challenge was to fly four F-86s in close formation and in different formation configurations representing actual fighter tactical combat conditions.

We lived two guys to a room in an old World War II barracks adjacent to flight operations and the runway. Wayne Czelno was my roommate and flying companion. He was a good-looking, strong athletic man, and we got along well. On our third mission, Wayne was on takeoff in front of me. I was beginning my takeoff roll and was watching Wayne rotate for his takeoff. I could see the whole top of the airplane from the runway, and it looked funny to me. As I reached rotation speed, Wayne's F-86 stalled back to the ground and started to burn as it skidded down the runway. The aircraft fuel tanks were full and burst into flame. I took off through the smoke and fire as his airplane exploded on the runway. I didn't learn much about aviation on that flight, but I learned a lot about loss and deep sadness. I no longer had this friend and roommate.

About half of the guys that I began pilot training with in the first part of cadet training had already washed out, but there were no deaths. Earlier there had been an accident in a T-28 where a man was burned badly, but survived. Wayne's loss was my first experience with a tragedy at this level. He over-rotated the airplane when it came off the ground, so it was actually in a stalled attitude when he took off. (In aviation *attitude* is the physical condition of the aircraft in the three-dimensional environment.) That was easy to do in the F-86. It was the first airplane to have a "flying tail" which functions as a dynamic flight elevator for pitch control but does not split to create or decrease lift. A flight elevator is the horizontal stabilizer of the airplane. It flies like a wing. The airplane is rotated for takeoff by controlling the horizontal stabilizer. In Wayne's situation, when the aircraft came off the ground, the basic wing was actually in a stalled attitude. Even if the pitch were overcontrolled, the ground effect would allow the airplane to become airborne to maybe 30 or 40 feet. But it would stall back into the runway. That's what happened to Wayne.

I don't know if this problem happened often, but it happened at Nellis and so became something we had to be very aware of. Because these were the early days of the F-86, problems did occur. Sometimes these problems either were not well publicized or the information was not adequately passed on to the young pilots in training. The F-86s were new, and the guys flying them lacked experience in this new technology. The early stage of the jet and accompanying problems created the necessity for a flying safety process to resolve these problems before more casualties occurred.

Each day we would fly very stringent tactics and formations, air-to-air gunnery firing 50 caliber machine guns into airborne targets and air-to-ground targets. These were very high-performance maneuvers with the F-86. We were learning how to use it as a weapon. This activity continued day to day, flying maybe three times in a day. About halfway through the program, a young fellow, Dick Nien, was on an air-to-ground target mission. He loaded the airplane wing near 5 Gs, and the right wing broke off. He was killed instantly as the F-86 struck the ground.

Dick's death surfaced another serious problem with the F-86. The holes where the rear wing connector bolts went through were too big, although only slightly, allowing the wing to shift a fraction of an inch. The shifting of the wing from loading a high-G force and unloading a low-G force could eventually create a crack. Until this new problem was fixed, we were restricted to 4 Gs. The problem was fixed quickly. The manufacturer redesigned and replaced the wing bolts, and we were back to full capability within a couple of weeks.

The program became more intense as the days passed. The instructors and commanders were seasoned, experienced combat pilots. My commander, Boots Blesse, was an absolute master of the airplane and a phenomenal athlete. I played handball with him on a regular basis. He wasn't really big — about five foot eight and probably one hundred fifty pounds — but he was a giant in most other ways. He was a fierce competitor, on the ground and in the air. He taught me a lot about being prepared to fly in a wartime environment. Major Blesse said the way to survive is to be the best. He instilled that challenge in all of us on a daily basis. Boots Blesse was a man of very high ethical standards. He was integrity personified. I thought the world of him. It was a marvel to fly with him and see how he piloted and used the airplane to its absolute maximum performance. He provided a strong foundation for my entry into the fighter world. He wrote the first book on combat fighter tactics, *No Guts No Glory*, which became a bestseller among fighter pilots.

We were about to finish up our program in December of 1954. One pilot took off and got lost on the gunnery range in a snowstorm north of Nellis. By the end of the day we knew he was down, but we didn't know where. It had snowed all afternoon in this area of Nevada. The next day several of us were assigned to go look for the fallen pilot. Two of my classmates searched the mountainous area. We don't actually know what happened, but it appeared that Lt. Henry Hildebrand flew too low into a valley area near Mount Charleston north of Nellis and didn't make it out the other side. He hit the mountain and perished. We had lost four so far out of the twenty-one who started the program. The lost pilot was not found until the following spring. Clay Tice's first-day premise that some of us might not make it through the program was beginning to materialize.

By my third or fourth flight, I had found my niche. I loved the performance of the airplanes, the disciplines of the Air Force, and the standards that were upheld. This kind of flying was a dream come true. When I went to Nellis I thought I had gone to heaven. Growing up as a child in Illinois, winters were cold, and keeping warm was always difficult. I went to Nellis Air Force Base in the middle of the winter and the days were sunny, 65 or 70 degrees, and I'm flying the world's greatest airplane. I had bought myself a red Mercury coupe to churn around in during my time off. I looked back on my previous life and found the change from my childhood was just monumental.

I was happy and proud to be a pilot in the U.S. Air Force. It was gratifying to serve my country, an honorable, responsible thing to do. I found flying the fast-moving jet one of the most satisfying jobs possible. The capability and the maneuverability of a supersonic jet fighter is something that is difficult to explain. It gave me a great sense of accomplishment. I think it all came together for me at the Nellis training grounds. Through the earlier flight training and the cadet program, I didn't have time to think about whether the Air Force was a good choice. I was so busy every day trying to keep up with the program. Suddenly at Nellis it all jelled. I was as happy as any young kid could be.

The loss of friends was hard to accept. One minute they were there, and the next minute they were gone. This experience was very difficult for me to deal with. It was hard for me to understand that deaths are the downside of a very dangerous occupation. In those days of new aircraft and new technologies, the fatality rate was pretty high. You learn to stand up to it. A fighter pilot establishes in his own mind the belief that it won't happen to him. It's going to happen to somebody, but it won't happen to me. Each person learns in his own way to accept the losses and realize that this is a business that has a certain amount of danger. I think the discipline, the commanders, and the old heads who had been around a while — many of them combat veterans of World War II as well as Korea — all played a part. These veterans believed in teaching future pilots that protection of their country was their duty as freedom-loving people. The possibility that one might die became secondary. It was certainly something I thought about, but I didn't rush out and get life insurance. There weren't many companies that would insure anyone engaged in a job with such a high mortality rate.

Ned Replogle was a remarkable person. He was one of those guys who could do anything. He was always at the top of the list in everything. Ned was so good that he received a short-term assignment to the research and development squadron, the 25th Fighter Squadron, at Nellis Air Force Base, just to see how fast he could advance. In a matter of three missions he could outshoot most of the instructors in air-to-air and air-to-ground. He was amazing.

When we were cadets we went to a carnival in Tifton, Georgia. One of the attractions was to have a fellow parachute out of an airplane. He didn't show up, and the organizers were at a loss as to how to keep the customers and the money coming. So Replogle said, "Give me 20 dollars, and I'll do it." He went up in a bi-wing airplane and jumped out of it for 20 bucks. It was the first time in his life that he had done such a stunt. I thought he was invincible, but as I learned, no one is invincible.

When we left Nellis, Ned went home to Pennsylvania for a visit. While there, Ned and another pilot decided to fly a T-6. Somehow they got the airplane in a spin and couldn't get out of it. The T-6 crashed, killing both pilots. I learned of Ned's death within days of completing the program at Nellis. Something was amiss, but the investigators never uncovered the cause. The T-6 was easy to get out of a spin, and Ned was very accomplished in the airplane. It was a tragic loss of a great guy and a close friend. That one I took very hard. We had been through so much together. Ned was the fifth loss of a friend I would endure, and it would not be the last.

The goal at Nellis Air Force Base was to prepare pilots for the complete combat envelope with the jet fighter as a major weapon in any air war. The training group assumed an assignment to Korea was imminent, but the war ended before the end of my training program. The armistice that ended the Korean War did not stop the potential for an outbreak in another part of the world or even in Korea for that matter. Every day for months it appeared that the conflict in Korea could re-explode and the United States would be back into full combat. Re-ignition of war was an iffy thing for several years. In fact, it has been iffy for more than 50 years in Korea. It has always been a tense environment. We were training as if when we got there, the war would be there.

During the cadet days, an aviation cadet lived under strict discipline and confinement to quarters with virtually no time off. Cadets were involved in either flight or ground training. There was no time for socializing as a cadet. During the last several weeks in training a Saturday afternoon or Saturday evening off was allowed, but usually cadets were too far behind in the curriculum to take advantage of any leisure time.

Time off for family and friends changed somewhat when I got to Nellis. We were commissioned officers now. I flew five days a week, sometimes on Saturdays if we got behind. But for the first time, in a couple of years we had evenings and weekends off to do whatever we wanted to do. Las Vegas, Nevada, was quite an entertainment city, with top shows to see. I remember seeing Frank Sinatra, Nat King Cole, Dean Martin, the Mills Brothers, all of those entertainment groups that came to Las Vegas on a regular basis. Las Vegas was a fun place for young Air Force guys to go, to meet girls, and to have a little leisure time.

As usual, drinking and gambling took its toll on some of our guys. There was one kid who became addicted to gambling and spent everything he had. We had to give him money to eat on in the last part of the month until he got his pay. When we graduated I was going back home to Champaign for a few days before going to Japan. A couple of the other guys, including him, were also going back in an eastern direction, so we took his pay and wouldn't give it to him until we got to Oklahoma City. We knew he'd just run down and gamble it, and be stuck in Las Vegas. He was very upset. Too much drinking also afflicted some of our guys. At that time I had not had a drop of alcohol in my life, and I saw no reason to start there. My experience with my father and alcohol had left a bitter taste. Moreover, I needed to be in top physical condition, and to my own mind alcohol was not conducive to longevity in high-performance fighter aircraft.

When Boots Blesse introduced me to handball, he said it was a great physical activity that taught good eye-to-hand coordination and quick mental reaction time. Blesse, as usual, was right. I played handball five to seven days a week, and continued to do so for the next 25 years. Handball kept you in very good physical condition and trained you for the kind of reaction time and physical requirements necessary to fly in a fighter role.

Nellis was a great learning tool from many different aspects. Air Force pilots were trained to protect their homeland and, when necessary, fight wars. I felt very self-confident as I completed the four-month program. I said to myself, "I can do this." Pilot training moved along at such a fast pace that it seemed you were always behind, but by the time I finished Nellis I felt I could go on to higher levels. I survived Clay Tice's rigorous Tiger Program, and I survived the loss of close friends in a dangerous occupation. I left Nellis with a strong commitment to duty, honor, and country.

CHAPTER 5

Fighter Jet Nuclear Capability

"The supersonic evolution was now in full stride."

As I remember, there were 14 from my class at Nellis who actually graduated from the Tiger Program. Seven of us were assigned to the Far East, and seven went to Europe. We were all trained in the F-86, and we were all to continue flying F-86s in our new assignments. When the Korean War ended with an armistice agreement in mid–1953.

U.S. wings in Korea were moved to better facilities in Japan. Locations from the northern extremity of Japan to the southern extremity were selected, including Chitosi, Misawa, Nagoya, and Itazuke. My first operational unit after I completed gunnery was the 7th Fighter Bomber Squadron, 49th Fighter Group, at Itazuke.

As the Cold War wore on the United States began to develop a capability for nuclear weapons delivery in tactical fighters. This set in motion a process to train fighter pilots to carry nuclear weapons worldwide. While the F-86 in which I trained at Nellis was a very advanced aircraft, it was not capable of carrying the Mark 7, a large nuclear weapon. The F-86 nose rotation was high, causing an F-86 carrying the Mark 7 to drag in the rear on takeoff. Because the F-86 could not fly with the weapon, we had to go to a more compatible aircraft. The older F-84G jet aircraft used in Korea was selected.

Early in my stay at Itazuke, Capt. Sam Milan, a World War II veteran, checked me out in the F-84G. He was a great pilot. Since there were no two-seat fighters in those days, the instructor flew wing on the student during the checkout phase, as was done with the F-86. Sam made lasting impressions on me. He reminded me several times during our briefings not to let the airspeed get low in the F-84 Thunderjet during the final turn for landing because the aircraft was heavy and the engine slow to accelerate from low RPM. I believe he thought I did not understand the situation. He said with emphasis, "Earl, do you know what will happen if you let the airspeed get low in the final turn to landing and you shove the throttle full open to attempt recovery?" He answered his own question, saying with even more emphasis, "The engine will be running just a little faster when you hit the ground, that's what." Now I definitely understood clearly.

The F-84Gs were redesigned for nuclear weapon carriage. This was the first time that fighters were made capable of undertaking worldwide nuclear missions. Refueling in the air was necessary to accomplish the worldwide mission. The fighters had to fly long distances to reach any place in the world, mostly up to the borders of Russia and other Communist countries.

The process of in-flight refueling was unusual in itself. Holes were cut in the outboard pylon tanks (tip tanks), and 18-inch probes were welded into those tanks. A long hose was hung from the bottom of the fuel-carrying KB-29 with a drogue to dispense fuel to the fighter. To refuel, the pilot had to line up directly in the prop wash of the KB-29 inboard engine and stick the drogue with the tip tank probe to fill up the wing tank, then go over and stick the other wing tank to fill that tank while pumping the fuel from the first tank inboard. When the second wing tank was filled, the pilot would go back and re-stick the first one and fill it again. The arrangement with the tanker on top, fighter just below, took three sticks to get a full load of fuel. There were some pilots who just couldn't maneuver the fighter to air refuel. You were right behind the props of the KB-29, sitting in the prop wash, trying to hit a little

2nd Lt. Haney was assigned to the 7th Fighter bomber Squadron, Itazuke Air Base, Japan, 1955.

drogue, 18 inches in diameter, with a probe while you are jetting along at 250 miles an hour. Not an easy task.

I had been home for a visit before leaving for my assignment in Japan. Shortly after I arrived in Itazuke, bad news came my way. Mother wrote me that my little dog, Skippy, had passed away. Even worse, much worse, a week later I got a telegram with the most unexpected and unwelcome news of my entire lifetime. Mother had died of a stroke. She was only 55 years old. The thought that my beloved mother would not always be in my life had never entered my mind. The shock was devastating, something I wasn't prepared for, nor did I ever think it could happen. With a quick emergency leave, I flew back to Illinois for a few days to attend the funeral. Over the next few weeks memories of my mother were constantly on my mind. Mother was given a small Bible in her early childhood. She gave the little Bible to me when I was assigned to my tour of duty in Japan and Korea. From the time of her death, that Bible and Mother's spirit followed me wherever I

2nd Lt. Haney is flying the center aircraft during an assignment with the 7th Fighter Bomber Squadron, Itazuke Air Base, Japan, during a checkout phase in the F-84G fighter aircraft. These were the early days of Lt. Haney's association with Colonel "Iron Mike " Meroney.

KB 29 Tanker refueling an F-84G with Probe and Drogue system, 7th Fighter Bomber Squadron, 1955.

went. Her gift and her faith had reached me. I continued to attend chapel services throughout my Air Force career.

Back at work, I had to not only fly a new mission in a new airplane but also at the same time carry the heavy sorrow of the loss of my mother and Skippy. I realize looking back that everybody has to learn to deal with bereavement and in time eventually move on. I had lost my two pillars in life, my mother and Skippy, in a matter of days. I felt very alone. My new commander, Virgil K. Meroney, helped me move on in life. He kept me very busy preparing for the future.

Colonel Meroney was the 7th Squadron commander. He was known as "Iron Mike." His nickname followed his legend, a man made of iron. He had tremendous strength and never backed down from a challenge. Iron Mike was absolute in drawing the line on excuses or mistakes. Perhaps because I was 22 years old, a second lieutenant, and the youngest, most inexperienced guy in the squadron, I was assigned to fly with the "Old Man" more than most. He drilled me from the minute I got up in the morning right up to quitting time. He flew every day and always took the most demanding missions. If the weather was really bad, he would manage to be taxiing in out of the murk as the rest of us were just coming in for work. "Just checkin' the weather to see if it is okay for the rest of you," he would say.

Iron Mike demanded that every pilot work to be as good a fighter pilot as he was. He seldom bestowed praise or compliments. Iron Mike, like Boots Blesse and John Frederick Howard, believed that top pilots learned by flying to perfection. He was a great leader and a great fighter pilot. He could do anything with the airplane. Because I flew a lot with Meroney, I learned from him how to survive in a fighter environment.

Iron Mike was an ace fighter pilot in World War II. One of his compatriots recounted several episodes in Meroney's military history. He told of the time that Meroney was leading a flight of P-51s going on a combat mission when he lost an engine shortly after takeoff. He bailed out at a very low altitude but survived because his chute opened just before he hit the ground. He ran back to the flight line, jumped in another P-51, and re-joined his P-51 fighter formation—without a parachute. Later he was shot down and taken prisoner. He spent the last two years of the war in a German prison camp. The Allies liberated the prison camp in the last days of the war. According to the account, Meroney was strapped to a pole ready to be shot by a firing squad when U.S. Army tanks broke through the gates of the prison camp, saving him from certain execution. Apparently, he had made so many escape attempts that the German prison camp officials ordered death by firing squad.

When we became combat ready in the re-designed F-84G, we had to demonstrate capability, versatility, and flexibility to meet new mission requirements. Colonel Meroney, two other pilots, and I, as "Blue 4," were assigned to intercept a British Navy fleet in the Pacific about 400 miles northeast of the Philippines. Our mission was to refuel en route, intercept the fleet undetected, simulate attack, and recover at Clark Air Force Base, Manila Bay. The refueling rendezvous did not go well. The tanker was 165 miles off point, and when we did rendezvous the number three fighter "snaked" the drogue hose while disconnecting and jerked it out of the KB-29. This left me, as number four, with no gas. Iron Mike told me to attempt to make Clark AFB while the tanker initiated rescue efforts. It appeared at first I could not make Clark with existing fuel. Because the mission was of extreme importance, Colonel Meroney and the two others continued on.

I dropped the external tanks and climbed as high as the "Old Hog" would go, about 49,000 feet. At this altitude, with a very clean, light F-84, fuel specifics and cruise were much better than expected, but I had 350 miles yet to go. At approximately 100 nautical miles out from Clark, I was down to 25 gallons of fuel. I decided to shut the engine down and glide as far as I could, restart, and give myself some flexibility for whatever kind of landing, or bailout, I would be facing. The weather was undercast below me, but Clark had forecast 2,500 feet broken for our original arrival. I was just a tad early.

When I shut the engine down at this high altitude, the canopy began to frost over on the inside, and I lost pressurization, making pressure breathing difficult. Things were getting scary. A nice feature of the F-84 was that it had a sliding canopy instead of a clam shell, and you could open it in flight at slow speed without tearing it off. When I descended through 5,000 feet, I slowed the air speed to 200 and opened the canopy. In the humid climate the ice dissipated quickly. I had the homer at Clark tuned up, and it was indicating straight off the nose. I just didn't know how far away it was. I broke out below the clouds about 2,500 feet, and I could see land. I restarted the engine and pressed on. Like magic, the runway at Clark came into view. I landed, but flamed out taxiing in.

I got out, walked over to the parking ramp, lay down in the sun, and waited for Iron Mike and the others to return. Col. Meroney never showed much expression nor gave any compliments, but I could tell this time he was glad to see me. He was tough, but again his impossible mission was a complete success and demonstrated a new worldwide mission capability in jet fighters. Dance lessons on the mahogany bar were authorized in the club on this night.

Antiquated ground systems that were not really capable of accommodating high-speed fighters were still prevalent. For that reason, fighter pilots flying over Korea and Japan relied on cockpit navigation, meaning basically dead reckoning navigation, calculating time and distance from point to point with respect to aircraft speed and forecast winds.

On one occasion Colonel Meroney and I flew in the middle of the night from Japan to the Philippines to evaluate a serious accident of one our fighters. We normally flew fighters in pairs or in fours for safety reasons, to support one another in combat or in day-to-day flight. In this scenario, as in many, Meroney himself needed to be on the scene, and I flew on his wing. We went in and out of thunderstorms for the last two hours of the flight and were almost out of gas. We shot the approach the first time into Clark Air Force Base, but it was raining so hard we couldn't make sight of the field. We went around and came back for the second approach. We had radar ground-control approach there, but it was it difficult in the heavy rain for the radar to pick up two small fighters. The controller said he wasn't sure that he could help us on our final approach for landing. The ceiling was about 200 feet, and the visibility about a quarter of a mile. Meroney crawled all over him. He said, "You have that radar there to get fighters down on the ground, so you better get these two fighters down, fella!" The controller realized he was dealing with one tough soldier.

On the second approach, we landed from the ground-control approach, where I flamed out, out of gas, taxiing in. After the ground crew brought us in, all Meroney had to say was that I must have been overcontrolling the throttle because I flamed out on the way in, and he didn't. He had nothing to say about the traumatic experiences we had just gone through coming across 1,200 miles of water at night in severe thunderstorms and landing with a 200-foot ceiling. But that's the way he was.

Our return trip to our base in Japan was not much better than what we had just gone through coming in. We were going to land and refuel in Okinawa. Meroney sent me to base operations to get the weather report and file clearance. The weather at Okinawa was reported as zero ceiling, zero visibility. We were told we wouldn't be able to get in there all day. Meroney looked at the report and said, "Well, let's go direct." This meant flying from the Philippine Islands all the way to Japan non-stop. I said,

"Sir, I don't know if we can do that." He just looked at me and said, "We'll make it." He signed the clearance, and I took it back.

I was almost certain we were not going to able to get all the way to Japan. I had figured the fuel with the drag co-efficient with external tanks on and knew we could not do that distance. We took off, reached desired altitude, and in the process burned the fuel out in the external tanks. Iron Mike signaled to drop all the underslung external tanks. The airplanes were now more drag free. We climbed to almost 50,000 feet, cruised all the way back, and made a long landing descent into Itazuke. I flamed out again rolling into the chocks, but Meroney never mentioned that one. It was just another day.

Colonel Meroney and I shared other unsettling experiences — unsettling for me, that is. He had an eye problem and had to have a surgical procedure done to correct it. He was taken to Nagoya, Japan, for the surgery. He was expected to stay in the hospital post-operatively, but he insisted he had to get back to Itazuke. He called for me to come and pick him up in the two-seat T-33 to return him to Itazuke. When I arrived his eyes were bandaged, but he said we were going. Weather conditions were terrible. The rain was so hard when I left Itazuke the water on the runway was actually slowing the airplane down. It took probably an additional thousand feet of runway to get off.

By the time we left Komaki Air Base, Nagoya, a tropical typhoon was closing in on Itazuke. Nevertheless, we proceeded to Itazuke even though the rain was coming down in torrents and the wind was 45 to 50 knots on the runway. I shot the Itazuke approach the first time without success because the torrential rain made it impossible to contact the runway. I shot a low-level instrument approach four more times but never could make visual contact with the runway. The T-33 was now down to about 60 or 70 gallons of fuel. I went around again and told Colonel Meroney that it didn't look like we would be able to land. He said, "Well, what are your options?" I told him we could bail out. To jump out of an airplane in that kind of wind and the torrential rain was not an especially good option. The chances of us landing in the ocean were pretty likely — and likely also to be a decidedly unsuccessful choice given the force of the typhoon.

I determined the last and only possibility was to land at a small island or peninsula off the coast of Japan called Brady Island. On Brady Island, a 3,000-foot pierced steel planking air strip had been built for transport planes — C-47s and that type of aircraft — to take off and land during the

Korean War. Pierced steel planking was not the kind of runway that would be suitable for jet fighters. I told Colonel Meroney I thought that was our only option. His instructions to me were, "You had better make it, Lieutenant."

I let down to about 100 feet over the water. There was a low-frequency homer right in the middle of Brady Island. I tuned it up and got it right off the nose. As we went across the island, still at about 100 feet, it was raining very hard, and visibility was virtually zero, but I could see vertically down. The runway was directly below me. So I did a 90–270 degree reversal turn back into the field. By this time the T-33 was down to about 10 gallons of gas. The engine began flaming out from fuel starvation, which meant we were going to land in a few seconds, ready or not. I was about 50 feet off the water. By the time I completed the turn and got the homer back on the nose, I could see down below the aircraft, and, as luck would have it, we were right over one end of the runway. I knew, however, that a 3,000-foot runway was not going to be long enough to stop the airplane once we touched down.

Somehow I managed to make contact with the narrow landing strip. I shut the engine down and opened the canopy to increase drag to the maximum. The airplane was sliding around on the slick steel planking, but it was slowing down far more quickly than I anticipated. I could see the end of the runway coming up fast, but I got the airplane stopped just as the nose wheel went off the end of the runway into the sand. At this time the rain was coming down in torrents and the hurricane force wind was about 80 miles an hour. Again as luck would have it, I had turned into this runway and the turn was right into the wind, so I had an 80-mile-an-hour head wind that slowed the airplane immensely when I touched down.

We managed to get out of the airplane, but the wind was so strong that we could not even stand up. I got underneath the airplane on one side, and Colonel Meroney got a hold on the landing gear on the other side. We sat through four hours of winds that got up to over 100 miles an hour. We clung to the main gear under the aircraft as waves 20 to 30 feet high cascaded up and over the aircraft. In the first onslaught all the bandages were pulled off Colonel Meroney's face. The waves were relentless, and every time the water swept over us we had to hold our breath to keep from drowning. After four hours of that, I was exhausted. What amazed me most is that Iron Mike showed no fear. I was scared to death. I was absolutely petrified. He was calm, as if it were just another day at the office.

When I thought the typhoon was spent, Iron Mike warned, "No, we're in the eye of the hurricane. We have another four hours to go." I wondered whether I could withstand another four hours. As always, he was right. It took about an hour for the eye to pass over us, and then we were back into the 100-mile-an-hour winds.

We again held on to the main gear of the aircraft. The nose wheel was buried into the sand clear up to the fuselage, so the angle of the wing was negative. It did not present a surface to catch the winds, which otherwise would probably have blown the airplane, and us, off the ground. It was just luck again. We sat underneath the airplane hanging onto the main gear for another four hours. By the time the typhoon finally passed over us, it was about six or seven o'clock in the evening, still daylight.

I thought, "What do we do now?" The island base had been dismantled after the end of the Korean War. The navigation aid, the low-frequency homer, was still active, but the base was closed. We were the only inhabitants of the abandoned island. As the weather cleared a helicopter crossed the bay and landed right in the middle of the runway. I ran over to the helicopter, and the pilot shouted they were looking for Colonel Meroney and a young lieutenant who they presumed had gone down in the ocean and were lost. I said, "No, I think we're the guys you're looking for." I told him Colonel Meroney was over there under the airplane, and we were both safe. The helicopter crew was as amazed as I was that we had survived. We caught a ride back to Itazuke on the helicopter.

Meroney never said much about our narrow escape from the storm. The next morning at a pilots' briefing, the operations officer, Herb Henderson, held a short inquiry regarding the incident. When the briefing came to an end, Major Henderson turned to Colonel Meroney and said, "Our trainer airplane is over at Brady. How are we going to get it out?" Meroney never hesitated. He said, "Haney flew it in; he can fly it out."

So here I am, a young second lieutenant trying to figure out how I was going to get that airplane out when its nose was buried in the sand at the end of a pierced plank runway. A C-47 crew offered to lend a hand. We flew two 55-gallon drums of JP-4 jet fuel to Brady Island. We hand-pumped the fuel into the fuselage tank and dug the nose wheel out of the sand. A couple of sergeants and I turned the airplane around and cleaned the sand off the nose wheel. I climbed in, closed the canopy, started the aircraft, and on takeoff made a victory roll as a gesture to the crew below. Back at Itazuke, Meroney said little, but the next day at a pilots' meeting, he looked right at me with those piercing blue eyes and said, "It's a goddamn good thing that roll was a good one." What Iron Mike was saying was that whatever I did, he would know about it. That was another lesson about discipline, but I also sensed a measure of pride that some of his teaching had rubbed off.

I had a run of good luck in the landing on Brady Island, but I had a run of bad luck the next year when I had to pilot three dead-stick landings in a row. Dead-stick landings were not all that unusual during the earlier stages of jet development. In the 1950s jet engine experience and technology were scarce. Much of our experience in fighter jets still was being learned by trial and error. The wear and tear on the earliest jets was beginning to show. The F-84s had just completed the Korean War with heavy use, since the war had been engaged in extensive high-speed, high-G flight training for the new worldwide nuclear fighter role.

"Dead stick" means the engine is out, leaving the aircraft to function basically as a glider. The airplane will have to land without engine power. In a high-performance airplane, this can be difficult because the pilot must maintain adequate speed coupled with enough air space to negotiate a landing from about 5,000 feet above the field. The pilot must set up a standard rate turn and make a 360-degree descending turn to land at a prescribed place on the runway. The aircraft must maintain minimal speed and still descend at a rate that will maintain enough energy to get to the landing strip but not so much energy that it overshoots the runway.

The first dead-stick landing occurred as my flight was leaving our deployment in Osan, Korea. I took off on the right wing of my flight commander, Capt. Don Pascoe. As we climbed through 14,000 feet, the engine began to vibrate violently. There was an explosion, and the fire warning light came on. During the severe vibrations the instrument panel came loose from its upper mount and fell in my lap. At this point, with all the smoke and vibration, my thought was to get out of the plane, as these conditions would indicate. But that idea was out because the instrument panel was in my lap, restricting control stick movement. The smoke cleared, and everything became very quiet. Clearly, the engine was dead. I was able to lift the instrument panel from my lap so I could move the control stick. I proceeded to nearby Osan and made an uneventful dead-stick landing. When I got out of the aircraft, I went behind and looked up the tail pipe. Some of the engine had gone out the rear with some turbine pieces going out the sides. I could see that I had lost a turbine blade.

The turbine, a huge steel wheel, causes accelerated gas to go out the exhaust pipe at the rear of the engine, creating thrust. These turbines are subjected to extreme heat through the power process of the engine, causing parts to wear out in time. In the course of day after day of cooling and heating, cooling and heating, the turbines show wear, and cracks develop. Apparently, the jet I was flying developed a crack in one of the turbine blades, and eventually broke off. The broken blades created a tremendous imbalance. A turbine back in those days would probably turn at about 11,000 RPM. Today the rate is much higher, up to 30,000 to 32,000 RPM. Regardless, when an engine loses one of the blades, as happened in this event, the engine quits and the pilot is without power. There are only two options: He can bail out, or he can attempt to dead stick the aircraft to the nearest possible landing field.

I hitched a ride from Osan back to Itazuke on a C-119 cargo plane. The following day I was scheduled to take an F-84 to the overhaul facility near Nagoya, Japan. My second dead-stick landing occurred when my flight commander and I were climbing out of Itazuke in solid weather. As we reached 24,000 feet, I realized the power was decreasing, even with the throttle against the wall. I was losing power rapidly. I glided to the Iwakuni homer and commenced a standard rate turn from the homer. At about 5,000 feet altitude, I hoped I would break out of the weather with enough altitude to dead stick into the Navy Airfield at Iwakuni. As I descended through 5,000 feet, making my turn away from the station, I began to break out of the clouds. I saw part of the runway, which was almost underneath me. From here this dead-stick landing was "a piece of cake." So again I needed a ride. Apparently the Navy appreciated my not splashing an aircraft on their turf, and they gave me a ride to Tokyo, where I was scheduled to take an aircraft from the overhaul facility southwest of Tokyo the following day en route to Bangkok, Thailand.

The next morning my flight companions and I took four F-84s from the Mitsubishi overhaul facility with a scheduled stop in Yakota, Japan. This short flight gave us the opportunity to check out the aircraft in flight, and Yakota provided a runway long enough to take off with the aircraft at maximum load: four 230-gallon external tanks, two wing-tip tanks, and two underslung tanks. It was a long way to Bangkok, and we needed the fuel. After briefing, we started and taxied to Yakota's long runway. Again, I was on the right wing of the lead aircraft. We had calculated a 5,900-foot takeoff roll. As we started the roll, I remembered that my last two F-84 takeoffs had not been too effective. "There ain't no way" it could happen three times in a row. But it did.

The takeoff took us over the edge of Tokyo. We stayed low, accelerating the heavy jets to climb speed. As we reached 270 knots, my jet started losing power very smoothly. My heart began to react very un-smoothly. The hex was on me. I attempted a quick restart without success. By this time, I could see the rooftops were very close. Although the flight manual procedure with engine out, no start below 2,500 feet, was to eject, it just didn't seem like the thing to do — to leave a fully fueled fighter in downtown Tokyo. I edged the Old Hog down a dry creek bed and reached for the external-store salvo switch. I felt the tanks separate with a heavy "whomp." I pulled the stick back to gain some altitude, and the aircraft went into an uncontrollable roll to the right. The right tip tank had not released with the other three tanks. As the aircraft rolled very low to the ground, I reached for the manual jettison release handle. The tank came off about two-thirds through the roll. The momentum threw the tank above the aircraft, and it hit the rear of the canopy and fuselage. I saw it coming. It looked more like a 230-*thousand*-gallon tank than a 230 gallon.

I had 250 knots to negotiate with. I eased up to about 500 feet, hoping for some sort of major breakthrough in the world of uncertainty I was in. The visibility along the coastline was not more than a mile, which was not uncommon in the fall when farmers burned rice fields and created large plumes of smoke. I kept my eyes focused on the windscreen, thinking, "What am I going to do now?" As I strained to see ahead, I made out what appeared to be a concrete slab slightly off to the right. I turned toward it and realized it was a concrete strip. I also realized I would probably not be able to make it because my airspeed was bleeding off too fast. I decided to try and make it to the overrun and go in gear up. As I approached the overrun, I saw it appeared to have a smooth surface. I quickly grabbed the emergency gear-release lanyard. The main gear dropped out and locked down a full second before they touched the ground. The nose wheel required air pressure to lock down in the emergency mode, taking a little longer than the main. I rolled onto the concrete with the nose wheel still unlocked. It locked down just as it touched the concrete.

I was at Atsugi, Japan, just south of Tokyo, on the coastline. As I rolled to a stop, I pushed the mike button and reported to my flight leader that I was okay. A couple of Navy fighter pilots close by had heard the radio conversations and observed my approach to Atsugi. One said, "You lucky bastard!" Truer words were never spoken.

Dead-stick landings happen, but it would be pretty unusual for one guy to have three in a row. After those three flights, one of my friends said to me, "Haney, you are an optimist if you take your lunch to work on your next flight." Thanks, I needed that.

The first two dead-stick landings were not quite as eventful as the last one. In the first one, the airplane vibrated so severely as a consequence of the broken turbine blade that the instrument panel came loose from the top mounts. Under normal conditions I would have ejected from the airplane because the cockpit was full of smoke and it was vibrating severely. As it turned out, I was able to land, albeit without engine power, without further incident. The second dead-stick landing was caused by engine failure, the most common problem in flying earlier jets. The compressor started leaking, interfering with adequate engine thrust. I was over Iwakuni, Japan, a naval air station, and landed safely. I was getting better at dead-stick landings.

The third one was really iffy. Air Force safety personnel threatened to take disciplinary action against me. By Air Force standard procedures, if engine failure occurs below 2,500 feet, the pilot has only one choice, and that is to bail out. I chose to attempt to land because of the existing conditions: I chose not to leave a fully fueled fighter to crash in a highly populated area. A lot of innocent people could be affected, or killed. Nevertheless, I was faulted for my decision to dead stick as opposed to the "by the book" direction to eject.

The case against me was being pursued by a flying safety "expert" from behind his high-speed desk. My case, with three back-to-back landings in engineless fighter jets, was not dissimilar to other unusual military cases. Someone wants to discipline, and someone wants to reward. The manual doesn't cover this kind of unusual situation, and cannot, because of the multitude of possibilities. The military manual has a rule for many possible situations, but the manual procedures can only be guidelines as to what should be done under normal conditions or under emergency conditions. How often does a pilot wind up with an airplane without an engine over downtown Tokyo? A disabled fighter jet over a large city doesn't happen very often; it's not in the book. But that's where I found myself.

Colonel Meroney heard about the dead-stick case and came to my defense. I was never interviewed by the Air Force Safety Board, other than by Colonel Meroney. He was highly respected within the whole Air Force community, and when he spoke, people listened. I don't know exactly how he handled it, but apparently he said, "the lieutenant made the correct decision, at risk to his own life, and that's the end of the subject." Apparently he argued that Lieutenant Haney used good judgment in very difficult circumstances and should be applauded not prosecuted. I know if he thought I had done something out of line, he would have landed on me with both feet himself. In the end, I received the Far East Air Force Able Aeronaut award for judgment and success under extremely unusual circumstances.

The week following the safety board hearing, Itazuke Air Base received the new F-100D jet fighters. The F-100 was the first supersonic fighter airplane fully designed for nuclear missions. The supersonic evolution was now in full stride. The F-100 was a very high-speed, high-performance airplane. The airplane was loaded with new technology. The flight control was more advanced. The airplane had an afterburner, more power, newly designed swept wings, and an improved air refueling system. The cockpit design, the instrumentation, and other features were a quantum leap beyond the F-84.

The F-100 had a lot of power; it was a good airplane to fly. But it also had all the idiosyncrasies of high-performance airplanes, which fly very well at high speeds but are difficult to maneuver at lower speeds. The stability of an airplane that is designed for high speed can become critical when flying at lower speeds and in landing patterns. We had accidents as we transitioned in the F-100 because the performance of the airplane, the controllability and stability, was decisively different from that of the F-84.

I always looked forward to the advent of a new airplane. I compared it to buying a new car. The new models looked good and smelled new. Best of all, I enjoyed the challenge of the new technology. Each new jet model was better than the previous one. And I loved flying with Meroney. He just had the natural feel for the airplane. In no time at all he could fly the F-100 to its maximum performance.

Our relationship with the Soviet Union and other Communist countries was strained in the era of the Cold War. Because East-West tensions could turn the Cold War into a hot war at any time, the United States and its allies were on constant war readiness, as was the enemy behind the Iron Curtain.

We continued to train in the new airplane. Our missions required flights as long as eight hours, designed to simulate wartime missions in the event of nuclear war. We trained for atomic weapon delivery. We dropped weapons that were exactly the same configuration as the real weapon but that would not be armed with nuclear materials unless and until we actually had to go to war.

In all tactical fighter weapons delivery there are tactics and maneuvers to insure target effectiveness and safety of the delivery aircraft. The tactic for delivering nuclear weapons from fighters is more difficult because of

The F-100D Super Sabre was the first supersonic nuclear weapon-carrying aircraft employed by the USAF. First Lt. Haney flew the F-100D during the Cold War era.

the thermal effects and radiation as well as the blast envelope of nuclear weapons. The delivery aircraft must exit the target area by several miles to insure he is outside the lethal envelope of the atomic weapon.

The maneuver most used in tactical fighter nuclear delivery is called the "Over the Shoulder" method. The fighter moves toward the target at high-speed low altitude, masking himself from enemy fire and radar detection. Over the target the pilot accelerates the aircraft to a vertical attitude, releasing the weapon at approximately 7,000 to 8,000 feet altitude. The weapon continues upward to approximately 20,000 feet before it reverses and commences earthward to the target. This allows the delivery fighter time to exit the target area before weapon impact, providing him safe return home.

Once a month we would have to fly a profile mission that exactly replicated the mission we would fly in actual wartime. We would fly the same amount of time with the same navigational problems that we would incur if we actually flew into a real target area. We did not ever infiltrate enemy air space, risking interception, being shot down, or worse. We took flights to controlled allied countries — generally destinations north and northwest of Japan — designed to simulate distance and conditions of an actual wartime mission.

My own mission was eight hours long, which would have taken me well up into Russia. I had to refuel every two or three hours, which would be at least two refuelings, sometimes three. I would go out and refuel, simulate the mission, go back and refuel about two-thirds of the way through the mission, and fly back to my final destination. Normally we flew in flights of four, but on these simulated wartime missions we usually flew single ship: one F-100, one pilot, alone, without support.

Missions of this nature required refueling in the air from KB-50 cargo air tankers. The KB-50 had a newly designed drogue that dispensed fuel from the end of the wing rather than requiring the airplane to maintain a critical position behind the tanker. With the drogues out on the end of the wing, we didn't sit right in the prop wash as we had in the F-84. In the F-100 we had to stick the drogue only once to get a full load of gas, compared to three sticks in the F-84. The KB-50 tanker could dispense fuel to the fighter three times faster than an F-84 refueling. It could take a full load in eight to ten minutes, compared to the 20 to 30 minutes needed to refuel the F-84. This was a great advancement for the fighter pilot.

The evolution of the era of supersonic flight started with primitive jets that advanced with each new iteration to the technological capabilities of the safer and more sophisticated jet aircraft of today. This was a very active and fast-moving two years for me. We were just beginning the mission of hauling nuclear weapons and achieving worldwide nuclear strike capability in jet fighters. A lot was happening. I flew probably 1,200 hours of fighter time during this two-year period. That's roughly 50 to 60 hours a month. I learned lessons from Colonel Meroney in these days of the development of fighters and fighter capabilities that have stayed with me forever. I learned a lot about aviation, character, and integrity. He showed me that there is no point at which you give up; you go on no matter what. I thought the world of him.

Ten years later in the Southeast Asian War I returned to the Far East as a fighter pilot assigned to the 8th Tactical Fighter Wing at Ubon, Thailand. Remarkably, Iron Mike Meroney was there, serving as vice commander of the wing. His effect on me had never faded through all the experiences I would have in the ten years since we had flown together in Japan and Korea. His strength and courage did not fade either, as I can attest from our combat experience together.

CHAPTER 6

Flight Test

"Trial and error."

In my last few months in Japan, I started doing flight tests on aircraft that had undergone extensive maintenance. Ground crews had gone through the aircraft with a fine-toothed comb, both for scheduled maintenance and for repairs, but the Air Force wanted the jets to have test flights before taking them on normal operations. In this way, the safety of the pilot and plane was assured by checking for any possible remaining mechanical failure or anomaly. The crew usually completed maintenance assignments by the end of the week, and on Saturdays I flew test flights in F-84s and F-100s. The aircraft would then be readied and released for operational use on Monday.

By early 1957 I was fully qualified in the F-100 and even more confident and comfortable in the fighter world than I had been when I left the F-86 at Nellis. Test-flying fighters in Japan triggered my desire to dig further into the envelope of the jet fighter. I was interested in learning more about how the airplanes fly, why they fly, and the technology behind them. When I completed my assignment in Japan — I had been promoted to first lieutenant in the summer of 1956 — I was sent to Bryan Air Force Base in Texas, where I was assigned to Flight Test. I spent eight months at Bryan and flew about 860 test flights before I began formal qualification as a test pilot.

At this time, aviation testing was largely a trial-and-error system; experience with high-performance aircraft and technology was still in short supply but in great demand. Aircraft were designed and built with existing technology and then flown to the limits of the required envelope to insure the machine was sound and operable in its flight envelope. Jet development depended a great deal on test pilots putting prototype jets under stressful flying conditions to see how well they would stand up. Many pilots and planes were lost in this process. This was a dangerous environment, very unforgiving for error and malfunction, and losses in flight test were very high.

Then, we did not yet know a great deal about the dynamics of flying jets. The slower propeller-driven fighters in World War II were easier to spin and easier for the pilot to recover in out-of-control conditions. But jet fighters were very difficult to get out of a spin, and the higher speed required a larger flying space in which to maneuver. Because of the design and extreme dynamics in the jet-fighter environment, high-performance aircraft do not react in a conventional manner when they depart from controlled flight. Out-of-control flight was sometimes encountered, usually resulting in the loss of the aircraft.

This problem, combined with the need for critical flight control and aircraft rigging, made out-of-control evaluation and knowledge a primary issue. Development of a spin program became a priority at Bryan Air Force Base, and the Flight Test crew was given the task. My first intentional fully developed spin was approached with great care. Spinning a jet aircraft is more nerve-wracking than any carnival ride known to man, but, like anything, once you learn the mechanics and become acclimated to the situation, it is not all that bad.

I learned a great deal about high-performance flight dynamics after hundreds of spins in every imaginable configuration and attitude. Attempts were made at Bryan to develop "out-of-control maneuverability" into fighter flight-training programs. On more than one occasion in Training Command and Tactical Air Command, we attempted to incorporate this training. We demonstrated this by taking well-qualified pilots (but untrained in high-performance spin) and exposing them to their first "out-of-control" situation. The first encounter was always disaster, but once the pilots were shown the mechanics and procedures for responding to an out-of-control situation, recovery became a walk in the park. However, because it was believed the expense and hazards of training were too great, the program has never been incorporated in fighter training. Considering the number of fighter aircraft lost in out-of-control spins over the years (in the hundreds) and the ease of training that could have avoided losses, I believe failure to provide this training was, and is, a mistake.

An out-of-control spin is critical whenever it happens, but it is better to experience it in a controlled environment than one day finding yourself flailing through the air trying to figure out which way is up, a situation that results in not only loss of the aircraft but also many times the loss of the pilot. This training might not save all the unintentional out-of-control incidents, but I would bet it would be up in the 90 percent range. There was also a great secondary, or maybe even the primary, benefit: the increased confidence the pilot developed by understanding how to fly the airplane no matter in what condition he found himself. It just made him a better pilot.

(Today, a new Air Force plane is subject to laboratory research testing and computer modeling before a test pilot actually takes the plane on a flight test. In this way the bugs in a new plane can be minimized in the laboratory, reducing the loss of life and the destruction of multi-million-dollar airplanes that occurred before the days of laboratory testing.)

I believe that the experience I gained in high performance flight dynamics in this exposure was one of the best life insurance policies I ever obtained. Flying, itself, is a dangerous environment. High-performance aviation in an extremely dynamic environment is unforgiving of error and malfunction. In combat, this is even more so. The more you can learn about flight and the better you train yourself for the extremities of the envelope, the better pilot you are and the longer you will survive. Unfortunately, formal training programs and the printed documents do not encompass all you are faced with in the total flight environment: ultimately the pilot is still responsible for controlling all situations in the air—and surviving.

At this stage of my Air Force career, I was experienced and comfortable in the air. I knew how to fly, but I wanted to know more about the principle of flight itself—the propulsion systems, the electronic systems, the hydraulics, and the very engineering process that allowed man to build a machine that can fly faster than the speed of sound. To go on and become a qualified test pilot I needed more engineering knowledge, and I needed some academic knowledge to be able to understand why the airplane does what it does. So, happily, I was assigned to attend the Maintenance Engineering School at Chanute Air Force Base, Illinois, to complete my flight test qualification. I arrived at Chanute, which was close to my home in Champaign, in January 1958. There I spent one year in intense academic training for all the engineering processes of tactical fighters. I had been married on December 28, 1957, before I left Bryan Air Force Base, and my twin boys, Mike and Max, were born in Champaign. Marriage and children made a big change in my life.

The Maintenance Engineering School presented a new challenge. It was a difficult year. I only had a high school degree, and most of the Air Force schooling was designed for a higher educational level. So initially the academics were not easy for me, as I had to get to the level they were teaching. Once I crossed that bridge I never had difficulty. I just had to spend extra time and work. Throughout my Air Force career, academics started out hard, but once I got up to speed I got along fine. I never had any trouble with the flying part. I stayed completely current and flew almost every day. I went to school in the mornings and usually would fly in the afternoons.

When I went to Chanute, high-performance flight activity in jet airplanes was in its early stages. All the technology in terms of the propulsions for aircraft and the flight dynamics of high-performance airplanes was being surfaced. So at Chanute I had the opportunity to get in on that ground floor and learn a great deal about what was known to that point. At this time there was increased development of experimental flight testing, and the Air Force was expanding the academic aspects of the Experimental Flight Test School (later to become the school for the astronauts). I received the Air Force Specialty Code (AFSC) as a qualified test pilot, which at that time was an F-4344 Flight Test Capable. (The AFSC 2865 for testing later encompassed the more complex aviation and space requirement including more computer modeling engineering evaluation than had the previous trial-and-error flight test method.)

When I graduated from school at Chanute there was a slot available at Edwards Air Force Base, California, and the home of the Air Force Flight Test Center. I asked to be sent there. I was now a qualified test pilot under the criteria at that time, and I received the assignment. Lucky again. In December 1958 I arrived at Edwards — the best place in the world for flight tests of high-performance machinery. The heated international competition in developing cutting-edge military jet aircraft, and later space travel, made Edwards a top national defense base. The Cold War with the Soviet Union and the launching of Sputnik had opened the eyes of our government leaders, and Edwards was becoming a beehive of activity. Flying aircraft at Mach 1 speed and beyond was accomplished at Edwards. Early training of astronauts for future space travel became a part of the Flight Test Center. The Air Force assigned top-notch pilots to Edwards.

I was associated with the best test pilots and programs in the world during this era. I was only 25 years old, and most of the guys at Edwards — Pete "Speedy" Everst, Chuck Yeager, Bob White, Ivan Kinchloe, Bob

Rushworth, and other pilots—were 10 to 12 years older. I was just a kid by comparison. Most of these men were also World War II veterans with battle scars and medals. But I had accumulated substantial jet time for my age and career so far. This experience was of great benefit in this new environment. My experience in several different aircraft was also beneficial in this test mission because aviation and flight test were expanding at a rapid rate during the 1950s and 1960s. There were many new aircraft to evaluate: rockets, fighters, bombers, cargo, and helicopters. This was another place where I learned every day, as the whole system of high-performance technology began to be developed also for space travel.

But there was another side to life at Edwards: as a young lieutenant and the youngest guy in the fighters, I was the one assigned to do all the little chores that nobody else wanted to do. For example, when a large party was planned at the club someone decided that we could buy liquor really cheap if we went to Mexico. I was assigned to fly to El Paso, Texas, cross the border into Mexico, and buy as much tequila and Oso Negra gin and vodka as allowed. Some of the liquor went for as little as 85 cents a fifth. I remember the tequila because each bottle had a little worm in it. To this day I won't drink tequila. I returned to the airplane and packed all the bottles in the gun bay. The gun bay of the airplane is not pressurized, so whatever the ambient pressure, that's what it is in the gun bay. As you increase in altitude that pressure decreases. I took off from El Paso en route to Edwards and encountered thunderstorms at about 23,000 feet. I climbed to almost 40,000 feet to get over the thunderstorms.

When I landed at Edwards and opened the gun bay all the corks and caps had exploded off the bottles and let the liquor out in the gun bay. I thought, well, the mission is over. I did what I was supposed to do. I reported the situation and was told, "Lieutenant, we don't have the goods, so you will have to return to El Paso and get what we sent you for the first time." I got in the airplane and went back to El Paso. This time I stayed below 25,000 feet regardless of the weather because I had been told that the pressure below 25,000 feet was adequate to keep the caps on the bottles. I got back to Edwards, all of the bottles survived, and we had a big party.

While I was at Edwards the older pilots had a great time playing jokes on me. One of the guys on the T-38 project used snuff all the time, and his oxygen mask reeked of it. Once when I was going out to fly a T-38, someone stuck his oxygen mask on my helmet. They all watched from a window while I put the mask on and realized I was wearing Swart Nelson's terrible-smelling oxygen mask. Hap Palaga, who ran the personal equipment section — parachutes, helmets, and other gear — planned another memorable prank. He had a menagerie of animals used for the survival school at Edwards. He had trapped two bobcats up in the mountains and caged them on the base.

One Monday morning when I was going out to fly, the pranksters placed a tarpaulin over the bobcats' cage, which was just outside the building window. They tied a string to the tarp and ran it inside the window. When I went out around the corner of the building with my helmet and parachute, they pulled the cover off the cage. I was right next to two snarling and growling bobcats. I threw my parachute and helmet away, and ran all the way across the ramp to the taxiway. When I felt safe, I turned around and saw all the guys standing in the window of the parachute shop laughing at this young lieutenant scattering himself all across the area. It seemed that I was destined to be the victim of the best of the local jokes, but I got a laugh out of them, too.

At Edwards I was a project officer assigned to a range of projects, taking on one at a time. My first undertaking was the F-108, a new Mach 3 intercept fighter built by the North American Corporation. I had this occasion to work with Bob Hoover, a test pilot for North American. I first met Bob in Japan when he demonstrated the technology of the F-86, a fighter employed in the Korean War. I developed a closer relationship with Bob Hoover as we spent time together working on the F-108 project at Edwards.

The F-108 was discontinued a year or so after it began because of the expense and because the United States was then becoming involved with ICBM missiles. The same thing happened with the B-70, a Mach 3 bomber. The B-70 was the aircraft that was going to open up supersonic travel for commercial airlines throughout the world. These two aircraft were so expensive that they never came into production. We did continue some development with the B-70 as a test bed for supersonic airlines, but the rest of the program was scrubbed. The one B-70 prototype test bed was lost in an accident, ending this most significant test program.

I was able to meet with Bob Hoover on a regular basis over the four years I was at Edwards. He lived in Los Angeles and flew the initial flights of North American airplanes, including the F-86 and the F-100. He also flew demonstrations all over the country for North American. He did an unbelievable demonstration in the P-51, a World War II fighter, and the T-39, a twin jet executive aircraft. If he couldn't answer a question, his staff or his flight test engineers could. Hoover spent his entire working life airborne as a fighter pilot and civilian test pilot. He went on to do demonstrations all over the world. He could take the aircraft to its outer limits, to an extent that even his contemporaries said couldn't be done. Bob led the way in making the new jet technology commonplace in the mainstream of the U.S. Air Force. He was an absolute master in the air, and his talent became known worldwide.

I learned every day from him. I followed him just as I had followed Colonel Meroney. Every day, if Bob Hoover did it, I wanted to do it. He once wrote an article that came out in an aviation magazine. The title was "Be an Old Smoothie." The theme of the article was to fly the airplane as smoothly as possible: to overcontrol high performance airplanes could end in disaster. He argued that even in out-of-control maneuvers, the pilot must be very smooth with the fast-moving jet. "Don't be a rough rider with the aircraft," he would say. "Be soft with the controls, and the airplane will fly dynamically." I applied the adage "Be an Old Smoothie" throughout my Air Force career. Hoover's thesis still applies in today's flying environment.

Bob was a daring test pilot, and test pilots were supposed to take the airplane to its outer limits. Hoover had over 30 accidents, barely surviving several of the more severe ones. Once he tried to dead stick an F-100 with a deficient emergency hydraulic control system. Because of the loss of hydraulics, things got a bit tense at the end of the flight. The F-100 crashed, and Hoover's back was broken in several places. But he had been able to bring in the lifeless plane under dead-stick circumstances and survive to continue test piloting. This event was a learning experience in the art of flying disabled planes. I experienced a similar dilemma several years later. Because of having learned how Bob had handled it, I was able to survive a similar dead-stick landing. When I had a mid-air collision on the way to Europe for Thunderbird shows, he heard about the accident and called me from Los Angeles in the middle of the night to see if I was okay. Bob was genuinely concerned about my condition.

I have often said, if you didn't like Bob Hoover, you didn't like anyone. He had an effervescent personality. He looked like he could have been president of a corporation — a tall, good-looking guy with a happy attitude that just absorbed people. He was never hard on others, and I never heard him raise his voice. He was always a team player, yet he was the guy who was the leader of the team. Hoover was a leader who led through example. In comparison, Colonel Meroney was a very strong disciplinarian; if Iron Mike asked you to do something, you had better find a way to do it. Hoover was a lot softer and easier on everyone. As much as I admired Colonel Meroney and now General Blesse, we were not "friends." They were hardened leaders. With Hoover it was a smooth friendship, and we accomplished things together. I had such great respect for him — for his ability, for his character, for his personality.

Bob Hoover has been a major figure in aviation, especially fighter aviation, for more than 50 years. He's the guy that everybody knows as the world's greatest fighter pilot. He and Chuck Yeager are close friends, but they have very different personalities. For years Bob led the air races at Reno, Nevada. He would fly the lead airplane to start the unlimited class. I used to go there whenever possible and spend the day with him. One of my last contacts with Bob occurred several years ago when I was consulting with the Federal Aviation Administration. I talked with him several times to seek his advice as he had had some previous difficulties with this agency. In my opinion, Bob Hoover was the best test pilot ever. A number of people might exceed him in aviation academics, but for pure guts and stick capability, I don't think anybody could get close to Hoover. He's one of a kind.

I moved from the F-108 to a unique aircraft called a helioplane, a short takeoff and landing aircraft (STOL) to be used in remote areas. It had a big turboprop engine and leading and trailing edge flaps for slow flights. The helioplane, the L-28, was engineered to take advantage of dynamic control for very low speeds at takeoffs and landings, while maintaining a reasonable cruise speed. I worked on the helioplane project for nearly eight months. As we went through the program, we came to the realization that the L-28 would not live up to the requirements and specifications of the Air Force. It was too small for carrying troops and heavy loads. The concept of the helioplane was good, but the aircraft just wasn't big enough. The Air Force needed something more practical like the C-130 or the C-123 — larger aircraft with short takeoffs and landings capable of carrying heavier loads. The L-28 program was cancelled in the early research stage. The aircraft was very different from the fighter jets that I was used to piloting, but it was a very fun plane to fly.

I later spent six weeks with the U.S. Navy VX-74 Squadron in Oceana, Virginia, evaluating the F-4 Phantom, which was being produced as a fleet interceptor for the Navy. The F-4 was a proven fighter, already operational in the Navy, and its reputation was such that the Air Force sent a special task force to analyze the F-4 to see if it would be suitable also for Air Force missions. The Navy's mission requirements for the F-4 weren't nearly as extensive as those of the Air Force. Our mission requirements included a nuclear mission, special weapons missions, and air-to-air and air-to-ground missions. The Navy's requirement for the F-4 was mostly fleet defense, to fly off of a carrier and defend Navy ships, or, in offense mode, to attack enemy ships or submarines. Our assignment, called Operation High Speed, was to analyze the aircraft to see if it could be modified to meet the Air Force requirements. The F-4 fit the bill in all cases. It was a good airplane, a safe airplane, high performing, and easy to train and maintain for this time and era.

We concluded that the F-4 lived up to its expectations. With some modifications for incorporation of the Air Force requirements, little transformation beyond the Navy's specifications was necessary. The airplane, we determined, would be a very suitable fighter for the Air Force. The rest is aviation history. The F-4 was produced in great numbers and was the backbone of high-performing tactical fighters for the Air Force for more than 20 years, completing thousands of missions in the Cold War environment and in the Vietnam War. I myself flew the Phantom in Tactical Air Command and in 214 combat missions in the Vietnam War. I also instructed, flying the Phantom, for two years in the Air Force "Top Gun" school. The F-4 Phantom is a rugged, mean fighter that will get you there and back if you will just be "an old smoothie," as Bob Hoover said.

On one of my flights into Oceana while working with the Navy there, I made a stop at Chanute Air Force Base. It was about ten o'clock at night, and there was a severe line of thunderstorms northeast of Chicago going all the way down into the Oklahoma-Texas area. During pilot training we were told that an aircraft couldn't be struck by lightning and absorb the electrical energy while airborne. I found out later that wasn't the case at all: I was a young second lieutenant leaving Korea en route to Japan crossing through a line of thunderstorms. Normally we did not worry about going through thunderstorms because the airplanes are very rugged. You might get some severe turbulence, but the aircraft, I thought, were never really damaged.

On this particular day I went right through a dark thunderstorm cell. Inside it gets very dark quickly. Lightning did strike, and it did penetrate my airplane. It burned out all the electrical systems in the airplane. It shattered the sight radar antenna. It shattered the running lights. It dismantled and destroyed anything that had the electrical source running through it. I had no instruments, no radio, no communications of any kind. The engine continued to run because the engine doesn't depend on electrical power. It gets started electrically, but fuel flow is all mechanically operated.

I received a severe shock physically, and was stunned to the point of losing partial consciousness for a few seconds. After I realized what had happened, it was back to work as usual. I flew out of the thunderstorm into clear skies all the way to Japan. I went on to Itazuke and landed without incident.

Now, in 1960, I was climbing out from Chanute and went right into another thunderstorm at a bad altitude of 15,000 to 16,000 feet. Thunderstorms are easy to see at night because lightning strikes are like lanterns lighting up the dark skies. I could see the flashes from the lightning and decided to weave my T-33 between the storm cells. I took my second lightning jolt while going between the two thunderstorms. As with my first experience flying into Japan, the lightning incapacitated me for a few seconds — I don't know exactly how long. It was quite a jolt. Again I had no electrical equipment whatsoever. No instruments, no navigation equipment, and no radio communication. I didn't really know what I could do from here. It was the black of night with cloud cover below me and no visibility in the darkened cabin of the T-33. I always carried a small pen flashlight with me in the cockpit, and it certainly came in handy this time. I used the flashlight to shine on the magnetic compass to turn south, assuming I would fly out of the line of thunderstorms and the frontal system.

I continued to fly south until I saw some lights begin to appear below as the cloud cover began to break up. I saw a good-sized city after about an hour and a half, so I started to let down, assuming there would be an airport around a city of that size. I did locate a lighted runway near the town. I committed to approach there, but I had no radio contact with anybody. I landed, taxied in, but did not know where I was until I

A T-33 Demonstration Team, Edwards AFB, 1960. The demonstration team performed local shows in the Edwards AFB area to represent fighter capabilities to the public. First Lt. Haney is flying the right wing position.

saw the words "Birmingham, Alabama" on the tower. I stopped the airplane, walked inside one of the airport buildings and called the tower. I asked, "Did you have an unidentified fighter just land on your runway?" Someone in the tower said, "Yeah, we're trying to figure out who it is." I said, "Well, it was me, and I'm right here, right below you, and all is well."

As in all cases, the aircraft was repaired and returned to service. I went on to Oceana, Virginia, and flew Navy aircraft for some of the remaining mission requirements on Operation High Speed. I thought a lot about my two experiences with lightning strikes. Nearly every day pilots encounter every possible weather condition, sometimes severe, sometimes not. After my experiences with lightning strikes I was much more cautious when penetrating thunderstorms and flying through turbulent weather.

In early 1960, I was promoted to captain and assigned to the new T-

T-38s in diamond formation, 1961. These were the first production aircraft that toured USAF pilot training bases demonstrating supersonic training aircraft. 1st Lt Haney is flying in the right-wing position over Edwards AFB, California.

38 trainer and N-156 fighter, a program that lasted a couple of years. The N-156 was the early version of the F-5 Freedom Fighter. By this time I had a fair amount of flight test and program experience at Edwards. This was an innovative program, coming at a time when maintenance of the aircraft was being evaluated with much more scrutiny and consideration. Creating easier maintenance and better reliability resulted in having flyable aircraft for longer time periods. The safety factors were beginning to get very strong consideration, too, given the high cost of losses due to accidents. Airplanes were not cheap to produce anymore, and preventable losses were not acceptable. The J-85 engine in the T-38/F-5 incorporated some new technology, including a newer lightweight, very-high-RPM engine, developing exceptional thrust for its size. It was a very efficient engine — too efficient. Most jet engines will reach "compressor stall" if the engine begins to overspeed. Not the J-85. It will continue to wind up until it self-destructs, which it did several times. It was a nerve-wracking experience when the RPM started crawling over 100 percent and the throttle was ineffective, knowing that it would not be long before the "big bang" (engine failure). Unfortunately, this problem did its share of damage and injury before it was fixed by installing an overspeed governor to automatically cut the fuel flow when throttle control was ineffective and maximum engine RPM was reached.

Transition into the new T-38, the Talon, was greatly enhanced by the new high-performance technology, especially in the instrument flight area. The new cockpit design and instrumentation called the "Flight Director" was easy to interpret and adapt to. The rapid accelerating engine and high thrust-to-weight configuration made things easy also. The T-38 became a major turning point in meeting the expanding training requirements in the new supersonic high-performance aviation world. During the test project, we took the four project T-38s (597, 598, 599, and 600) and toured USAF training command bases demonstrating this new versatile supersonic airplane, soon to be incorporated into the Air Force inventory. For over 50 years the T-38 has been a backbone aircraft for pilot training, test support, lead-in training for fighter pilots, and astronaut flight proficiency. The F-5 (the T-38 sister aircraft) was also successful with the USAF, as well as for other countries throughout the Free World, during this same period.

Many notable events occurred at Edwards AFB during this era of aviation expansion. The first woman to go supersonic accomplished this in a T-38 in the early 1960s with then–Col. Chuck Yeager as her instructor.

Jacqueline Cochran, the famed aviatrix from World War II, performed this extraordinary feat. This added requirement to the T-38 test project was not easy to absorb. Her checkout in the Talon took limited project missions away from us until she could go solo and break the sound barrier. We had to "double-up to catch-up" to keep the test program on schedule. We finished the T-38 Talon test on time; Jackie Cochran was the fastest lady in the world; all was worthwhile.

Developing the instruments in the T-38 supersonic trainer and F-5 fighter was among my projects. The instrument and navigation systems in the earlier airplanes were not well developed, but I had gained a great deal of experience using cockpit instruments in navigating inclement weather over the past several years. My instrument skills gave me an opportunity to engage in my assignment to improve instrument flying in operational, training, and research programs at Edwards.

During my time at Edwards, I had completed the USAF instrument instructor course. New instrument development programs focused on three jet airplanes: the T-38, F-5 and T-39. In these aircraft, we replaced the round dial instruments with newer technology, the Flight Director system, a state-of-the-art upgrade for high-performance airplanes. The new instrument system consolidated the position of all the instruments needed to fly in poor weather conditions. The instruments were placed in the center of the instrument panel in clear view of the pilot. In the previous arrangement, the instruments and dials were configured in different places. The lack of centralization of the instruments required the pilot to crosscheck all over the cockpit for flight information. This presented a real problem, especially when flying in low-visibility conditions at high speeds and lower altitudes. Correction times for making a precision approach were limited. The more accurate and newly centralized instrument panel allowed the pilot to save time by relieving the need to crosscheck instruments in different locations.

As new instrument systems and cockpit designs were incorporated in this new supersonic jet, experienced pilots became a part of the cockpit design and configuration. This area has improved with each new aircraft design, permitting easier and more realistic pilot workload in the rapidly expanding fighter aviation mission environment. The Flight Director system remained the next iteration in fighter instrumentation for the next 20 years. Because of the development work in new flight instruments and my completion of the USAF instrument instructor course, I gave most of the annual pilot instrument checks done in the fighters.

I spent most of my assignment at Edwards on the T-38 program and on the upgrade program to bring the seven test T-38s to a standard configuration to be used for pace-and-chase test projects and for use in the test pilot school. To prove its reliability and maintainability, we flew all seven test aircraft in formation on the last T-38 test mission. This final formation culminated in 1,200 flight hours of experimental test in the T-38 without the loss of an aircraft. I remained on this follow-up T-38 project to modify and upgrade the test aircraft for flight test application plus test pilot school utilization until July 1962. The T-38 has been monumental for 50 years. I felt elated to have had a part in some of that development.

Test piloting is a dangerous business; there is no doubt about that. The attrition rate was high during my four years at Edwards. We had a lot of accidents: failures of engines, failures of structures, and failures of instrumentation. The mission at Edwards was to put the prototype plane to the extremes to see if it could pass the test for safety and soundness. The whole idea was to weed out problems so the airplane could go into production for operational use in the Air Force.

During the development of the F-104, the losses were heavy because the new engine was lightweight, coupled with a high-thrust, high-RPM engine. It only had three main bearings. Most of the jets at that time had four major bearings, two of which were thrust bearings, holding the load of the engine in high–RPM, high-heat conditions. The J-79 engine was problematic. It had one thrust bearing, so the whole thrust load of the engine at high RPM was absorbed through one major bearing. The J-79 had an afterburner controlled by hydraulics in extreme heat conditions in the aft section of the engine. We had difficulty with the afterburner system and the hydraulic system that controlled the burner. It seemed that about every week we were losing another 104 through engine problems. We developed the T-38 and F-5 with the new J-85 engine, which was similar to the J-79, but with more reliability. With our J-79/F-104 experience, we learned a lot and applied it in the later aircraft.

In this period there was a stronger and stronger concern for safety in all aviation. There were just too many costly, tragic accidents. More emphasis was placed on what caused each accident and what could be done to prevent another and yet another. While at Edwards, I attended a newly developing accident investigation school. Its purpose was a very technical approach to evaluating aircraft accidents and incorporating all the findings — from the physiology of the pilot to the technology of the machine — into future aviation safety improvements. Most jet accidents left only pieces to work with, but it is amazing what information is available with an organized approach. And most accidents have much greater depth than the old standby "pilot error." Lack of training, maintenance, supervision, and overstressing of both aircraft and crew members are usually the real problems.

Unfortunately, I had to participate in investigations of many accidents from this time on. I liked each one less and less because of the tragedy that accompanies every accident. But I learned immeasurably from each one. The safety and performance of aviation have been enhanced significantly by this "leave no stone unturned" approach to accident investigation. This in-depth approach was invaluable as long as integrity was maintained and truth was accepted.

Flying at supersonic speeds became routine for me. I was flying every day, sometimes four or five times a day. From that point on through my career I maintained my status as a test pilot, even in operational units. From then on and for the rest of my Air Force career, I flew different jet aircraft out to Mach 2 almost daily. With each airplane that I checked out, I always took it out to its maximum velocity to test the movement of engine control mechanisms accomplished by mathematical sequence and angular change. For example, the compressor blades in the engines have to move properly in order to keep the airflow through the engine at a rate that will support burning, and the airflow coming into the intake of a supersonic airplane must be regulated. The air coming into the intake has to be subsonic so it won't create a shockwave that will destroy the airflow. This is done by movable ramps in the intakes. At Mach 2 speed, as the airflow channels into the engine the force of the air must be reduced to below Mach 1 levels. The dynamics of the airplane change dramatically from subsonic speeds out to Mach 2. Most of the new fighters are Mach 2 capable. Air Force technology has reached the point that going faster than Mach 2 will not significantly improve flying under combat conditions. Most of today's fighters can get up to around 1,700 miles an hour, about Mach 2 to Mach 2.2, which is about the same as it was when I was a test pilot at Edwards Air Force Base.

For use at appropriate occasions such as Veterans Day, Memorial Day, and open house displays at Edwards AFB, we formed demonstration formations in T-33, T-38, and other aircraft to demonstrate fighter flexibility along with demonstrations of new high-performance aircraft being evaluated at Edwards. I was current in the T-33 and T-38. These demonstration flights were fun, relaxing, and were great tools for exposing new advancements to the rest of the world.

There were other lighter moments during my stay at Edwards. One of them was the Model A Ford Club. The fighter pilots drove Model A Fords of every style and vintage. I had a rare five-window coupe with 16-inch spoke wheels and a rumble seat. We would have various activities with these unique cars: fighter-type formations out on the dry lake bed, or even formal social events with style and prestige, arriving in our magnificent machines. One of the advantages of the desert is the fact that due to the dry desert air the old Fords were well preserved with little rust. My kids loved the car and had so much fun sitting in the back in the rumble seat. All of the pilots in the club met Monday mornings at the base operations snack bar. Many times on the weekends, we would go out on a nearby lake bed and do formations and other fun stuff with our 1928–1932 Model A Fords. This was a great entertainment thing, driving around and letting off steam. These were cherished moments, and it was a uniquely enjoyable activity I had not seen before or since.

Another lighter moment is firmly etched in my mind. Lute Eldridge, a friend I met in cadet training who had become a Lockheed test pilot, called me to say he was flying a P-51 into Lancaster Fox Field near Edwards AFB. The P-51 is a World War II prop fighter and one of the best fighters ever built. I had always wanted to fly the P-51 and the P-38, another famous World War II fighter. I had never flown either and thought this at last was my chance to fly the P-51. Lute owed me a favor, so I said, "Let me fly the airplane," and he agreed. I went to Fox Field, got into the cockpit, had help starting it, and took off on my first flight in a P-51. I was tickled to death. I went out over the test range in the airplane and decided to make a run over to Edwards. I let the P-51 down at a very low altitude and made a pass over one fairway of the Edwards golf course. There were four guys standing on the tee block staring at the P-51 coming up the fairway. I didn't know who they were at the time but found out later that one of them was my superior officer and another was the base operations officer.

The next Monday morning, the pilots' Model A Ford club met at the base operations snack bar with our cars parked outside. The discussion of the day was who had dragged the golf course in a P-51 on Saturday. Nobody had any idea of the identity, and I never said a word. I was still the kid in the crowd, and it would not be wise to admit any youthful pranks. But around ten o'clock that morning, Ted Rodgers, the base operations officer, called me and said, "Earl, that was you in that P-51!" As best that I can remember, here is the gist of the conversation:

"Earl! That was you in that P-51, wasn't it!"
"What do you mean?" I said.
"Earl. That *was* you in that airplane, wasn't it?"
"Sir, I've never been checked out in a 51. I've never flown one before."
"I know it was you. I know it was you!"

He didn't get a straight answer from me that morning. I never gave a clue until about a year later. Rodgers was reassigned to another base, and at his going-away party he came over and asked,

"Earl, that was you in that airplane, wasn't it?"
"Yes, Ted, that was me," I said.
"I knew it! I knew it!"
"Well, how did you know?"
"You're the only guy when the 'A' club met that morning who never said a word, and that was because you knew the answer to our questions. Everybody had a comment but you. So you had to be the guy!" Ted was right on, but being a young captain among lots of high-ranking officials, I did not offer the answer.

I had the opportunity at Edwards to become associated with some very remarkable individuals, many of which went on to do great things in the Air Force and the world of space. Swart Nelson was the operations officer in charge of the T-38 activities. Jim McDivitt was also on the T-38 program. Jimmy and I became very good friends. We seemed to have a lot in common and liked the same sort of things. Jimmy was a highly experienced fighter pilot and test pilot before entering the Gemini and Apollo space programs and completing two space flights. He established the criteria and the baseline for the astronaut school, an augmentation of the test pilot school at Edwards. Jimmy was on the space program, and I had gone back to tactical fighters when we met later on at McDonnell-Douglas. He was working on the Gemini capsule, and I was developing the F-4E configuration to be used for the Thunderbirds. We spent a couple of weeks together, giving us time to recount the things we had done since leaving Edwards Air Force Base.

Pete Knight was on the T-38 program. We flew together in the T-38. Pete stayed at Edwards and spent most of his career with the X-15 and ultimately became the vice-commander of the wing at Edwards. He went on to do many great things in the X-15 and other programs, including speed records that still exist. He was an extraordinary person and test pilot. I thought the world of him. We were together on a team to select the astronauts for the Apollo program. We also became very good friends and remained friends until his death. I also flew with Al Crews, a very good test pilot who later went to the Manned Orbital Laboratory project (MOL), which folded after only a year or so. I worked with him throughout the T-38 program. Hank Gordon, an experienced test pilot, flew the T-38 with me. He also went to the MOL program, and when it was cancelled, moved on to other programs.

My youngest son, Steven, was born April 8, 1960, at Edwards Air Force Base. My twin boys were almost two years old by then. At this time we lived in the World War II Wherry housing area. When a new housing area called Capehart was constructed just a few blocks away, we were moved to a four-bedroom Capehart house at 6905 Balchen Drive. It was a beautiful house, but had no landscaping. There was not a tree in sight.

At this time Rosamond Dry Lake, adjacent to Muroc Dry Lake where Edwards Air Force Base is located, was being landscaped to enhance safety procedures for the X-15 test missions. A row of trees along Rosamond Boulevard was being cleared in case the X-15 should have to make an emergency landing from north to south on Rosamond Dry Lake. I asked if I could have one of the uprooted trees. I chose one with the limbs removed. I dragged it home to begin my landscaping project at 6905 Balchen Drive. All my neighbors laughed and kidded me about my silver oak tree skeleton. It will never grow, they chided. I dug a large hole and planted the stripped tree trunk in front of the house. I watered it daily, but nothing progressed, except the neighbors' jokes. I had almost given up hope when, early one Saturday morning as I was leaving to fly a test mission, I spotted a small branch with a green tip protruding from the top of the skeleton. I woke the neighbors for them to view my landscaping miracle!

When I left Edwards Air Force Base in 1962, the silver oak had grown into a beautiful shade tree—the focal point of my landscaping. As the years rolled by, I did not have time to visit Edwards and see how my tree had grown. While assigned to the Air Force Test and Evaluation Center around 1975 I was sent to pick up Senator Barry Goldwater at Edwards AFB and take him to Washington, D.C. I had met the senator at Edwards in 1961 while on the T-38/F-5 project. He was a World War II fighter pilot. He had maintained a devout interest and influence in USAF fighter aviation, remained committed to the future of fighter aviation, and was a vocal advocate in Congress in support of the Air Force. I thought I would have time to run up and see my tree before leaving Edwards with Senator Goldwater. But on final approach to landing at Edwards I was informed the senator was ready to go and was advised not to shut the engines down.

The aircraft would be refueled with the engines running, and we would immediately depart. I didn't get to see my tree. Again, in 1980, I was asked to pick up Senator Goldwater at Edwards. Again, he was ready to go, and, again, I did not get out of the aircraft.

It was not until 2005, after my USAF retirement, that I got back to Edwards AFB. I went to 6905 Balchen Drive. The house was easy to find because of the *huge* silver oak that had been planted in 1960. It towered over all the other trees on the block. I took pictures and sat under the tree for a long time, remembering wonderful days at Edwards as my three boys began to grow along with the era of supersonic fighters — as did the silver oak. Miracles really do happen, I thought. That day the current occupants of the house asked me in and told me that everyone wondered how that tall tree had happened to take root in a neighborhood where there was no other tree like it.

The Air Force Flight Test Center was a unique education in aviation for me, and I will always be grateful to all the great aviators and technicians I was associated with. There were many advancements and achievements in the 1950s and 1960s that created significant aviation performance and safety during this evolutionary era in aviation. Much credit goes to those dedicated "never know when to quit" people in the Flight Test mission at Edwards.

I could probably go on forever about my four years at Edwards. I look back at it now and can't believe the Air Force would let a young pilot fly under those test pilot conditions. I was just a kid but learned so much. I flew many different airplanes and met some very exciting people. It seemed that every day was a holiday. Every day I wanted to meet the standards established for me. It was a chore to measure up to some of the more seasoned and older test pilots, but I survived, and it is something that I look back on with great satisfaction and sense of accomplishment. I was the happiest kid on the block, and felt I was the luckiest guy in the world. The years at Edwards were the best time of my Air Force life.

CHAPTER 7

Return to Tactical Fighters

"Felix Fowler is Superman, not Clark Kent."

In late 1961 the confrontation over access to East Berlin escalated into what became known as the Berlin Crisis, resulting in deployment of U.S. Air Force squadrons to Europe to be in readiness in the event of armed conflict. While I had expected to continue at Edwards working on the F-5 program, I was selected to go back to tactical operations, probably because of my experience in Korea and Japan in the F-84.

In mid–1962 I left Edwards Air Force Base for my new assignment with the 366th Tactical Fighter Wing, consisting of four squadrons known as "The Gunfighters." I had learned a great deal in the flight test programs at Edwards, but the new assignment turned out to be a good move. It was time for me to return to the fighter world. Our assignment was to protect the Berlin corridor from four vantage points in France, none of which was far from our mission requirement near Berlin. For several months our mission was to remain proficient, maintain our position, and be a visible threat to the Soviets as negotiations proceeded. During the next year, as we watched treaty agreements being made, I was able to have my family join me, and we had some time to travel together. We bought a sports car and toured Europe, skiing in the Alps, Germany, Austria, Italy, Switzerland, and France.

When the threat of hostilities eased and the immediate crisis was resolved, the 366th was returned to the United States and deployed to Holloman Air Force Base in New Mexico. The plan was to fly the aircraft with refuel stops rather than air refueling. There were 18 fighter jets in a squadron, 72 in a wing. In addition to the 72 airplanes, two attrition F-84Fs were assigned to each squadron, as were two T-33 trainers. To fly this number of airplanes with enough tankers to support such a huge fleet was logistically unfeasible. The flight-schedule refueling stops were France to Scotland; Scotland to Iceland; and from there to Sondrestrom, Greenland. We were to fly from Sondrestrom to our fourth refueling at Goose Bay, Labrador. The next three stops were in the United States: Goose Bay to a Strategic Air Command base in New York; New York to Little Rock, Arkansas; and Little Rock to Holloman AFB. The deployment took place in July of 1963 over a period of about seven days. During the deployment, movement control teams were located at each of the bases. These teams were responsible for handling whatever support requirements we needed: fuel, maintenance, and logistics for the airplanes.

A traumatic situation for me occurred on the stop at Sondrestrom—something unlike anything I had been faced with in my life. One of the F-84Fs had an electrical fire shortly before landing at Sondrestrom. My duty as wing movement control officer at Sondrestrom was to insure that all the airplanes were in commission before continuing on to the next leg. My inspection of one F-84F indicated fire damage around the nose section, so I grounded the airplane. The 366th Fighter Wing had to report the flight status of each aircraft to the Sondrestrom command post, which would then report to an airborne command post ultimately in charge of the deployment of the fighter wing. General Albert W. Schinz, a one-star general aboard the command post, was in charge of the movement of the entire fleet. The F-84F I had grounded was still at Sondrestrom, but the local movement control people had erroneously reported it flying on to Goose Bay, Labrador. Their mistake created confusion because the airborne command post assumed the airplane was in the air when in reality it was still at Sondrestrom.

The movement control officer at Sondrestrom, a Major Cook, soon realized that the flight status had not been properly reported. To cover up the reporting error, he sought me out and ordered me to release the aircraft.

"It is not safe to fly. It has had an electrical problem requiring repairs," I said.

"It has to join the rest of the airplanes," he told me.

I said, "I'm sorry; it's not going to fly until it's fixed." He ordered me to put the airplane on flyable status. I refused.

"I'm giving you a military order," he said.

I replied, "I don't care what you're giving me. I'm not going to launch an airplane that's not safe." I left to return to the barracks. It had been a long day. I went to bed.

About an hour later Major Cook with three other officers arrived at the door and bodily dragged me out of the barracks and up to the command post, which was about a quarter of a mile away. Their intention was to commence an in-field court martial and put me in jail. I later learned that the four men had been drinking in the base officers' club. The aircraft had been misreported, and the intent was to cover up their dereliction by convicting me of disobeying an order. An in-field court martial is a serious matter. They set up the procedure and began to record it.

About ten minutes into the scenario, Felix Fowler, a six-foot-three, 235-pound officer, broke down the locked door. Major Fowler was a flight commander in the 390th Squadron. I had been attached to the 391st Squadron, so I didn't yet know Felix. But he had heard these four guys talking in the club about what they were going to do to this young captain. He followed them to see if they were going to try to carry out their plan — which they indeed were. So he intervened. Felix was a monster of a man. He grabbed them up, sorted them out, and threw them back down in their chairs. As a major, Felix had equal rank to any of the other guys, so not only did he have physical authority, but he also had military authority. And he was one tough hombre that night. I assisted Felix when necessary.

Felix and I then contacted the airborne command post and informed them of the true status of the airplane in question. When the misreported aircraft had not landed at Goose Bay, it was assumed that the airplane had gone down in the water; the command post was preparing to set up a search-rescue operation. We informed them that the airplane never took off from Sondrestrom. This upset General Schinz, who wanted to know how the airplane could have been so misrepresented. He was informed that the airplane had a maintenance problem and was under repair and scheduled for takeoff with the next flight of aircraft. When the repairs were made it was evident that the airplane could never have made it from Sondrestrom to Goose Bay. The electrical system would have totally failed, disabling fuel transfer and instruments. General Schinz flew into Sondrestrom himself to analyze the situation and undertook whatever disciplinary action was indicated. I later learned that the officer who had instigated the cover-up left the Air Force. None of the four belonged to the 366th, and I never saw any of them again. Nor was I looking forward to any further encounters with these guys.

In a strange twist to the story, it turned out that the aircraft in question was Felix Fowler's airplane — the very airplane he had landed at Sondrestrom. He had written the airplane up, noting that it had an electrical problem in the air. In some cases that might not have grounded the airplane, but as an engineering test officer I was responsible for insuring that any discrepancies on an airplane would be corrected before the aircraft could move along. I grounded the airplane because I could see that there actually had been a visible fire in the electronics bay up in the nose. I had put a big red "X" in the record, which means that the airplane cannot be flown until appropriate repairs had been made and the aircraft upgraded to flight status. It is a formal process.

At the time that Felix intervened to stop the so-called court martial, neither of us realized that the issue involved his airplane. He only knew that the situation he had overheard at the officers' club indicated that something horribly wrong was about to occur, and he intended to correct it. There are few people who would have had that kind of strength — who would intervene regardless of any risk to himself— to stop something that he knew was wrong. He had absolutely no concern for his own comfort or safety. Ironically, my grounding of Felix's F-84 very likely saved his life, as almost certainly his airplane would have gone down in the water somewhere between Sondrestrom and Goose Bay. When I got to Holloman the wing commander, Colonel James S. Coward, asked me to explain what happened, although he knew that I had been cleared of any wrongdoing. He looked me straight in the eye and said, "You know, if it hadn't have been for Felix, no one would have believed you." I said, "Colonel, no one knows that better than I do. Felix Fowler is my hero. He's Superman, not Clark Kent. Felix is a fearless, amazing person."

There was a mission report filed about the entire deployment of the airplanes from Europe back to the United States. I wrote a factual report concerning this very unusual incident. There probably is some mention in the mission report of this discrepancy at Sondrestrom, but I doubt that there is anything in great detail. There were never any actual formal charges made against me, so there was no legal activity. The problem was solved by the actions of the appropriate people. Felix and I were both at Holloman, so from time to time we laughed about the court-martial story. It certainly wasn't funny at the time, but after the fact, it became a good story when it was told around the club.

The incident didn't have an impact on my career, but it did on me personally. I didn't think things like that could happen in a controlled, disciplined organization like the United States Air Force. It opened my eyes to realize that there are no holds barred under certain circumstances. When people are afraid for their own careers or want to protect themselves in other ways, they may do indefensible things. Crazy things happen when people are under the influence of alcohol. I had learned lessons about alcohol from my own father.

Unfortunately, the episode at Sondrestrom was not the last time I would witness a lack of integrity. Later on in my career there would be were similar incidents. The leavening factor was that at the same time I was witness to the behavior of a man of extraordinary courage and integrity. There aren't many people who would do what Felix did in this situation. His selfless actions left made me determined to stand up for what is right, no matter what the circumstances. When a life is at stake or a severe issue needs to be corrected and you are in the box, you step up to the responsibility. I attempted from that time on to emulate Felix Fowler. I said, "Man, when I grow up I want to be just like him. I'm never going to be as big as he is, but maybe I can be as strong."

Felix never changed. He was like that for as long as I knew him, which was the remainder of my Air Force career. I never worked with him again, but we continued to stay in contact. We met up in 1967 during my Thunderbird deployment to Europe when he was the 390th Squadron commander. It was great to see him again. Some years later, however, I got word that Felix had been killed in an O-2 liaison aircraft, a small prop-driven airplane used for forward air control. When I heard he had been killed in an airplane I was absolutely devastated. I didn't sleep all night. I just couldn't figure it out. What was Felix doing in such a small airplane? He could hardly get in one. He was so big, he could *carry* that airplane.

At about four or five o'clock in the morning I got a phone call from Europe. It was Felix! I was stunned. "I thought you were dead! I thought they had buried you yesterday." He laughed and said, "No, I got out at the end of the runway. I was flying with a young captain, and I decided not to go on." He explained that the airplane was cramped and uncomfortable and he was looking at a four-and-a-half hour flight. "So when we got to the end of the runway I decided not to go. I just got out of the airplane and walked back home." The airplane crashed, and the pilot was killed. It took authorities several hours to sort it out.

"They assumed I was still in the airplane," he said. "I knew you'd be worried."

"If it ain't one thing, it's another," I said. "You scare the hell out of me every time I turn around." We talked a long time. I gave him an order as we got off the phone: "Don't you get in any more little airplanes, period. If it ain't a big airplane that goes fast, stay out of it." He said he would do that.

When we were at Holloman with the 366th Fighter Wing, Felix and I saw each other on a regular basis because all four squadrons were on the same base. In France they were scattered in different strategic locations. At Holloman we talked on an almost-daily basis and enjoyed a close rapport. I patted Felix on the back, and he patted me on the back. I last saw Felix at a reunion. He was living in Cleveland, Ohio, where, perhaps not surprisingly, he had been a vice police officer before he came into the Air Force.

Early in my assignment at Holloman it became obvious that we were going to transition into the newly produced F-4C Phantom, the aircraft that I had worked with at Edwards some two years earlier. The 366th Fighter Wing was designated to receive the new aircraft in 1964. We were one of the first wings to transition and become combat capable in the airplane. My initial duty at Holloman was wing quality-control test pilot, but I also was a fully qualified fighter pilot. In other words, I was a fully qualified test pilot under the F-4344 Air Force Specialty Code, and I was a fully qualified 1115, which is the fighter pilot qualification. I had both AFSCs, and exercised both missions almost every day. As I had experience with the F-4, I was one of those sent to Davis-Monthan Air Force Base in Tucson, Arizona, to become fully combat capable in the F-4C and in all its mission requirements. I was then assigned to ferry the new airplanes to Holloman from the McDonnell-Douglas factory in St. Louis, Missouri, *and* to do the flight tests and acceptance tests on them. Those were some joyous days!

The Phantom had unbelievable performance. The aircraft was a pilot's dream. It had all the innovative Flight Director features we had developed at the Edwards Flight Test Center. It had very strong radar and a versatile fire control system capable of handling any sort of combat mission known in the 1960s. The aircraft went from brake release to Mach 2 in no time at all. It could fly straight up and straight down and roll your socks down any time you stoked up the afterburners. The new capability in weapons, radar, and expanded aircraft performance added new roles and missions to the fighter pilot. He could now launch non-stop to any place in the world and fight any level of war then in existence. This was another quantum leap in the evolution of the supersonic fighter.

It took about six months to complete the transition from the old F-84F into the new F-4C, that is, to get all the airplanes in place at Holloman and all the pilots transitioned into the F-4. Usually in a transition of that magnitude, you can expect some losses, but we never scratched an airplane.

The airplane was so well designed and had such flawless flight dynamics and unbelievable power that it was hard to get the airplane in trouble. It was simply a major jump in performance from the F-84 to the F-4. Most of that was due to the improved technology and design as well as the emphasis placed on safety and performance, not only in VFR but also in all flight conditions. The F-4 was just a very well-constructed, very well-prepared airplane. It was a busy time for me. As the wing flight test officer I was attached to the 389th Squadron at Holloman, and during this period I flew every day to meet the flight test requirements of the entire wing as well as the mission readiness requirements of a fighter pilot.

On one of my last flights in the F-84 — a routine test flight out of Holloman — I took off, rotated, and when the aircraft came off the ground I pulled the gear up. When the gear came up, the flight controls locked. The stick jammed and wouldn't move. I had no control over the aircraft, except power, speed brakes, and flaps. I had no aileron, no elevator, and very little rudder. Normally, a flight control adjuster for pitch control (horizontal stabilizer) sets flight control for slow flight, and when the gear comes up, it readjusts for high-speed flight. I later learned that the mechanism had been installed backwards, and when the gear came up the flight control systems were damaged to the point that they were rendered inoperable.

I was in level flight and had the flaps down, but I had enough of a nose-high attitude that the airplane continued to climb. I started bringing the flaps up at about 200 knots. By the time I got it up to 300 knots it would fly pretty well, but I still had no flight controls. I called the command post and explained what was wrong.

"You're going to have to bail out," I was told.

"It's full of gas," I said. "I don't want to just jump out and leave it to crash no telling where." So I said, "I'd like to fly around a little, burn some of that gas, and get in a better position to get out of it." Working with the situation, I found I could control the pitch attitude with power manipulation and by raising and lowering the gear. I climbed to a safe ejection altitude, about 20,000 feet, and continued to practice with the power, the speed brakes, and the flaps. I began to think that perhaps I could land the airplane. I did have minimal rudder control. The rudder would move about 15 degrees to either side of center, so I could probably control the roll axis with the use of rudder and pitch axis with the power and flaps being able to round the airplane out. I figured that when I was ready to touch down for landing, I could put the flaps down, which would cause the nose to rise up slightly. I already knew that the gear was usable and that I had brakes once I got it on the ground.

Although I had been advised to eject, ejection in those days was an iffy situation. You could get hung up in the parachute, hung up in the seat, or hit the airplane. There were a multitude of things that could happen. If that is the only option, you go ahead and do it. But I always looked at it this way: Your responsibility is to fly the airplane if you can do it. To just dump a very expensive fighter is something that should be a last resort. I felt that as long as you could fly it, you fly it. Moreover, you don't want to turn an airplane loose in the air that could wind up in downtown Dallas or someplace. Should a falling jet hit a populated area, then that is something you have to live with for the rest of your life. If it is your responsibility to fly the airplane, and if you don't do that when you could have, you haven't met your responsibility. You have done less than what you could have done.

So I told the command post that rather than jump out of the airplane I was going to try to land it. I said, "I think I'm going to be okay with it."

"The book says jump out of it," they said.

"It's flying now," I said. "I don't want to jump out and leave it to go fly no telling where and come down in somebody's back yard."

Holloman has a long, wide runway in the White Sands Missile Range, with ten miles of lake bed at the approach end. "I'll make the approach out over White Sands. If it lands a little short, I'll just land in the desert and control it up to the runway," I said. As I flew around and discussed the situation with the command post, I thought about a similar situation Bob Hoover had once experienced. He was not successful in the final portion of the landing and got banged up pretty badly. Understanding what had happened, I believed I would be able to alleviate that problem in my approach. I was almost wrong.

I set the approach up. It was a long, straight-in approach out over White Sands to land on runway 030. I was descending, and everything was as smooth as it could be. I had about 200 to 210 knots on final. I put the flaps down 20 degrees to decrease air speed. I dropped the speed brakes and full flaps. As the airspeed started to slow, the nose started to rise. I hadn't calculated ground effect, and because I lowered the flaps a bit late, the nose didn't quite get to level flight. The nose wheel hit the ground first and caused the aircraft to balloon back up in the air at about 45 degrees. I still had about 170 to 180 knots of airspeed, and though I had never considered using the drag chute in the air, that suddenly was the only option I had. I dropped the chute, nose high and climbing to about 100 feet in the air. The chute deployed, decreasing the pitch attitude back down to almost level flight and slowing the airplane down. The main gear touched the ground just as if I had known what I was doing.

The wing commander and all the counts and no-accounts were out at the end of the runway as I completed the roll out just like another day at the office. In fact, I was shaking in my boots. I stopped the airplane at the end of the runway and got out of it. Colonel Coward, the wing commander, picked me up, and as we were riding back in, he said, "Boy, that was an amazing piece of aviation right there near the end. How did you know exactly where to drop the drag chute?" I told him the absolute truth: "Colonel, it was just blind-ass luck." He was silent the rest of the way because he realized that he had just about lost an airplane.

I got a lot of recognition for that because it was unusual to land a fighter with a locked-up flight control system. I received the Air Force Well Done Award, the Tactical Pilot Distinction Award (an Air Force commendation medal), and a letter from the Chief of Staff of the Air Force. I appreciated the recognition, but my primary feeling about the incident was simply being glad to have survived. During an emergency situation like that, I never had time to be scared. I was too busy trying to figure out how I might save the airplane and myself. I usually get nervous after an emergency is over, and I start thinking, "Why did I do that?" If I had that one at Holloman to do over, I probably would have jumped out. There is always the unforeseen circumstance that surfaces at a very bad time and leaves you with your pants down. In this case, I didn't consider there would be ground effect; in other words, that radiation from the ground would affect the dynamics of the airplane. That is what almost bit me in the end. By this time in my career I had been flying high-performance fighters almost every day for ten years, and I was used to extreme dynamic conditions. In the fighter world you are faced with the extremes almost every day, though not necessarily a total loss of flight control or loss of engines. But in this case I felt comfortable in the airplane and felt that I would know the time when I couldn't control the situation.

There were a lot of very good, very experienced aviators at Holloman — guys who, like me, had been flying jet fighters for ten years. But moving into the F-4 was really a major thing for me. It was a fun airplane to fly. It was a very safe airplane: a high-performance, 7.33 G airplane, with Mach 2.2 capability. Because I flew the test flights as well as operational missions with the squadron, I designed a test profile that would exercise every system and every capable parameter of the airplane, as I did in every test situation. So every day I flew a test flight, I would go out to Mach 2 to make sure that when it did land it was a serviceable airplane.

Mach 1 is the speed of sound. Supersonic is anything over Mach 1, that point where you exceed the speed of sound. You hear the term "sonic boom" all the time. That is the point where the airplane releases a shockwave. There is an actual shockwave coming off the wing and fuselage of the airplane that has a pretty strong impact—four or five pounds per square inch (psi) of pressure—whenever you go through the speed of sound. Supersonic is not an absolute number. It changes with temperature or altitude. As you get into more dense air, sound travels faster. It's about 710 miles an hour on a standard day at sea level. At 40,000 feet on the same day, it's only about 670 miles an hour. So it is variable. The F-4 would accelerate out to Mach 2 and leave you breathless. In the F-4 aircraft you had to be careful because the engines could push the airplane faster than the dynamic capability of the aircraft. The F-4 had amazing power, more power really than it needed, and was capable of going beyond Mach 2. I had it out to about Mach 2.3 many times, but a pilot has to be aware of the dynamics of the airplane. As you go supersonic, the lift vector moves rearward on the wing. As you go faster, the lift vector moves farther rearward on the wing until it exceeds the limits of the aircraft and the airplane becomes unstable. And that's the end. The aircraft tumbles and destructs.

Award presentation by Wing Commander Col. "Spot" Collins for Capt. Haney's successful landing of the F-84F under flight Control failure conditions.

One of my most interesting projects involved the

U.S. Army during the latter part of the F-84 days and into the F-4. The main purpose of this project was to use our fighter capabilities as air support to Army ground forces and for delivery of air firepower to support the Army under combat conditions. These training missions were successful in demonstrating how two branches of service can develop rapport and cooperation in mission accomplishment. In this period I spent a lot of time with the Army at Fort Lewis, flying out of McChord Air Force Base, just north of Tacoma, Washington, in support of the 4th Infantry Division. During the Cold War and the transition to fighter jet nuclear capabilities, the Air Force also worked a lot with the Army for close air support. Conventional warfare was as viable as ever, and the military was aware that the Air Force would be called upon to provide air support to the Army in the event of armed conflict. Joint training missions such as this proved to have been of great benefit; as the Southeast Asian war developed in the mid–1960s the Air Force did supply close air support to the Army on a regular basis.

I would take a flight of four to eight fighters from Holloman for the training exercises on an average of one week out of a month. I usually went along because I was flight test qualified and we needed that capability to keep the airplanes in commission while we were deployed and because I was then a senior captain with supervisory responsibility. We had a two-seat trainer airplane that we sometimes deployed with us. I was qualified in both the fighter and the trainer, and from time to time I would fly an Army general in the trainer to demonstrate the flexibility and the capabilities we had in the air. They were often amazed to see firsthand how much ground a fighter could cover and the ordnance we could haul in support of Army ground missions. The dual engagement between the Army and Air Force turned out to be very successful.

Holloman was a good assignment for me and for the family. We had a lot of fun in Southeast New Mexico, skiing at a resort near Ruidoso in the winter and enjoying the many things a family could do together in the White Sands area. I worked hard as in all my other assignments but was glad to be able to enjoy this family time.

CHAPTER 8

USAF Thunderbirds

"Keep the Light on the Star."

My career took another course in 1965 when I was selected to fly on the Thunderbirds, the Air Force Flight Demonstration Team. I was on leave in Champaign, Illinois, from Holloman Air Force Base when I ran into Billy Hosmer, a friend I had known well in the F-86 program at Nellis. At this time the Thunderbirds were flying the F-100, and Billy suggested I should apply for a place on the team. He said, "Earl, you have F-100 time, and the Air Force is considering using the F-4 as the next airplane for the Thunderbirds. Since you are already in an F-4 wing, you would be a good candidate for the new generation in the F-4s. You should apply for the team." I said, "No, I've got enough to do." "No, you've got to apply." So I put the necessary records together and gave them to Billy. Several months after my application was submitted, the Thunderbird team landed at Holloman. I met and interviewed with them. A little later, I received the good news that I was selected to become a Thunderbird in June.

The qualification criteria were rather tough in the early days of the Thunderbirds and may be more so today. An applicant for the Thunderbirds in 1965 had to have in excess of 2,000 hours of fighter time and have an exemplary name in the fighter world. Air Force officials used a selection process to pick the best pilots, and there was always a large number of aspirants to draw from. Personality and ability to get along with people was a strong consideration because the mission of the Thunderbirds is to communicate the capabilities of fighter tactics and fighter aircraft to the civilian populace. Physical exams were not required since applicants had already met these requirements as fighter pilots. Candidate Effectiveness

Reports had to be close to the top on a 9–4 scale. The ER has nine places ranging from unsatisfactory to outstanding and four blocks for potential consideration. There is also a short narrative stating the officer effective results on the performance report. A 9–4 index is an outstanding score and, other criteria being equal, leads to promotion ahead of your contemporaries. I had a 9–4.

To make the final cut, each candidate must fly with the existing team to demonstrate his ability to meet the flying conditions of the Thunderbird organization. The final decision is based on the total results of one's physical, mental, social, and fighter flying capabilities. One hundred to two hundred guys might apply each year, a number that is narrowed down to the four who will be accepted.

I gathered that one of the strong points in my favor was my flight-test background. The Thunderbirds had had difficulty with maintenance of airplanes, and they needed somebody with extensive engineering experience. I think that the selection team felt my experience with the F-100 and other aircraft qualified me. The team had been in the F-105, but in 1964 there was an accident at Hamilton Air Force Base in which Gene Devlin, who was the left wing at that time, was killed. A severe deficiency in the F-105s was found, and the aircraft had to be grounded. This problem forced the Thunderbird team to move back into the F-100. At that time it was the F-100D model, with which I had experience, but it would be necessary to improve the F-100Ds for the Thunderbird mission, as these F-100s were older, high-time airplanes with nearly 4,000 hours per aircraft. This involved the rigging of flight controls for the best dynamics, stability, and control of the airplane. To assure flight formation safety, all controls had to be almost perfect. This was to be my first job on the Thunderbirds.

I arrived at Nellis Air Force Base to join the Thunderbirds in July of 1965. At that point we had nine aircraft — eight F-100 single-seat D models and one two-seat F-100F model. I flew at that time in aircraft number 8, my first number as a member of the Thunderbirds. I was in charge of all the flight tests and maintenance of the aircraft. My first task was to establish a very rigid test profile to bring all of the aircraft up to the best configuration possible for the Thunderbirds. I emphasized specifically the stability and control of the airplane. Thunderbird aircraft had to be rigged almost to zero so there would be no infractions in the air. There were many times the team would go down below stall speeds in the air to facilitate a maneuver. During those periods the dynamics of the airplane had to be nearly perfect so the airplane would not drift off its line of flight.

When I came on in July, the January and February beginning-of-the-year training was already over, so I didn't get many checkout flights. I had to hit the ground running, and I had a lot to do in a very short time. I had to learn to fly the positions without many missions for training. I had to bring the maintenance people up to have confidence in me, believe that I knew what I was doing, and have faith in my decisions. During that early period I had to get up to speed with an organization that was moving very fast. I was probably the most experienced pilot on the team at this point in terms of number of fighter aircraft flown and flight hours, and the only pilot who had a flight-test background. I did most of my re-indoctrination into the F-100 and my indoctrination into the Thunderbird formation as we traveled from point to point, so it was "earn while you learn" again. The Thunderbird training was fast-moving. You are experienced and expected to move into the position quickly.

My first couple of weeks on the team were dedicated to test flying and maintenance. Maintenance of the airplanes had not previously been handled well — not the fault of any individual, just too much to do and too little time to do it, as well as having old aircraft with extensive utilization. Every pilot performs some administrative duty within the organization. The officers run the organization, but also fly the aircraft. All team members, officer and enlisted, demonstrate tactical capability and flexibility every day like any other Air Force fighter squad. There were 38 enlisted people who handled all of the maintenance as the team traveled from one point to another.

Major Paul Kattu was then flight leader and led the formation in 1965. In August 1965 a new commander, Lt. Col. Ralph Maglione, came on and began to prepare to become flight leader when Paul left at the end of the 1965 season. I flew a lot with Maglione. At that time the team flew from point to point in the eight-ship formation called the "Outhouse." During these flights "Maggie" and I would break off the formation and practice the demonstration maneuvers, with me flying in different positions. I flew the left wing and the right wing and the slot almost every day from that time until Maglione became the new flight formation leader.

As we ended the 1965 season, we went to Central America. We spent about one month in several countries — Guatemala, Nicaragua, Panama, and others. It was a very difficult time because we had so much flying to do. In jet fighters you are always short on fuel because of the consumption rate of fuel in supersonic jet engines. During the early period of the supersonic evolution, navigation facilities were barely adequate even in good weather and smooth terrain. These fuel and navigation frailties became apparent on this Thunderbird out-of-country deployment.

On the second leg of the trip we were to travel one thousand miles from Guadalajara, Mexico, to Guatemala City, a long trip for an F-100 without external fuel tanks and no air refueling. There was only a low-power, low-frequency navigation homer for the approach to Guatemala and no ultra-high-frequency voice communication or weather forecasting. A C-47 was to fly from Panama to Guatemala to monitor and assist our approach and landing at Guatemala. It aborted at Howard Air Force Base, Panama, and we were unaware of this. We arrived over Guatemala with undercast below, no communication, and less than 1,000 pounds (150 gallons) of fuel per F-100. We made an unorthodox approach into Guatemala, arriving over the landing runway with nine F-100s in formation and out of gas. It was a spectacular arrival, a little close for comfort, but somewhat normal for the early days of the supersonic evolution.

We completed the 1965 season at Howard Air Force Base, Panama. When we departed that day we had all nine airplanes with us because the narrator who normally flew ahead of the formation was now going to join the formation to proceed back to Nellis Air Force Base and end the 1965 season. The leader, Paul Kauttu, wanted to exit Howard AFB in the Nine Ship Diamond formation. The first four aircraft took off, and then the two solos, Bobby Morgan and Clarence Langerud, took off behind them. Colonel Maglione and I took off as number 7 and number 8, and Russ Goodman, the narrator, took off in number 9 position. The plan idea was to take off and make a 180-degree turn, and be in the Nine Ship Diamond formation as we exited at about 100 feet off the runway. It was a difficult join-up as we reversed position descending for the pass. We had almost com-

The "Outhouse" formation, one of the travel formations used by the USAF Thunderbirds.

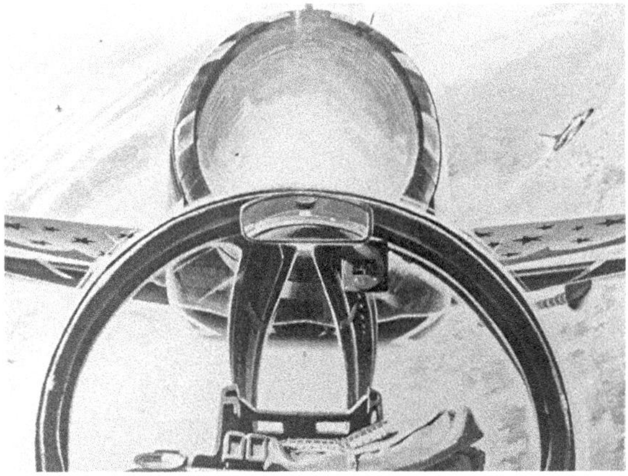

Pilot's sight picture in a rear flight formation position.

pleted that 180-degree turn and Russ, who was an unusually good pilot, now had to make it into the second slot position to complete the Nine Ship Diamond. As we began the join-up, I didn't think Russ would be able to make the turn and be in number 9 position in time. I was wrong. In full burner, he came directly at the eight ships and rolled to decrease his angle off with respect to the formation direction. His shadow went across my canopy as he completed the roll, ending in perfect position as we passed over Howard AFB in salute. Absolutely amazing. We called Russ "Mr. Wonderful" because he could do anything and do it well. Russ went to war in Southeast Asia and was killed in combat, a terrible loss.

To my knowledge that was our first exit demonstration with the Nine Ship Diamond. We normally used six airplanes during the scheduled 30-minute air shows. Colonel Maglione liked the nine-ship formation. He intended to use it on a regular basis during the 1966 season. We went back to Nellis and began to train for the 1966 season. This was going to be an exhaustive season, with over one hundred scheduled demonstrations as well as the unscheduled flight activities that occurred on a regular basis, such as fly-bys for memorials or special occasions.

The Thunderbird training period starts the first of January and continues through February. Training takes place with a runway marked off at Thunderbird Lake, just north of Nellis Air Force Base. The final practice is completed at Indian Springs, an airfield 35 miles northwest of Nellis. The demonstration season starts the first of March and ends sometime in December. Thunderbird personnel changes are made every year. Assignment is normally two years. Half the team leaves each year. The training process never ends, as half the people on the team are always new.

We were solid in the F-100 in January 1966 when Colonel Maglione took over as the new commander/leader. In addition to flying with

The Nine Ship Diamond formation, a demonstration and travel formation employed during the 1966 show season.

Maglione as he prepared for the flight leader position, I helped train new team members. For 1966 Charlie Hamm (left wing) and Clarence Langerud (solo) had been replaced with Chris Patterakis and Bob Beckel, respectively. Frank Liethen became executive officer to train as Maggie's eventual replacement. Buster McGee was right wing, and Hank Canterbury was slot. Number 9, the narrator, was now Hal Dortch, an F-105 combat veteran.

The Thunderbirds' mission is to demonstrate tactical capability and flexibility to people all over the world. The team demonstrates publicly what every fighter pilot does every day. Thunderbird spectators were very enthusiastic about the fighter demonstration. Flying the Thunderbird formation is not difficult, but it must be done exactly right. The hard part is moving from one place to another on a daily basis. It is a constant challenge each day to acclimate to new places, social activities, and flying environments.

My hours were long. In addition to supervising maintenance as we traveled from place to place, I had to complete test flights. I might get up at four o'clock in the morning to roll down the runway at six o'clock and complete a test flight to prepare an aircraft for demonstration that day. I established a test profile that exercised the limits of the aircraft envelope, as hard a mission as you could fly in the airplane. This was to insure that the aircraft were maintained to perform at maximum level by flying a very rigid test flight. Duty hours were long for the entire Thunderbird team. The maintenance crew, highly trained, experienced jet aircraft mechanics, worked day and night. These skilled technicians work behind the scenes and receive little publicity compared to the officers flying the airplanes. This team of hard-working, dedicated people is the real foundation of the Thunderbirds. Without them the Thunderbird operation could not function.

The whole essence of tactical fighter aviation is teamwork and trusting the people flying around you, especially the leader. Each Thunderbird pilot must maintain position in the flight, no matter what, and wherever the leader goes, you go. The wings in flight formation are overlapped about three feet, sometimes more. Flight safety depends on maintaining precise formation position for each aircraft. There is no room for error. It is a precise operation and a demonstration of the fighter pilot's daily life in the tactical aviation world.

From left to right: Lt. Col. Ralph Maglione, Lt. Chris Patterakis, Capt. Buster McGee, Capt. Hank Canterbury, Capt. Bob Morgan, Capt. Bob Beckel, Maj. Frank Leithen, Capt. Earl Haney and Capt. Hal Dortch.

The Thunderbird demonstration is a sequence of three-dimensional maneuvers in formation. On the F-100, there is a running light on the end of each wing and a star on the fuselage of the airplane. The pilot positions the running light on the star of the fuselage and maintains the "light on the star." As long as the light is lined up on the star—and the "light on the star" is maintained—the aircraft is in proper formation. If you don't have that light right in the middle of that white star, you're not in position. Every fighter pilot that flies puts that light on the star and keeps it there. There is little difference in one wing position or another so far as the pilot is concerned. The slot pilot keeps his aircraft lined up with the leader at approximately three feet below the leader's tail pipe.

We began the 1966 demonstration season the beginning of March. I will never forget our first trip to Malstrom Air Force Base, Montana. When we left Nellis the temperature was about 65 degrees. We got to Malstrom, and it was 15 degrees below zero. I thought, "Who is going to come out at 15 below zero to see a flight demonstration?" When we landed I couldn't get the canopy open because it was frozen shut. A crew had to come out with a heater to melt the ice on the canopy so I could get out. I was amazed the next day when 100,000 people came out in subzero temperatures to see the Thunderbirds. I realized then how important the Thunderbird mission is. This small group of people can circle the world, demonstrating tactical formation and combat capabilities in a language everybody can understand. When the crowd sees those red, white, and blue airplanes, they know where they belong. When they see what those airplanes can do in the air, they realize their capability is about as good as it gets, and they love it.

The Seven Ship "Stinger" formation, one of the travel formations used by the USAF Thunderbirds.

During the early part of the 1966 season, we would travel in a Seven Ship Diamond formation called the "Stinger." The narrator would precede the formation to solidify team arrival requirements. The diamond would take off with the spectacular move by aircraft number 4 from fingertip formation to slot position, creating the "diamond." The solos would take off shortly behind the steep-climbing diamond, and each would roll the aircraft low over the runway. I decided to do the roll between and behind the solos as they completed their rolling maneuver, to put a "pigtail" on the dynamic Thunderbird departure. No one in the formation could observe the pigtail, as they were all out in front of me. On one departure, Maggie had commenced a left turn a little early. He looked back and did observe the pigtail. He said slowly, "That looks good." I don't know if anyone else in the formation knew about the pigtail, but I continued the maneuver when appropriate until I left the team.

Colonel Maglione was very good to people and had an effervescent personality. In the mid–1960s, the Thunderbirds were adding more demonstrations and going to more places throughout the world. Maglione wanted to express to the public that not only could the Thunderbirds fly, but as U.S. Air Force officers they were also personable, honest, and strong. Maglione wanted to promote the Nine Ship Diamond, a difficult formation not used in prior air show demonstrations. He wanted to enter a demonstration base with a Nine Ship Diamond, roll the formation, reverse, come back, and do a loop with the whole Nine Ship Diamond. This is a spectacular thing to see: nine fighters in a diamond formation do a loop in which the top does not get over 5,000 feet. We would reverse direction and perform a roll, then reverse the formation and pitch up from 50 feet off of the runway for landing. Every four seconds an airplane would pitch up from formation to land. The string of nine fighters would land about 2,000 feet behind each other. The Nine Ship Diamond was very impressive and a crowd pleaser. Colonel Maglione liked the attention drawn from using the nine F-100 formation. He flew this formation during arrivals and often let down at bases in the nine-ship formation for special occasions to honor or pay respect to a particular occasion or memorial event. We used the Nine Ship Diamond a lot, which was probably the most spectacular of all the formations used over the years.

Colonel Maglione decided one day he wanted to take off with seven airplanes in a single formation, which is a lot of airplanes rolling down the runway at one time. A significant problem was the width of the runway. The F-100 has a wingspan of over 40 feet, and seven of them made it necessary to overlap the wings about ten feet just to keep all seven airplanes on the runway. With the wing overlap, I was looking out of the cockpit right down onto the wing tip of the adjacent airplane. We would roll down the runway and get airborne with the entire Seven Ship Wedge formation at one time. It was stunning to see because of the number of airplanes and the closeness of the formation. This Seven Ship Wedge got a lot of attention throughout the 1966 season.

The nine-ship formation created challenging maintenance circumstances in 1966. We had a requirement to fly all nine of our airplanes each day. I did some consulting at Trans World Airlines, asking TWA how they maintained airplanes given their very high utilization rate. Sometimes the airlines would fly airplanes 20 hours a day, every day. That left some four hours between flights to complete the maintenance requirements. I talked with the director of TWA maintenance, and he explained that they did part of the maintenance requirements every time the airplane landed. They would do as much as they could, and then fly the airplane, and do as much as they could on the next stop.

This had never been done in tactical fighters. I decided to try it. In this way we would not have to put the airplane down for a week at a time to do the required scheduled maintenance. In the new plan, a maintenance schedule was followed every day. Engine change was required every one hundred hours. At the one-hundred-hour increment I would have an engine flown in to our location. The engine would be changed that night and a test flight on it performed early the next day. This procedure worked extremely well because we found that looking at an airplane a little each day accomplished the required maintenance in a better manner than flying it for a hundred hours and letting it sit on the ground for a week while scheduled maintenance and an engine change were done.

The end result was that in the 1966 season we had all nine airplanes in commission to fly every day, seven days a week, while we maintained the airplanes in between the flights each day. As a result we had fewer write-ups and fewer problems with the airplanes. At first it was said, "Can't do it; it's never been done." I said, "I don't want to hear 'Can't be done because it hasn't been done.' We're going to do it." Once we got into the rhythm of it, the concept and procedures went like gangbusters. That year we flew nine airplanes over five thousand hours a year. This is an abnormally high amount of flying time for tactical fighters.

In 1966 we flew extemporaneous missions. For example, "Can you go by Pocatello, Idaho, and do a memorial?" Maglione would say, "Well, sure." So we'd take off, let down over Pocatello, and do a fly-by. Sometimes we would get air-refueling support to help. There were Air Guard units in Fort Worth, Texas, and Sioux City, Iowa, with KC-97s that could refuel us with short notice. The commander of the Thunderbirds made those decisions.

We did a lot of flying just getting from one demonstration site to another. What do you do when you are moving rapidly along at 45,000 feet, hour after hour? We had UHF radio for voice communication and a squadron frequency that we used to talk with one another without interference or interruption from outside radio. Many times we would tune up low-frequency radio stations through the low-frequency navigation system, which was the same frequency band used by local broadcasting stations. I took advantage of the opportunity. For example, I might leave San Francisco and ask to hear some Dave Brubeck from the local radio station. By the time I got to Denver I could get Buddy Greco and his piano. By the time I got to the East Coast I could hear Barbara Carroll play "I Love the Piano."

It was a means of making the boredom of hours and hours at altitude a little more pleasurable. Even when practicing out at Thunderbird Lake or doing a test flight, I would sometimes call the local station and make a request. I liked to listen to "Rhapsody in Blue" when we were in formation. It seemed to enhance the flying activity and just make it more rhythmic and smoother. I would always ask for particular kinds of music that I liked, and the stations always accommodated. A disk jockey would say "This one is a special recommendation for the Thunderbirds." The DJs were happy to help us out when they could, and their efforts were appreciated. Music often made a flight a whole lot more enjoyable. The view of the Earth as it passes beneath you at 600 miles per hour is beautiful. From mountains to desert, city to city, sea to sea, it is like an endless colorful movie.

Another responsibility during my Thunderbird days was taking celebrities for a ride and getting them supersonic. Wherever we would land, the people in that particular town or activity would select somebody they wanted to ride in a tactical fighter and experience supersonic flight and maneuvers we did during the demonstrations. Each of us had to take our turn flying these celebrities. I flew with Frank Sinatra, Jr., for several days on one trip. I took Robert Lansing, who was a "Twelve O'clock High" TV and movie actor, on another trip. Throughout the country I flew mayors and senators and other politicians.

I think one of the most extraordinary individuals we flew was Yvette Mimieux, a famous movie actress at the time. She was sponsoring a program called "Operation Bedside," a documentary for a nurse recruiting program. Yvette asked if she could ride with us. It was my turn, but I did not know at the time that my passenger that day would be someone so prestigious and beautiful. I sat down and briefed her on the mission. She was very unusual, not just beautiful but also pleasing to talk with. She speaks French beautifully as well as English. At that time I could speak a little French, and conversation in the two languages can be an almost-mesmerizing combination.

After the briefing, we went to the airplane. I thought to myself that if Colonel Maglione, the commander, finds out that Yvette Mimieux is here, he's going to roar out and take the flight over. I was hoping if I got the airplane moving down the runway, I wouldn't have to stop in the event that Maglione did show up. Well, as luck would have it, we were just starting to taxi out when I looked up and saw a cloud of dust barreling down the taxiway at a high rate of speed. Sure enough, it was Maglione coming to exercise his command authority and take Yvette on the ride. So I had to get out of the airplane and let Maglione take over. After the ride was over I met Yvette for lunch. This was probably one of the most pleasing experiences that I can remember. She was such a pleasure to be around.

However, the Yvette Mimieux ride created some serious difficulties over the publicity given to such a high-profile celebrity. General J. P. McConnell, the Air Force Chief of Staff at the time, was upset because it appeared we were taking movie people to help publicize their films. I met him at Chanute Air Force Base a few days after Yvette's ride, and he was abrasive with me about flying this movie star to support her movies. I tried to explain to him that it was a nursing recruitment documentary and well within our authority. But General McConnell didn't pay a whole lot of attention to that explanation. The general did not know I wasn't the person who took Yvette on the ride, and I wasn't about to tell him. I took the heat for some time after that. Still it was a nice experience, and I will always remember it. Yvette Mimieux was one of the first distinguished celebrities to fly with the USAF Thunderbirds. She added a new dimension to our appearance and prestige in the eyes of the public.

There were a couple of noteworthy events during the early part of the 1966 training season. I was skiing at Mount Charleston with my three boys when I took a hard fall and broke my left arm. I didn't know at the time that it was broken. As we drove back home, it started to swell up fast, and it didn't look very good. I went to the flight surgeon at Nellis, who told me it was broken in two places. I thought, "This is not going to be easy." I called Colonel Maglione and said, "Sir, I broke my arm skiing today." He only hesitated a couple of seconds, and said, "So?" A couple of seconds more and he added, "Brief at seven o'clock in the morning." I wasn't sure what I was supposed to do, but I did know that at 0700 hours I would be in a briefing. I went back to the flight surgeon and told him I would have to be prepared to fly. He said that was out of the question. Just in case, we modified the cast on my left arm so I could operate the throttle on the F-100. He took the still-wet cast off, and gave me a shot of cortisone at the break to enhance healing. He put on a cast that would fit over the throttle and leave my thumb free to use the speed brakes and microphone controls. I flew, a little sore, the next day.

As it happened, we were also scheduled to take pictures for team publications that day. For the photos I put my hand in my helmet so the cast would not show. That first morning when I reported in, Maglione never said a word to me, never asked how I was doing. After the briefing, I got in the airplane and flew with the broken arm. This was something a little unusual, as normally you don't fly with a cast on. I glued the back of my leather flight glove on the back of the cast, so it was a little less conspicuous. I continued to fly with it until mid–April and actually had no difficulty.

I played handball on a regular basis and continued to do that, too. I taped a small metal strip to the inner side of the cast, over the palm. That cast was a threat on the handball court because I could take the ball off the front of the court and it would come off my arm as quickly as it came off the wall. It was a decisive advantage, believe me. But that didn't last. I was sent in late February to the Air Force semi-final handball tournament at Mountain Home, Idaho. I went all the way through the semi-finals before one of the players complained that I had an unfair advantage with the cast. I was eliminated. But I hadn't lost a game up to that point. When I left Mountain Home that night I beat that field up pretty good with my racy F-100. A flight surgeon in Columbus, Ohio, saw that I had a cast on and said that I could not fly with a cast. When I returned to Nellis from that trip it was time to take the cast off anyway, and I continued to fly as normal.

About midway through the 1966 season, Buster McGee, the right wingman, broke his right hand during our daily handball competition. Unlike the broken arm episode from which I had recently recovered, Buster's break was in his right hand and could not be cast in such a way that he could still fly. There also had been repercussions from my flying with a broken arm. Major Frank Liethen had joined the team. He was an

Capt. Earl Haney with an F-100D. Capt. Haney's left hand is in his helmet to hide a broken arm from a skiing accident, 1966.

old friend from Nellis, a great aviator, and an accomplished test pilot from Edwards Air Force Base. He was to replace Colonel Maglione on completion of Maglione's tour with the Thunderbirds. Frank didn't have much to do until it became time for him to train as the new leader. It was decided that Frank would replace Buster on the right wing until Buster was back in medical condition. To prepare, Frank and I left the demonstration team and went back to Nellis Air Force Base. I flew with him three times a day for seven days. We went to Indian Springs and flew air show after air show until Frank was ready to join the team on the right wing. We rejoined the demonstration team in Florida, and Frank flew his first demonstration after only seven days of our extensive training, with me flying as the leader and Frank flying as the right wingman.

Many said it could not be done, that we could not train a person that quickly. I think under normal conditions that might be true. But Frank was an exceptional guy — a very good aviator and a very strong person. My only concern was that he had never done the "Bomb Burst" with more than two airplanes. The Bomb Burst cross is done with four airplanes at 500 miles per hour at 50 feet off the ground opposing one another from four directions. I was a little concerned about how he would do in an actual situation with four airplanes. But it was just another day at the office for Frank. His first air show was letter perfect. Frank stayed on the right wing until Buster got his hand out of the cast and resumed the right wing position. After that we went on with the Nine Ship Diamond with Frank as number 7.

During the 1966 season we flew some night demonstrations on return to Nellis AFB. At one time we were returning to Nellis and had extra gas. We came across Sunrise Mountain east of Nellis. It was dark, and as we approached the runway Maglione for some reason pulled up and did what's called a "Whifferdill." That's a reverse of direction by using altitudes and direction change to reverse direction in minimum time and distance. He did a Whifferdill, came back down the runway, and decided that he wanted to do a limited demonstration at night. Demonstrations at night are much more difficult than under daylight conditions. High-performance maneuvers and changing position with respect to the ground at a very rapid rate are a tricky things to do at night. Maglione had this idea, so we did night demonstrations under his supervision.

On one of these night demonstrations we were almost vertical coming down at the runway. Maglione said on the radio to turn the air refueling probe light on. The air refueling probe light was actuated by a toggle switch underneath the right canopy rail. This light would shine on the air-refueling probe so the probe could be seen when you refueled at night. We were coming down, and he says, "Probe lights on." I've got to take my hand off the stick, get over to the switch, and get my hand back on the stick before I kill myself. We were still coming straight down, and he says, "Probe lights on." It was hectic for us in the airplanes, especially those of us in the rear. The sight picture you have when you are flying formation at night — changing direction, changing altitudes and attitudes second by second — is out the front windscreen, right at the tail pipe in front of you. It's visual when the afterburners are on, such as going up over the top in a maneuver, but with afterburners off you aren't able to see beyond the lip of that exhaust pipe. It was difficult to change any kind of cockpit configuration when you are fighting to stay in formation and with the difficulty of doing it at night. Consequently, when I heard "Probe lights on," I did not take my hand off the stick and did not get the air refuel probe light on. We got back and landed, and Bobby Morgan and I were walking across the ramp. I said, "Bobby, I didn't get that damn probe light on." He said, "I didn't either." By the time we walked in, we all figured out the only probe light that was on was Maglione's.

Those night formations were only done on the return to Nellis. People at the base would see the formation, and our families would be watching waiting for us to return. The people in Las Vegas could see it. This got a lot of attention. All that could be seen in the black of night were the wing running lights and the afterburners in formation. The aircraft were not visible. Those who saw the night demonstrations said they were truly spectacular. A favorable comment once came from the control tower, which fueled Maggie's enthusiasm. For me, it was like anything you do at night in the air: Be very attentive and careful. We did not do this often, which was probably best, and I doubt the night demonstrations have been done since the 1966 season.

On many of our returns to Nellis we would fly below the Grand Canyon Rim, from east to west, crawling up over Sunrise Mountain to enter our arrival sequence at Nellis. The formation in the canyon was very close for obvious reasons. Safety became of more concern after accidents. Night demonstrations would only enhance the chances of putting the Thunderbirds in harm's way. We were ordered not to do any more night demonstrations after one late-night return to Nellis from the East Coast.

Our final refueling stop en route to Nellis many times was Kirtland Air Force Base, Albuquerque, New Mexico. This left just short of 500 miles to Nellis, a reasonable flight under normal conditions. Accurate high-altitude wind forecasting was inadequate at best during these early days of high-altitude flight. We departed Kirtland about 11 P.M. with no unusual winds or weather reported en route to our destination. As we arrived at Prescott, Arizona, we were 44 minutes behind our planned flight schedule. We had flown into the jet stream, an unexpected phenomenon at this time in the early high-altitude supersonic era. The head winds at our altitude were around 200 miles per hour. This extreme wind condition meant we would not be able to make Nellis AFB under existing conditions. Colonel Maglione elected to commence an early descent to exit the jet stream.

Generally the weather in the Las Vegas, Nevada, area is pretty clear, which would allow us a fuel-saving visual approach into Nellis AFB, ten miles north of Las Vegas. On this night, however, Las Vegas was overcast with a 2,000-foot ceiling and light rain. We would have to make an instrument penetration and weather approach into Nellis using fuel we did not have. We arrived at 20,000 (high cone) over the Las Vegas approach fix. We were in the eight-ship Outhouse formation. Our procedure was to break into two four-ship flights for instrument penetration, with Colonel Maglione leading the first four aircraft and with me leading the second four. Maggie would commence penetration as I would do a 360-degree turn for spacing and then commence penetration with my flight.

I did not have the fuel for this, so I turned the flight 15 degrees off the outbound heading and commenced penetration behind Maggie. We were in the clouds, with most of the penetration breaking out at 2,000 feet on final approach. Maggie elected to land from an overhead approach at 1,500 feet. I, again, did not have enough fuel for this. I faced the fact that the engines would flame out with excessive bank angle, as we were now down to 100 pounds of fuel. We landed in formation on a wet runway directly behind Thunderbird number 4. We operated on minimum fuel often, not uncommon in jet fighters, but this episode was off the safe scale. "Speedy Pete" Everst, my old friend from Edwards AFB who was now our wing commander at Nellis AFB, was not happy about our low-fuel arrival.

We continued through the season, successfully overcoming obstacles that were before us, such as weather, heavy schedules, impromptu fly-bys, and anything else that came our way. Then in late October, again at Indian Springs, unthinkable tragedy struck in an instant. Frank Liethen was to fly with Bobby Morgan in the two-seat F-100F for indoctrination in solo routine. Bobby Beckel was in a one-seat F-100. At the top of the opposing Cuban 8 (four Gs over the top and roll out), the two aircraft collided.

Bobby and Frank were killed instantly. Two remarkable humans were lost in that moment over Indian Springs. Bobby Beckel flew in with his airplane — it had some damage — but he was able to get it back on the ground. As always with a tragedy like that, news of the accident was transmitted on television and became a very public thing. We had another mid-air collision in 1966 while training at Indian Springs, just previous to Frank Liethen and Bobby Morgan's accident. In this case Buster McGee and Chris Patterakis ran together at the top of a loop and were able to bail out. Both got out okay, but we lost two airplanes.

People were saying, "The Thunderbirds are having accidents, and maybe it's too expensive to keep the Thunderbirds in motion." It was near the end of the season, and it was decided to complete the season. We would continue with a Four Ship Diamond and one solo until the end of the season. Colonel Maglione would move on to the rest of his Air Force career, and a new leader would come on. I led the team from Maxwell Air Force Base, Alabama, back to Nellis after the final demonstration in 1966. We began the training for 1967 but did not yet have a new leader. The bigger question was what the Thunderbirds would develop for the 1967 season, if anything at all.

There was discussion that the Thunderbirds would transition into the F-4E soon. In late 1966, I went to McDonnell-Douglas, St. Louis, Missouri, where ten F-4Es without fire control systems were located. These aircraft would be ours. I worked a couple of weeks on the requirements to accommodate the Thunderbird mission. The modifications were few, but the Thunderbird transition was delayed because of political differences between the Navy and the Air Force. The transition to the F-4 was completed in 1969.

With the completion of the 1966 season it was time for me to leave the Thunderbirds and go on to my next assignment. I had volunteered to go to the war in Southeast Asia, but now this would have to wait. In 1967 we were going to bring four new pilots on with a new flight leader. I had to stay. Stan Musser came on as the right wingman. He was instantly ready. Jack Dickey replaced Hank Canterbury, and Mike Miller was the new narrator. Tony McPeak, a man of great strength, was the new solo pilot. We began the training season with the four new guys, and waited for the new commander, Major Neil Eddins, to return from a Vietnam combat tour in the F-105. Neil had been on the Thunderbirds earlier as a pilot and had been selected to lead the Thunderbird organization for the next two years. He would now be replacing Frank Liethen who, until the accident, had been scheduled to become commander.

Neil came in early February, about halfway through the training. I flew with him two to three times every day, much as I had with Frank Liethen and Ralph Maglione. I flew in each position until he became comfortable with the whole air show sequence and the requirements that he would have to meet. Neil had added pressure because of the accidents and

In the center is Capt. Jack Dickey. Going clockwise from extreme left are Capt. Tony McPeak, Major Earl Haney, Capt. Mike Miller, Capt. Bob Beckel, Lt. Chris Patterakis, Major Neil Eddins, and Major Stan Musser.

need for quick acclimation to the dynamic Thunderbird mission. We did not have an executive officer to handle the day-to-day personnel and mission problems for the commander. During this season I acted as the commander's exec when necessary to give him the time he needed to concentrate on mission accomplishment and future development as a commander should. I flew number 7 this year.

The Nine Ship Diamond was no longer allowed. We began the normal demonstration season as usual in March 1967. The new season would be no different from the previous two. Five new guys on the team, another heavy schedule, the same long days, and the same long hours made it so.

While I was on the Thunderbirds I acquired a name that would stay with me for the remainder of my career. My full name is Robert Earl Haney. My mother always called me Earl after her favorite brother. In the Air Force I was known as Bob or Earl until the weekend in 1967 when the Thunderbirds did an air show at my hometown, Champaign, Illinois. In high school my friends called me "Speed," a reference to our football coach's comments about the quick adjustments I made completing tackles as a defensive player. My acquisition of a Harley Davidson motorcycle added to that reputation. In the mid–1960s the song "Speedo" ("*They used to call him Speedo, but his real name is Mr. Earl")* became popular. One of my Thunderbird friends, Mike Miller, a good singer and guitar player, got up at a social event that weekend in Champaign and sang the "Mr. Earl" song to all my buddies, who then began calling me "Mr. Earl." The name caught on. In Air Force circles from then on I was known as Mr. Earl. Correspondence would come through the administration mail system addressed simply to "Mr. Earl," and I would get it.

We were gone around 250 days out of the year, usually seven to ten days at a time. We would be home for maybe one or two days, and then we were off again. We worked at doing a good job as we traveled but also worked as diligently as possible to spend the best time we could with our families. When I came home I would hit the ground running and use the time I had with the family in the best way we could. My three boys were just little fellows. When we arrived at Nellis in 1965 the kids were just beginning grade school, but even then they enjoyed sports and outdoor activities. Lake Mead, east of Las Vegas, was close by. We spent lots of time water skiing year round, even in the dead of winter. We would start off the beach with our ski boat, and the boys seldom ever touched the water. Snow skiing was a part of winter life. Lee Canyon, about twenty miles up to Mount Charleston northwest of Las Vegas, was an ideal recreation area. We sometimes would venture all the way to Bryan Head, Utah, about 150 miles north of Nellis, to winter ski. We returned from skiing a very weary lot. Even today my boys remember the fun that we had during the three years with the Thunderbirds.

When the team was home, we socialized a lot together and had fun planning events with the families. When we were traveling we lived together seven days a week, almost 24 hours a day. Working as a team was top priority, and for the most part the guys got along very well together.

Capt. Haney's three sons: Mike, Steve, and Max in a photograph taken during Capt. Haney's tour with the Thunderbirds, 1966.

Very seldom was there any sort of confrontation. The commanders, Ralph Maglione and Neil Eddins, were good leaders and did their level best to keep the continuity and the good spirit flowing. But over the years an occasional incident did occur. It seems in any organization there is always somebody who wants to be a bit of a hero or a prima donna, and eventually that becomes an irritant. Sometimes differences would just erupt. I got mad one day about some complaints. I jumped up on a table and offered a few of my inner thoughts. I believed we were given much, maybe too much. Occasionally something would occur in public that was less than acceptable conduct for an officer or a Thunderbird. We did our level best to minimize those things, but they do happen with aggressive fighter pilots.

While members of the Thunderbirds are given a great opportunity, it is important to remember the mission — not one individual or an elite group. People know the Thunderbirds fly flashy airplanes and do some spectacular maneuvering. The members of the team should look and act exactly like all Air Force fighter pilots. The Thunderbirds belong to a larger, more important organization: the United States Air Force. If the Thunderbirds transmit to the public the character of our country and capability of our fighters, they have done a good job. Once at Sacramento, California, an elderly woman approached me and took my hand. She said, "Today you have made me proud to be an American." I thanked her with sincerity. As I walked on, I thought, "Today I have done a good job."

Sometimes when we were going from the West Coast to the East Coast and had to be there in one day to meet a requirement the following day, we would have to refuel en route two or three times. When we didn't have time to stop at bases along the way to gas up the F-100s, we would have tankers meet us in the air for an air refuel. Anytime we went overseas — deployments to Central America, Europe, Alaska, or wherever — we normally would air refuel because there were no fueling stations available to us. Air refueling flights often were eight- to ten-hour flights. I had been doing six-, eight-, ten-hour missions as a fighter pilot since I was a second lieutenant. You can't move around much in a fighter, so after about three or four hours you get a little bit restless. Eventually you sort of settle in knowing you are going to be there for a long time. I used to take my G-suit and fold it up and put it underneath my seat to get more comfortable. It had a little test valve that you could test the G-suit with. I would roll it up and sit on it, and every now and then I could push the test switch and get the G-suit to inflate and massage my lower body a little.

In early May of 1967 we were en route to a 30-day deployment in Europe, air refueling all the way. About 100 miles north of Wichita, Kansas, our eight F-100s were refueling off two KC-135 tankers. Colonel Maglione and the new leader, Major Neil Eddins, in the F-100F took the first four airplanes to refuel on the first tanker. Normally I would lead the next four airplanes — the two solos, the narrator, and myself— and refuel on the second tanker. When we came off the tankers, we would join up in the eight-ship formation and continue on our next en-route leg.

On this day, however, Bobby Beckel had asked to lead the second element and the change was okayed. The second element came off the tankers in a fast join-up with a little bit of G-load on us. We were in the wrong formation. We were in a fingertip formation when we should have been in a right-echelon formation so no lateral move would be required when we moved into the Outhouse formation. We were in a turn as we moved underneath the first flight. The man on the left wing, Mike Miller, moved laterally across the formation. The vertical stabilizer of his aircraft raked across the underneath of my F-100. I lost control of the aircraft, and it immediately caught on fire. I ejected instantly. As I did the airplane exploded, scattering debris all over Kansas. I really didn't have time to be scared when the collision occurred. Your first thought is how to survive, and my priority was to get to the ground safely.

We were going between 400 to 500 miles an hour when I ejected. I flailed around violently in the slipstream. The collision completely tore off the survival kit that hangs below the seat. The survival kit is connected to a 25-foot cable and survival dinghy in case you go down over water. Immediately after I bailed out, that 25-foot cable wrapped around me, tying me up like a mummy. I was pinned and couldn't get loose. I flailed through the air until I slowed down to a terminal velocity of somewhere around 180 to 200 miles an hour. I started getting the cable unwrapped, enough that I could get the chute opened. I fell for a while before finally getting the cable off and the chute opened.

The first thing I saw when the parachute opened was a TWA 707 airliner. I *knew* it was going to hit me. The airliner was not far away, and I was descending to a point where it looked like the 707 was going to hit me right between the eyes. I actually started climbing up the parachute lines thinking I might be able to clear the airplane. It was like trying to crawl up a wall to keep a mad dog from getting you. It just seemed the only thing to do at the time. I went right behind the 707. It wasn't as close as I had thought. I cleared it by about 100 feet. But I got caught in the slipstream of the airplane, and it caused me to oscillate. I was oscillating almost 180 degrees in the air. The winds on the ground were about 35 knots, which is strong to be landing in a parachute. I didn't want to land in that oscillation, so I took a survival knife, and I cut some of the parachute lines so I could get the chute to bubble on one side and stabilize it. If you can get an equal flow of air going through the chute — in other words spilling out one side of the chute evenly — it will stabilize, but make you fall a little bit faster.

I landed in a 35-knot wind, which is a hard landing, and the wind dragged me across the ground into a barbed wire fence. I finally got the chute disconnected, and it collapsed, tangled in the barbed wire. I got skinned and banged up a little bit. My flying suit was singed from the fire, and the epaulets were peeled off. Otherwise I was okay. I got up and started gathering up the chute. I will never know if the pilot of the TWA 707 saw me. I don't know exactly who reported the collision. It could have been the 707 pilot or the other pilots when the two F-100s went down. Commercial jets are not looking for some guy sailing down in a parachute. I don't think they ever saw me, but they may have.

There was a small dirt lane running between two fields. I saw an old pickup truck coming along the road. I hailed the driver to stop. He was stunned, because here's this guy with a big orange and white parachute standing there with a bloody nose. He had no idea who I was or where I came from. He was an older gentleman, and he never spoke a word, never said a thing. I asked him if he could take me to a telephone, and he nodded at me, but still didn't say a word. I threw my chute in the back of the truck, got in, and we proceeded down the old road at about 30 miles per hour. We got two or three miles along, and a state police car comes with siren on and lights flashing. So we stopped. The state trooper obviously was looking for the pilot who had bailed out. I thanked the old gentleman and transferred from his pickup truck to the police car. I tried to get my rescuer's name and address, but he remained totally speechless. I never did find out who he was.

We went about a hundred miles an hour down this old dirt road in the state police car. I never did figure out why we were in such a hurry. I thought all the trauma was over. We proceeded to a state police post. They thought I was the only one involved in the accident. I said, "No, there's another guy. There is somebody else down." At the moment the accident occurred I didn't know whether it had been a mid-air collision or an engine explosion in my aircraft. I realized, however, that there was more than one airplane involved when I saw two smoking holes on the ground while I was in the chute. A helicopter arrived on the scene, and I jumped on board to search for the missing man. We found Mike Miller in an open field. He was banged up, and I knew he was hurting. He had a broken leg and broken back, although we didn't know that at the time. The helicopter pilot and I put him on a stretcher and flew to McConnell Air Force Base, Wichita. I didn't look all that good, but compared to Mike, I was in fairly good shape.

The Thunderbirds landed at McConnell AFB, where Mike Miller and I were taken by helicopter from the accident site to the base hospital. All the Thunderbird pilots joined up there. Mike and I were on hospital beds with a couple of doctors and nurses around. They were attending first to Mike, realizing he had some serious injuries. The guys came in, but there was not much exchange beyond assuring one another that we were okay. It's just part of your life. It's what you do. Tony McPeak was a pretty hard guy, never showing much emotion. Tony was on my right wing when the collision happened. I got out just as the airplane exploded, so I was actually in a ball of fire when I ejected. I think Tony doubted I could have survived. When he saw Mike and me still alive, he was surprised and actually appeared to be glad to see us.

I was sitting on the hospital bed, with a burned flying suit, and a bloody nose and mouth. Maglione walks up to me and says, "You gonna be able to fly tomorrow?" I said, "If I can get up the airplane ladder, I can fly." He said, "Well, okay, we're going to have to leave tomorrow. We've got engagements in Europe." He looks at me, and he says, "Well, you scrub up a little bit, you'll be okay.

That evening, I jumped out the hospital window and went to town. I didn't have any clothes other than the burnt flying suit. Everything I had went down in the airplane. So I went to a clothing store—a nice place in downtown Wichita. I looked terrible. My flying suit was a mess. I walked in this clothing store, and the man standing at the counter couldn't take his eyes off me. I walked around the clothes and up to his desk. I said, "Sir, I need some clothes." He says, "Yeah, you *really* need some clothes." I said, "I'm going to tell you a story. You're not going to believe it." I said, "I had an accident and have no money with me." He said, "Don't worry about it; we'll take care of you." I said, "I jumped out of an airplane a little while ago and lost everything. I'm on my way to Europe, and I need to get some clothes."

I picked out a suit for the evening. We always had a black suit and a blue blazer and gray slacks. I picked out six hundred dollars worth of clothes and a small suitcase to put them in. I said again, "I don't have any money with me." He said, "Don't worry about it." He gave me a ticket. I said, "As soon as I get through this trip, I'll mail you a check for all this." I signed the ticket, gave it to him, and picked up the bag. I kept that bag. I gave it to my son Steve a few years ago. Yes, I did send the check for payment to the Wichita clothier.

Events such as the one I experienced over Kansas happen. It is something you know can happen. One is never totally prepared, but it is part of military life. You expect at any time that conditions will occur at a rapid rate and you'll have to react quickly. You train for it. I had practiced for ejection over and over, knowing I might have only a second to react. When the fire shot up between my legs, I ejected.

That night I was really upset about the accident. I realized it was just another one of those stupid things. We lost two more airplanes and almost lost two more pilots. The join-up was bad, and we were not in the right re-join formation. As usual, there was much discussion and "Monday morning quarter-backing" over this Thunderbird accident. Like all accidents, it should not have happened. Thunderbird flight is close, fast, accelerated and sometimes unforgiving for small errors. The accident was investigated. The investigators never interviewed me. I left the next day to go on to Europe, and Mike stayed in the hospital.

As I look back on this incident, I am not sure what really happened. I know we were moving into formation, and then all of a sudden my airplane was on fire. I didn't know whether I had been hit or the engine exploded. All I know is that the fire shot up between my legs and the cockpit filled up with fire, and I was able to get out. To this day, I have never read the accident report. I led the flight from then on. Mike was in a cast for several months. He was able to rejoin the Thunderbirds later in the 1967 season. In the meantime, we had to go on to Europe to complete the demonstrations.

After the accident I picked up a spare airplane. It belonged to a combat wing, which loaned it to us. They didn't have a red, white, and blue airplane, so I took a camouflaged F-100, not the typical color of the Thunderbirds. It looked like a lizard with the camouflaged paint. While it looked funny, the fighter pilots loved it because one of their airplanes was now in the Thunderbird formation. It proved a big hit as we traveled around Europe, with me in the "Lizard." There were now six red, white, and blue F-100s and one recently acquired lizard. We continued a very rigorous tour in Europe, although we were two airplanes and one pilot short. We completed demonstrations from point to point, some 20 as I remember. We either were flying in demonstrations or going from show to show every day. I don't know if we ever had a day off. At least I didn't. Keeping the airplanes maintained and meeting all the flight test requirements demanded very long days.

The fourth of June 1967 we were at LeBourget Airport, Paris, France. We left at about three o'clock in the morning to fly non-stop to Colorado Springs, Colorado. This was one of the longest single-engine jet aircraft flights ever made. We flew nearly 14 hours and had nine refuelings in the air, as I recall. We landed at Colorado Springs in the afternoon of June fourth. The next day we did a Thunderbird show for the graduation of the Air Force Academy Class of 1967.

As we returned from a grueling trip to Europe, we settled down to a consistent pace, free of unusual events until we arrived at Del Rio Air Force Base at Laughlin, Texas, in October 1967. A spectacular accident occurred during an air show demonstration. The mishap occurred as Tony McPeak was pulling up through the Bomb Burst maneuver. The aircraft in the Four Ship Diamond formation split to four cardinal directions while flying straight up. The solo, Tony, accelerates through the diamond. (This is similar to the "Over the Shoulder" bomb release tactic employed in the release of nuclear weapons.) As Tony accelerated to the vertical, the wings broke in the center, and his airplane burst into flames. Tony immediately ejected, making a quick descent to the ground and landing directly in front of the crowd. Definitely a tough act to follow. Tony was lucky to survive. He was a close friend and my daily handball competitor. I didn't want to lose him. He went on to gain four stars and became the Air Force Chief of Staff.

This accident opened up a serious problem with our aging F-100Ds. We found cracks in all of the main wing structure of the aircraft. They all required major structural repair/modification. Again it was a very difficult period of time. We moved on through the rest of that season, waiting for the modified F-100s. I had intended to leave to go to my duty in Southeast Asia during the early part of the season, but because of the accidents, the training requirements, and the repair of all airplanes I stayed on to help meet these commitments.

By 1965 we had begun to fly worldwide, and knowledge of the team's mission expanded to where more and more people wanted to see the demonstrations. Many people at that time had not seen a jet fighter. As interest in the Thunderbirds expanded, so did the requirements to demonstrate, to be visible to the public at many different places. As responsibilities increased and the exposure time that we had to fly increased, so did the accident rate. Eventually, there had to be modifications to arrive at a sensible number of air shows each year and carry out a very stringent training process that would eliminate, or at least minimize, the possibility of accidents. The evolution of the program through the 1960s was costly in some respects, but that was the mission, and that was the duty.

During the 1965 season, we completed 121 scheduled Thunderbird shows, as well as doing extemporaneous fly-bys as we got back into the F-100. We did in excess of 100 scheduled shows for each of my three years on the Thunderbirds. Those three years were the highest number of demonstrations ever flown by the team. In the present day the average air show season is around 60 per year with no extemporaneous fly-bys or nine-ship formations. This is about half of the number of demonstrations we completed in the middle–1960s. We probably did way too many shows and overworked the crew in the process. We had eight pilots or nine pilots for those years, and 38 maintenance people. The Thunderbirds today have eight pilots, a maintenance officer, an executive officer, an administrative officer, and about 120 enlisted maintenance people. Somewhere around

A celebration of 1,000 air shows since the formation of the Thunderbirds. The landmark air show was performed at Wright-Patterson AFB, Ohio, 1967.

150 people are involved as compared to our total of 50. The number of people has increased in order the meet the mission, even though the number of demonstrations has decreased. We just wore guys out. The maintenance people and the pilots during my three years were tired, a factor that no doubt does increase the accident potential.

Now more concern is on safety, with more rest time for both the pilots and the support people. The Thunderbirds are better managed now, more disciplined. I think the whole operation has improved each year, and that is as it should be. The requirements today are still stringent and have more restrictions. There is more down time. While on duty, pilots cannot go to social events that last beyond six in the evening if they are required to fly the next day. Today I don't think the Thunderbirds do anything more than a six-ship demonstration. In comparison, we flew from point to point in a seven-ship formation, the Stinger, and would arrive at a new show site in that formation. Normally the narrator would go ahead to provide all the necessary FAA requirements and social requirements prior to the team's arrival, but we sometimes flew the eight-ship formation en route. I don't think this is done anymore. We also flew the Nine Ship Diamond during the 1966 season, doing fly-bys and impromptu demonstrations going from one show site to another.

An F-100 in flight refueling. Air refueling allowed worldwide non-stop flight capabilities. Photograph of one of the F-100s in Capt. Haney's Thunderbird formation near Cedar Rapids, Iowa, during deployment, 1966.

In 1966 and 1967 we lost six airplanes and two pilots. Those were the bad years in terms of losses, but this was also the time when we were flying the most demonstrations, the most hours, under the most stringent conditions. In the early days, the Thunderbirds did not go outside the limits of the United States, and only flew four airplanes, followed by five airplanes, and then six airplanes. As the number of airplanes and the number of air shows and the demands placed on the Thunderbird mission increased, the responsibilities and the requirements increased. So did the potential for accidents, to a point that there had to be some change.

Other accidents happened in succeeding years. Several pilots have been killed in the 20-some years since I have been out of the Air Force, but overall the accident rate has decreased. During the training season of 1982, the whole diamond formation was lost at one time. The four pilots crashed into the ground at Indian Springs and were killed instantly. The 1982 season was the worst in the memory of the Thunderbirds.

I used to worry about the enlisted people working beyond their limits during the three years I was on the Thunderbirds. They never quit until the job was done. If it took 24 hours a day, they worked 24 hours a day. They were all proud members of the Thunderbird team. I never heard a complaint. There were a lot of four-letter words used, but "quit" wasn't one of them. They were soldiers personified. As an example, one morning I came into my office and found one of the men asleep on my couch. He had worked most of the night on maintenance, which was not unusual. My arrival scared him because he realized he had been caught on my big office couch. I said, "You're welcome to that couch. You're certainly doing more good with it than I am." The couch became a bed for many of those guys from that day on. I told the crew my office was open and it was theirs whenever they needed.

Sometimes I just stayed out of the way as they worked because I didn't want to get in the path of progress. I didn't really need to supervise them much. When we went to flying nine airplanes all the time, most people thought that was impossible; you can't do that. They never uttered a word of negative response. We just sat down and figured out how to do it, and we did it. That's the way we got things done. I usually was in contact every day with my crew, but there were periods when I had to spend a lot of time flying the airplane and was away from them. They continued on with the same rapport and hard working conditions whether I was there or not. When they had social events, I would often visit them, but we were never on a first-name basis due to the military organization. They liked the professional formality better than I did.

The maintenance crew flew in a C-130 when traveling from show site to show site. Everything went aboard the C-130, equipment and repair gear. Maintenance is hard to do when you don't have a permanent base with ground facilities. There were some things we could borrow from base to base, but for the most part, we had to bring in our supplies and equipment with the crew in the C-130.

The maintenance crew and I became very close. I can't say enough good words about them. We had great respect for one another. I did my level best to support them, no matter what the conditions were. If there was a mistake made, we shouldered the mistake as a team. We never did point one guy out or make one guy punishable or remiss if something went wrong. Whatever happened, good or bad, we did it together. I had bought an expensive bottle of liquor in France while we were on tour. I don't drink much, but for some reason — maybe because it was a pretty bottle — I bought it. When I left the Thunderbirds, all 38 members of the maintenance crew and I had a swig, and I extended my salute to them. These people are a rare breed, with a level of integrity unknown to most humans. When I left they gave me a plaque with my airplane model on it and some very much appreciated words engraved in gold letters:

To:
Major Earl Haney
Great Boss, Outstanding Officer, Loyal Friend
In Sincere Appreciation for Your
Outstanding Leadership, Your
Devotion to Duty, and Your
Fairness and Loyalty to All E.M.'s.
We Will Miss You "Boss"
Your Boys

During the 1967 season I had gone to Palmdale, California, to test and pick up a newly modified airplane from North American Aviation. I had ferried airplanes from Nellis to the factory and back, or from wherever we were around the world, and from time to time, I also would do solo demonstrations. That was what we were assigned to do. When I departed that day I flew through the archway gate at the entrance of the Palmdale plant. It was somewhat spontaneous, but all I had to do was put the pitot boom (a long tube that protrudes in front of the aircraft to measure air flow for air speed and altitude indicators) on the white line of the highway and get as low as I could and fly through the gate. Whenever I left a base by myself I departed in Thunderbird fashion if possible. Depending on where I might be, I would roll on takeoff and fly through the gate or maybe do an inverted flight by a tower. I would do some sort of farewell gesture on a regular basis.

Many of the maintenance guys that worked for me were at the Palmdale plant that day. When I left the team they gave me a painting of my F-100 flying through the arched gate that enters North American Plant 42 in Palmdale. They presented the painting at my going-away party. Gen. R. G. "Zack" Taylor, the Nellis Center commander, was there. He wanted to know a little background on the gift. He walked up to me after the presentation and said, "Mr. Earl, I want to see you in my office at 0700 Monday morning." Then I realized, looking back on it, that my flying through the gate wasn't a very smart thing to do. It was a little irresponsible, and I was about to be landed on for it.

I didn't sleep much all weekend. General Taylor was a combat-seasoned leader, and a fine commander. I had no idea what he was going to do but thought that whatever he did, I deserved. I got to his office in my dress blues and shiny shoes early on Monday morning wanting to be there

The 1967 Thunderbird enlisted personnel support team.

before General Taylor arrived. He arrived at the office at precisely seven o'clock. After a few moments his secretary said, "He will see you now." I walked in, saluted, and reported military fashion. We were very friendly normally, but he did not speak for the first several minutes. He was scribbling on some paper. Finally, he looked up and said, "Mr. Earl, how was your weekend?" I said, "Well, Sir, I haven't slept since Friday night." He smiled, looked at me directly and said very sternly, "Get to work. I don't have time to socialize." His message was loud and clear — the one between the lines. Another good lesson from another great leader. It was a dumb thing that I did, and I wouldn't do it again. I think he felt that I had punished myself enough. He also knew that I had volunteered to go to the war in Southeast Asia. He must have thought it might not be wise to punish a pilot who is going to combat. I never forgot his fairness in response to a young guy who had done something stupid.

The Thunderbirds was a good assignment, a fun assignment, but it was not the most difficult assignment in my Air Force career. It was not as difficult as some of the normal operational fighter missions I had already flown, nor was it the hardest thing I faced as a test pilot or later in combat during the Vietnam War. It was a good mission and an important mission, and I was proud to be a part of it. But the Thunderbirds do not have a great deal of emphasis in my mind over and above other assignments. It just fit in my life where it was. It is part of the puzzle that fits but that has no more particular color than any of the other pieces.

Characterization of Maj. Haney's flight through the main Gate, Plant 42, Palmdale, California.

The Thunderbirds began in early 1953 with just four

airplanes flying a Four Ship Diamond and doing just 15 or 20 minutes of maneuvers and demonstrations. The organization developed through the years with the addition of more airplanes, other flight members, and larger formations, until in 1966 we had nine pilots and nine airplanes and flew in the spectacular Nine Ship Diamond. The demonstration had become more than an air show. The Thunderbirds had become a very important organization because they transmitted throughout the world a language of tactical capability and actual authoritative war capability. They carried that particular red, white, and blue theme throughout the world in a language everybody could understand. Whether you could speak English or not, you could see that those red and white airplanes stood for freedom and authority.

Every flight and every movement of the Thunderbird aircraft is a demonstration of some sort of tactical capability. Even when we would fly across country at 35,000 feet or above, we would remain in close formation because somebody would be watching. Wherever we went, whoever would look up in the sky and see the contrail of a very close formation would know it was probably the Thunderbirds. It would always demonstrate the way and the manner that the Air Force handles itself in whatever kind of flight activity it is in, whether from cross-country to actual demonstration to actual combat. The end result of all that is accomplished by the Thunderbird demonstrations is what the overall Air Force can do in combat situations. That is what the Thunderbirds are for—not just a few minutes of demonstration but rather an everyday opportunity to show the rest of the country, the rest of the world, the tactical fighter capabilities of the U.S. Air Force. The Thunderbirds demonstrated to the public the aviation advancements made during the evolution of the supersonic fighter.

Every time the Thunderbirds start the engines it is a demonstration because you can't hide a 50-foot long, red, white, and blue fighter that makes enough noise to wake up the dead. It was a flamboyant assignment where you got a lot of attention as you traveled around in your shiny red, white, and blue fighter. You had a tremendous amount of freedom as you traveled—a small group of guys in some flashy airplanes. But in no way did the importance and attention belong to any individual. It belonged to an entire organization involved in an important mission with a great deal of value to the United States of America.

CHAPTER 9

Southeast Asian War

"The memory of the tragedies never goes away."

While in the Thunderbirds, I had volunteered for combat duty in Southeast Asia. Although my time with the Thunderbirds was extended, the government didn't forget. As it turned out, it just took a little longer than I expected for me to get there. I had elected to go back to the F-4 Phantom rather than stay with the F-100. It was necessary that I become current again in the F-4 aircraft before going to Vietnam. The F-4, which I had flown with the 366th Fighter Wing at Holloman, was fighting the air war—the fighter pilots' war—in North Vietnam, where I wanted to go. If I had stayed in the F-100 that I flew with the Thunderbirds, I would have flown missions in South Vietnam.

Unfortunately, I severed an Achilles tendon while playing handball during the re-current process. I had to have it surgically repaired and ended up in a cast from my toes to my hip. Because it was going to take several months to recover from this injury, I asked to be assigned to the USAF Fighter Weapons School in the F-4 aircraft at Nellis Air Force Base. My plan was to go through the academic course as I recovered from the injury and pick up the flying part as I became capable. I started in the Weapons School in March of 1968 and spent approximately six months at Nellis. The Fighter Weapons School, sometimes known as "Top Gun," was the most difficult academic course I have ever encountered, bar none. It encompasses the absolute corners of tactical fighter capabilities, requiring candidates to master the limits in fighter weapons and high-performance flight dynamics and energy maneuverability, both academically and in airborne performance. It taxes your authority and capability with all the weapons that are carried on a fighter and tests your ability to perform to the limits of the tactical fighter envelope. This is a very intense program and very few — usually only two of the best fighter pilots in each fighter wing — are assigned each year to train in the Weapons School.

I was still in a cast as I neared the end of Weapons School. A pilot must be grounded if he goes longer than 120 days without flying and must be formally reinstated to get back on flying status. I wanted to maintain my flight currency. As the 120-day limit approached, the big cast was replaced with a smaller one. I wanted to fly with the leg cast. General R. G. "Zack" Taylor, the Fighter Weapons Center commander, was not convinced that this was the thing to do. I mentioned that while I was on the Thunderbirds I had flown for six weeks with my arm in a cast, and that turned out not to be any big deal. Eventually, General Taylor agreed to let me fly. I took an instructor in the back seat of an F-4 and flew three landings, the minimum required to maintain my currency.

By the time my leg was strong enough to take out of the cast, I had finished the academic part of the Fighter Weapons School. After the cast was removed, I went back to flying all the missions that I should have completed while going through the academic requirements. I was a highly experienced fighter pilot by this time, so I did not need to fly all of the missions. I was able to bypass some of the usual requirements and move to the next phase until fully qualified. At this point, I had a very unusual Air Force Specialty Code, an AFSC F-1115-S, qualifying me as a fighter pilot, a test pilot, and a fighter weapons instructor.

I still limped badly because when the tendon healed it wasn't as long as it had been before the injury. As far as I was concerned I was ready to go on to Southeast Asia, but the flight surgeon thought that because of the limp I should not go into combat. There was a discussion, and I said, "Well, I'm as strong as I ever was. I just limp a little bit." The medical personnel came to an agreement that if I could successfully complete survival school for the second time (I had received escape, evasion, and survival training during my Japan/Korea assignment in 1955), they would approve my assignment to Southeast Asia. In October 1968 I went to Fairchild Air Force Base in Washington State for 14 days of survival training in the wilderness. Much of the training involved what to do in the event you are shot down and become a prisoner of war. The training helped acclimate downed pilots to the probable conditions they might face and ways to survive if captured. I then proceeded to Clark Air Force Base in the Philippines and went through another four days of survival school to acclimate to jungle survival. My Achilles tendon injury was now a thing of the past.

In November 1968 I went to Ubon Air Base, Thailand. I was assigned to the 433rd Tactical Fighter Squadron (Satan's Angels), which was a part of the 8th Tactical Fighter Wing, called the "Wolf Pack."

The shortage of people in the fighter world was then becoming evident. At that time a pilot was sent home after completing 100 combat missions, but it was taking longer than the 100-mission interval, which was about six months, to train a pilot in the F-4; that is, pilots were being sent home, but there were not enough trained pilots available to fill the empty slots. From the day I hit the ground at Ubon, I was assigned to fly. My first missions were normal air-to-ground tactical missions, just conventional-type activities. Normally you flew the first 15 missions on someone else's wing before being assigned as a flight leader or strike force commander. I had over 3,000 hours of fighter time in tactical fighters in the F-84, F-86, F-100, and all the way through to the F-4. I was a major when I went to Southeast Asia, with a lot of fighter experience, and a Fighter Weapons School graduate, and so was expected to be a combat leader. Those who have experience as leaders in the world of fighter aviation move to lead missions with four, eight, sixteen airplanes. I was immediately moved to a flight commander's position.

During one of my first combat missions I had a memorable experience in the exercise of authority and judgment. We were assigned to do a mission known as "Operation Road Cut" to cut some of the major thoroughfares from North Vietnam and slow the traffic of weapons into South Vietnam. This was my third combat mission, and I was assigned to fly as an element leader, position number three in a flight of four. I could see that there was a problem with the mission design: We did not have the right weapons for the mission. We were carrying "high drag" weapons — weapons equipped with speed

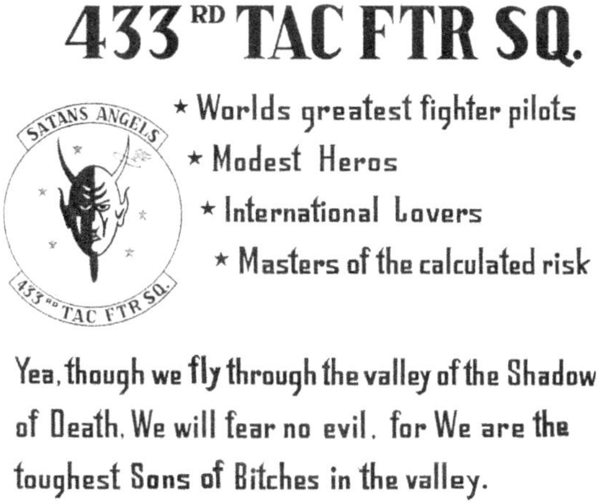
433RD TAC FTR SQ.
SATANS ANGELS
433RD TAC FTR SQ.
★ Worlds greatest fighter pilots
★ Modest Heros
★ International Lovers
★ Masters of the calculated risk
Yea, though we fly through the valley of the Shadow of Death, We will fear no evil. for We are the toughest Sons of Bitches in the valley.

Motto of the Satan Angels, 433rd Tactical Fighter Squadron. Major Haney flew with the Satan Angels for all of his 214 missions.

The 433rd Fighter Squadron, Ubon, Thailand, 1969. Major Haney is sitting in the front row, seventh from the left.

brakes to keep them at a slow rate of speed when they leave the airplane. This was not a good weapon to cut a major road because it does not have the velocity to penetrate the ground. The weapon explodes on top of the target and does nothing more than dust the road off. I was a new guy in the organization, but an old guy as far as fighters were concerned. I said, "We're using the wrong weapons, and we're using the wrong tactics to succeed in this mission." We were going to a very high-threat area near Mugia Pass where antiaircraft batteries and surface-to-air missile (SAM) sites were known to exist. The director of operations, a colonel, who designed the operation, disagreed with me. He directed me to do it as designed. My prediction was we were going to lose some airplanes.

We arrived in the target area. The leader of my flight rolled in for a dive-bomb weapons release, and the 37-millimeter enemy fire started coming off the ground at a very rapid rate. The dive-bomb attack is designed to launch lethal weapons from fighter aircraft to destroy targets on the ground and survive the attack. The fighter approaches the target from approximately 10,000 feet allowing the latitude to dive toward the target at approximately a 45-degree angle. The altitude and the angle of attack allows the fighter to accelerate to a high energy level to avoid ground fire

Maj. Haney completed his 100th combat mission in the F-4, Ubon, Thailand, 1969.

as much as possible and have the energy level necessary to exit the target without being caught in the explosion or fragment envelope of his own weapon, or running into the ground. As the pilot accelerates in the dive he has sight picture called a "pipper" that tells him when to release his weapons. Air density, winds, and release speeds all affect the weapons' travel to the target, creating inaccuracies. The later development of terminal guided weapons corrected these inaccuracies.

When the second aircraft rolled in, the two crew members in the F-4 took a direct hit from the ground fire. Because of the antiaircraft artillery (AAA), I had to rotate my airplane in a little bit closer to the center, or focal point, of the target, rather than follow the number two fighter. I went to a point where I would fly almost vertically into the target. As I rolled into the vertical and began rapid acceleration, I saw number two take the hit right between the engines. The aircraft exploded in front of me. I knew the airplane was a loss. I could also see the pilots had been able to get out. Because of their position at ejection they didn't hang in the chutes long. That was good for both of us, considering the firepower coming at us. They landed in rough terrain in a very dense jungle area. I stayed in close proximity, knowing if I lost sight of them a successful rescue mission was unlikely.

There was a lot of ground fire coming up, so I kept the airplane in a very high-G turn (six to seven Gs) and watched the two men hit the ground. I started calling for a rescue effort. I don't think the lead aircraft saw the situation unfold, as he was already pulling off the target during the initial dive-bomb attack. My wingman scattered because of heavy fire from antiaircraft artillery. When I took a look at some of the antiaircraft artillery — the 37-millimeter and 23-millimeter firepower — that was coming off the ground, my first thought was, this is not going to be easy for a hundred missions. I'm sure I wasn't the first pilot to look at a dangerous combat mission and say, "There ain't no way I'll ever survive this." All missions weren't like that, but I got a good taste of it on this day.

There was no Air Force rescue helicopter in the vicinity, but eventually an Army helicopter made contact and headed into the area. I radioed the helicopter crew that I would stay and try to pinpoint the downed pilots. During this time the bad guys were moving in toward the point where the two men landed. I used what ordnance I had to keep the North Vietnamese from converging on the two pilots until the helicopter could get in. I launched one 500-pound bomb at a time to stretch the firepower out as long as possible. The helicopter sneaked in over the hills and dropped a rope out of the back of the aircraft. The two guys hung onto the rope as the helicopter flew across the mountains to a safe area called a Lima site, built with a short runway mostly for Army and Marine use. There were several Lima sites throughout Southeast Asia, used mostly for troop transport, equipment transport, and other supplies ferried in and out of the combat zones.

By this time I had used just about all the fuel I had. I was down below what I normally would have gone home with. I was in emergency fuel by then, and I didn't know if I could make it back to Ubon. It was going to be close, so I zoomed the airplane up to almost 20,000 feet. By the time I got to 20,000 feet, I had about 80 or 90 miles to get back to Ubon. So I pulled the throttles back to idle and essentially started a minimum fuel letdown into Ubon. By this time I was becoming ever more certain I would not have enough fuel to get back and I was going to wind up jumping out short of Ubon. As in the past, old luck came through. As I got close to the final approach at Ubon, I had maybe a hundred pounds of fuel left. I held the gear until I got very close to the ground, put the gear down, and landed under power on the runway. I had to shut the airplane down in the armament area at the end of the runway because there wasn't enough fuel to taxi all the way in.

The director of operations, with whom I had discussed the mission earlier, met me at the end of the runway. The mission had not been well planned, and he was responsible for that. To divert attention from the bad mission, he redirected the attention to me. He was waiting to jump on me because I had stayed in a target area below the minimum fuel requirement. He said, "You jeopardized your aircraft and your life with it." I explained that I had used the emergency fuel in an emergency, and I felt that was within my authority. We had two guys down. This situation *was* an emergency. He was very hard with me, saying that I had not followed appropriate procedures and told me the other two pilots in the flight had returned and landed while I had not. We got into an argument, and he grounded me, saying that I wasn't going to fly until further notice. I told him I believed the rescue of the two men downed was worth the risk, and under similar circumstances I would do it again. Had I not been successful on that mission, my aviation career probably would have been over. If I had to jump out of the airplane, out of fuel, it would have been the end for me. The truth of the matter is, it was a poorly designed and directed mission and the official who designed it was looking to hammer a fall guy as a diversion.

By the end of the day the mission was discussed with the wing commander, Colonel Charles C. "Buck" Patillo. He believed I had done exactly what I was supposed to do. Two guys were down who would have been killed or become POWs, and we got them out safely. By this time the two pilots had been flown back to Ubon in a C-130. They were back okay. I was immediately reinstated to flight status. But I had made an enemy in the director of operations, who felt his authority had been overridden by the wing commander, never mind that my decision had been the right one. I felt I had to be careful around him, and was told so. I flew a few more missions and then was assigned as a flight leader and flight commander of strike forces.

The two rescued pilots remained at Ubon for a short time. The crew member in the back seat of the downed airplane refused to fly after that. He went to a medical center for psychiatric evaluation and dismissal from the Air Force. I saw the other pilot, Lieutenant Colonel Clemens, occasionally until he went home. I saw him again in 1975 when we served on a board, together with Pete Knight, Tom Stafford, and Bob Titus, to select the thirteen Apollo astronauts. He retired a major general.

The director of operations, although very hard nosed with others, made mistakes himself. One time he was coming off a target area and the leader signaled the flight to shut off the switches controlling the armament, which is necessary before you rejoin formation and return home. He didn't shut the switches off, and when they joined up he fired a whole pod of rockets through a formation, his own formation. He was never held accountable for that. He would not even attend the debriefing. He had a reputation for meeting less-than-acceptable mission responsibility, yet tagging others with severe consequences for the slightest infraction.

Later on, after all the dust settled, I was awarded a Distinguished Flying Cross for my part in the rescue of the two downed pilots. I never knew for sure how the award occurred, but I knew a letter had been written to my wing commander saying this guy deserves recognition for a distinguished piece of flying. My guess would be the writer was the helicopter pilot who would have known that I was able to keep the bad guys off the downed pilots by providing cover for them until the rescue mission could get them out. That made the difference in saving two of our pilots.

All missions required tanker support for air refuelings. Usually an outgoing flight, north of Ubon, required refueling to reach the mission area. Refueling was needed again on the return trip. A lot of flexibility was needed in case of bad weather or other circumstances, such as if a crash occurred on the runway at home plate and we had to divert to another base. You always wanted to have enough fuel to be able to meet any unforeseen condition you might be faced with.

The fighter pilot is always flying in formation. You may be flying within feet or even inches of another airplane in your flight. Formation is a continuous flight of correction. You are correcting all the time to maintain position. As long as you keep those corrections very small the probability of an accident is minimized. It is a matter of maintaining absolute control over the airplane all the time. It is a matter of being very good at it and being very conscious of conditions all the time.

This discipline is equally important in refueling except the formation is on the tanker rather than on another fighter. The other fighters in the flight stay on the wing of the tanker until it's their turn to move into fueling position. Refueling takes place at about 300 miles per hour. The faster-moving jets must adjust their speed to that of the tanker so that the tanker and the fighters are all moving at the same speed. It is up to the pilot in the airplane being refueled to make corrections continuously while he is on the tanker boom. If he doesn't maintain adequate control all the time, a serious problem can develop. If the boom on the tanker, or the tanker itself, is damaged, a lot of guys are going to be left with no fuel to get home. There is a high potential for accidents on the tanker, especially at night when you have a number of airplanes flying on a big tanker and all are going to have to cycle through the boom to get fuel. Night refueling in heavy weather is an even more difficult situation. It's doable, and we did it all the time, but refueling at night in the rain or with heavy clouds can be particularly hazardous.

Air refueling is a tedious process and unforgiving of mistakes. It takes about ten minutes to get 2,000 gallons of fuel from a tanker and about 40 minutes to fuel a flight of four airplanes. The amount of time spent in refueling becomes significant if you have a strike force of 16 airplanes to refuel. The number of tankers depends on each day's circumstances. There might be one strike force or more. Tanker support is not over-abundant. A good deal of the process in planning a mission is the amount of time needed for refueling. If the mission can be accomplished with four airplanes, four are employed because to run eight or more airplanes across the tanker will consume more time and enhance the chance of mistakes while refueling as well as the total mission. All things are considered in planning a given mission: the route and target conditions, the weather, and tanker availability.

Not every circumstance can be anticipated. I led a strike force on a mission with a pilot that was new to the squadron on my right wing. He was a fairly experienced pilot, but he had no combat experience. We got into the target area, and as the shooting started we became a little disorganized in the flight. As we collected ourselves out of the target area, I noticed that the new guy was missing. At first I feared that he had been shot down, but I hadn't seen an airplane get hit. Usually you can see it; there is a pretty good explosion when an airplane is hit or hits the ground. I looked to the north of where we were and saw an airplane off the target area going the wrong direction. I figured it must be the missing guy, but I couldn't get him on the radio. I went after him, to try to bring him back in to rejoin the rest of the flight. I intercepted him, but by this time I had used about a thousand pounds more fuel than I should have, and I was concerned about whether it would be possible to rendezvous with the tanker to refuel. I had left the other airplanes to loiter. They were low on gas but not as low as I was. I was able to bring the missing airplane back to join the rest of the flight to proceed to the air refueling rendezvous. He had just been scared and had gone off in the wrong direction. I had made a mistake: I went to get a flight member, and as a result I left all the airplanes low on fuel.

I realized as we exited the target area that we'd never make the tanker area, which was a couple of hundred miles away. I called the tanker and asked him if he could come north. He replied that he was not allowed to come into the combat zone. I said, "Well, if you don't come north, we're going to lose this flight of airplanes because I don't have enough gas to get to you." He asked me to go to another, discreet frequency and said, "I'm turning north." I knew what he meant. We had radar in the F-4s, and were able to pick up the tanker about a hundred miles out. I was now down to just two or three hundred pounds of fuel. I called him and told him when to start to turn for our interception. We were nose-to-nose with each other until we got to within about twenty miles, and I told him to start a 180-degree turn. When he completed the turn I was right underneath him. I was down to about a hundred pounds of gas. He stuck me with the refueling boom and filled my airplane up with fuel. We all refueled on the tanker, and it looked like we were going to make it. I was never told the tanker pilot's name and never found out who he was. I thanked him over the air, but I never saw him on the ground. He was not stationed at Ubon. He saved us that day. If he hadn't come north to meet us, we would never have made it home.

This had been an unusual day, and we were very high on nerves. It had been a tough mission and a tough exit. Right in the middle of Thailand is a huge golden Buddha. It's a religious shrine that the Thai people visit regularly. The shrine is huge, several stories high, and it's polished gold. I took the guys down and flew them around the golden Buddha as a reward for a job well done. At least we made it, although I don't know how good a job we did. When we got back to Ubon we had begun to feel more relaxed. We went as a group to the club to relax a bit more. The guys were complaining about the mission and all the hostilities. I said, "Shut up; get happy; we made it." Because I was the leader, they threw me up onto the bar and said, "Make us happy." I don't tell jokes very well, and that must have been quite apparent because one of them later gave me a joke book to provide me with a little better material. They also gave me a pair of white kangaroo flight boots that were acceptable for table-walking and other social occasions. I kept them for years. The meeting at the bar at the end of a mission, especially the hard ones, was an outlet, a way to try to relax from a difficult day.

There is a disciplined sequence that must be followed when a flight is in the target area. These sequences, the weapons you use to strike a target and tactics, are different for every mission, depending on whether you are delivering weapons from air-to-ground, or in an air-to-air environment, or day or night. You are trained to do whatever the mission requires. In combat a USAF command control system directs pilots into a combat area. A ground control center and an airborne control facility work together to warn strike aircraft of changing weather conditions, airborne threat, and threat of antiaircraft artillery, as well as provide control assistance in and out of strike areas and coordinate rescue operations.

Air command control in a combat zone can be difficult. In good weather, directing the aircraft to the target is not too bad. But if the weather gets bad or a flight is delayed coming off the refueling tanker, or if heavy enemy ground fire is encountered, it takes longer to accomplish the mission. Often we had aircraft from several stations or different wings aiming for the same target. Timing becomes difficult when trying to synchronize a number of fighters to one target. Problems occur if one flight arrives a little early or late, catching another flight leaving or going in. We tried to design tactics so we would enter the combat zone in one manner and exit in another to avoid conflict with other incoming or exiting aircraft as well as to confuse the enemy. That doesn't always work completely.

A routine strike force is made up of 16 airplanes: four airplanes to suppress the ground threat, four airplanes for top cover to suppress the air threat, and eight airplanes to carry the ordnance to destroy the targets of your mission. The air-to-air threat, however, is minimal compared to the ground threat. In the history of fighter aviation in combat, 85 percent of aircraft shot down are shot down from ground fire, with about 15 percent shot down from enemy aircraft. We often faced both airborne and ground threat. When both occurred, a flight of four airplanes goes in and suppresses the surface-to-air missiles and the antiaircraft sites. This first wave strikes the gun sites to help protect the strike aircraft designated to deliver the ordnance on the targeted area. At the same time, a flight of airplanes stays high to make contact with any airborne threat in an effort to keep those guys off of the strike airplanes.

This three-prong approach was routine. The enemy can put up all kinds of firepower from the ground. A fighter in the air can't carry a heavy load of weapons so it is not as great a threat as fire from the ground is. It has always been like that, from World Wars I and II to Korea, and to Southeast Asia. It is the ground threat that gets most of the airplanes. This can be insidious. You may not know where the ground placements are until they start shooting at you, and that may be too late. You've been hit before you realize it. But if you keep your eyes open you can usually see an airborne threat coming at you. The airborne attack usually comes out of the sun. The fighter flight elements are positioned to protect each other from all angles of attack.

After the arrival at the target, the commander of the flight takes control and is responsible for the attack on the target. Everything has to be right if you are going to get the job done. You must have the right weapons, and you must have the right tactics for the conditions that exist in the target area. You don't have much time to strike the target, and, if the munitions against you are severe, you can't hang around very long in the combat scenario, or you are going to get shot down. The pilot goes by a designated pattern to strike the target at a given time, but weather conditions and ground and air attack can upset the timing, especially if flights are coming in from other squadrons. Heavy firepower coming off the ground can create confusion and chaos. In the Southeast Asian war, the antiaircraft artillery was severe. The North Vietnamese had perfected the guidance and the lethality of their weapons to the point where they could just load the area of flight with munitions. Sometimes it appeared you could get out of your aircraft and walk across the flak. Their artillery had radar-sighting devices to lock on our aircraft. Because the AAA fire was disbursed based on radar contact and control, not only could the AAA hit you over the target but there also was a good chance that you could fly right into the storm.

We always debriefed after each mission, doing a review and evaluation of everything that happened. Sometimes the debriefings were difficult because in the combat arena things are happening so fast and so much is going on that it becomes almost impossible to recount everything that occurs in that period of time. To come back on the ground and be able to discuss events in detail is difficult. Sometimes it is almost a subliminal thing. I would see something a second time that was like something I had seen the day before or a week before — a similar scenario — and my mind would merge the two experiences. Often the debriefings were spotty, because no one sees it all, or in the same perspective, and no one recalls all of it. The puzzle doesn't always fit. In the debriefings, we learned as much as possible from the completed mission, which may or may not have significance the next day because tomorrow is going to be different from today. No two engagements were alike. The scenario usually was different, the weather was different, and the firepower was different. Every engagement was a new experience.

Night missions are more difficult than daytime missions due to darkness and distortion of normal spatial orientation. If the pilot can't see or decipher a level horizon, the sensory system becomes confused. This loss of orientation and ability to detect the attitude of the airplane becomes a serious problem in a matter of seconds. In night bombing missions the pilot must rely on instruments that provide information about attitude and condition of the airplane. Without this information, the pilot risks losing control with quick, disastrous consequences. The strike aircraft is usually moving at a rate of speed greater than 1,000 feet a second. In the air-to-ground attack, if weapons are released at 4,000 feet, the pilot has only a couple of seconds to control the airplane to a position to keep it from running into the ground. Gunfire and explosions from enemy anti-aircraft artillery coming up from the ground are another factor. At night, an explosion that goes off in proximity of the aircraft will instantly disorient pilots. The effect of AAA ground fire is similar to lightning strikes in a thunderstorm and can affect the stability of the aircraft and the pilot's equilibrium, leaving him momentarily confused. Night combat can be like Fourth of July fireworks, except you aren't a spectator; you are the deadly center of attraction. Hurling yourself at the ground you can't see, at a speed of 1,000 feet per second, to deliver your ordnance is no walk in the park. Night combat is just plain spooky.

The 497th Squadron did the night missions exclusively. They were more successful at destroying enemy targets because they were doing it every night. They became experts at acclimating to the night combat conditions. At times the 497th did not have enough aircraft and pilots to support an entire night mission. When this happened aircraft and crews from the other three squadrons were used. If I was going to do a night mission, I wanted to do it every night, and I wanted my crew to be properly trained to minimize the accident potential. I volunteered to do night missions with the night-owl squadron for a period of six weeks. I took inexperienced pilots under my supervision on night missions, with me on their wing. We discussed the frailties, the idiosyncrasies, and the dangers under night conditions in briefings. I then flew with them until I believed they were trained. We flew night missions every night in this period and never lost an airplane. I believe the personal training paid off: we concentrated on the dangers of night missions and how to make adjustments to compensate for these difficulties.

Often night missions were more effective than daytime missions because the enemy had an equally difficult time seeing to attack our airplanes.

Normally at night we flew in formations of four. There might be other airplanes, other flights, in the area, but usually the night mission would be designed around four airplanes, sometimes just two, depending on the mission and the weather. We always had to air refuel, so if there were not enough tankers available to handle more than one flight of airplanes, only one flight would go. Night missions usually used fewer airplanes because of the greater difficulty and increased danger inherent in night missions.

Most missions were significant for the target importance and the firepower and danger in that arena. But sometimes another kind of danger emerged on the return home. There was always the problem of damaged aircraft attempting to air refuel and recover. There was always the threat of severe weather (which could be a very significant factor in Southeast Asia) in the refueling area and at your return base. Sometimes you would relax a little coming out of the target area in one piece believing the hard part was over, only to discover that the hard part was just beginning. There always were the hidden hazards.

Once, after coming off the target without a hit, I believed we were home free for that day. As we neared the tanker area it was apparent that the weather had developed to a level that air refueling would be more challenging than the target scenario. The rule was that you must be able to visually see the tanker from 2,000 feet behind and below before commencing air refueling. I was leading four F-4s, and I had a new guy in my back seat on his first combat mission in the F-4. He had been a radar observer (R/O) in an F-101 all-weather fighter in a previous assignment.

We arrived at 2,000 feet from the tanker on radar, but I could not see the tanker because of the dense clouds. We did not have enough fuel to make an alternate base, so we had to take on fuel. It looked bleak. My new R/O said, "Sir, I can put you right on the tanker boom if you will follow my instructions." It was like Tiger Wood's caddy taking over on the final shot for the Masters. I had no other options. The young R/O advised me to start moving up to the tanker. I followed his instructions, advising him, "We cannot ram the tanker." He said, "I have the situation under control." He was controlling this critical situation through radarscope interpretation. At 1,000 feet from the tanker I said, "I do not have visual contact." As we continued, the R/O continued his dialogue: "You are at 900 feet, 800 feet, 700 feet, 600 feet ... I said, "I don't have contact," trying to maintain a steady voice. He continued, "500 feet, 400 feet, 300 feet, 200 feet." I believed it was futile, but he went on: "100 feet, 75 feet." At 50 feet I saw the end of the refueling boom, but not the tanker. I pressed the mike button and said, "Tanker contact." We all refueled in very close formation. From then on he was my ace in the hole. On this one mission he saved eight souls and $50 million worth of F-4 fighters. Not a bad day. On return, I gave my precious "caddy" his first view of the Golden Buddha and the shot-of-the-day reward at the Ubon club.

On another occasion, under conditions of ceiling and visibility unlimited (CAVU), I exited the target area with all four aircraft in my flight in good shape, but eight other fighters had faced problems and were arriving late in the refueling anchor area. Several of these aircraft had battle damage, complicating the situation even more. There were only two tankers available to refuel the eight fighters in front of us, and I realized that it would be at least one hour before I would be able to get my flight of four on the tanker. The existing conditions would place us extremely low on fuel. I calculated that I could make a minimum fuel dash to Ubon and make it, provided we did not encounter other complications. It was iffy, but I decided the home-plate dash was the best alternative. Adding a little pressure to the scenario, my wing commander, Colonel "Skip" Stanfield, was on my right wing. He offered no advice. No one else did either.

I commenced a climb from 26,000 feet (air refueling altitude) to 50,000 feet. I went to minimum cruise to conserve fuel. It was going to be close. As we approached Ubon at about 50 miles out, I could see that one end of the runway was clear and the other end was becoming obscured by cloud cover. The visible end of the runway was opposite to traffic landing at the time. I elected to make a minimum-time, minimum-fuel descent and land against traffic in visual conditions rather than attempt an instrument approach the opposite way, using more fuel than we had available. I called the control tower and informed them that in four minutes, I would land four F-4s against traffic, in Visual Flight Rule (VFR) conditions, and would turn off on the mid-runway taxiway so as not to disrupt on-coming traffic. The tower response was, "We cannot approve the approach." My response was, "I am not asking for approval; I am informing you of my approach under emergency conditions." I am sure the tower was aware the wing commander was in the flight, so there was no further discussion.

I began a minimum-time rapid-rate descent (25,000 feet per minute), pitched out, landed all four fighters, and turned off the runway at mid-field. When we got out of the fighters, Colonel Stanfield approached me and said, "Good decision, Major." I said, "Colonel, what would your response have been if it had not worked out?" He smiled. I thought, "No one argues with success." As Colonel Maglione, my former Thunderbird commander, would say, "In every endeavor you need a little luck."

Flying in combat is like any other activity in life: you have to learn a little bit about it before you get better. By the time I was halfway through my tour I felt I was pretty good at it. The F-4 had unbelievable performance. I knew how to fly the airplane, and I felt if I used that performance correctly, I would survive. It helped that I already had a good foundation: before my tour in Vietnam, I had flown every tactical jet fighter the Air Force had up to that time. I knew the performance of the vehicle, and I learned how far I could go with it to evade the enemy. I learned early to keep a high energy level and keep the airplane moving all the time. If you are going into a high-threat area, you need a lot of energy and dynamic capability to maneuver the airplane. You keep all three dimensions in motion all the time, making it difficult for ground munitions to lock on and hit you. An F-4 fighter moving at 1,500 feet a second is a hard target to hit. If you are slow and in level flight you are a very easy target.

The tactics you use are very significant to your survival. As I gained combat experience, I learned where the heaviest threat areas were, and I learned what kinds of tactics were necessary to engage in those areas. I learned specific circumstances to stay away from and specific tactics to employ to evade the enemy's capabilities. By the time I was 50 missions into my tour I knew how to avoid the enemy. I knew how to strike the target. I knew how to minimize the threat. And if the threat looked too great, I knew how to engage in a different way. I knew that you don't drive right into the enemy if you know they have you overpowered. You have an aircraft that can move at Mach 2. You can cover a lot of distance. I knew we did not have to strike the target from the position that was briefed earlier. If the defenses are so severe that you are going to get shot down, there is no sense in driving in there. Attack from another position, or just come back another day.

I never lost an airplane when I was the commander of a flight, although I was in flights where airplanes were lost. While I did not lose an airplane as flight commander, I came close a number of times. There were men who took hits in flights I was leading, but they all made it back. This doesn't mean that I was better than the next guy. It just means that I was lucky on flights when I needed it. It is extremely important to be a good aviator in combat, but you also have to have some luck. There is always that "Golden BB" out there waiting, that one round that you can't maneuver out of and that will get you if you're not careful.

I used to sit on the end of the runway with a flight of F-4s, and before I released the brakes I would wonder, "Will we all make it back today?" With all the engines going, there is so much heat that there is a parallax effect around the airplanes. I would look in the rear-view mirrors and see a kaleidoscope of wavering shapes. Before starting our roll, I would see this eerie picture from the heat of the engines, and I would always think, "Don't let me make a mistake today." Then we would begin the familiar pattern: we would take off and shortly thereafter join a tanker to get a maximum load of fuel to accomplish an assigned mission. We would complete the mission and then refuel on a tanker for the final leg back to Ubon.

I remember how scenic it was flying over Southeast Asia. So much of this was beautiful country with rugged mountains and steep canyons, marked sometimes by waterfalls that would fall 2,000 feet. We would fly over herds of elephants, families of tigers. The beginning of a mission could be remarkably picturesque — sort of like taking a vacation flight for a couple of hours. Then we would enter a combat zone where for 15 to 20 minutes the mission could turn into stark, raving terror. Firepower is going on all around you along with the chaos that goes on when guys are scared about where you are, what you're doing, and about somebody getting shot down. Then you would leave the target area, hopefully having all your marbles with you, to make the flight back home. The whole mission from beginning to end was a unique experience — to go from the beautiful terrain and magnificent flight in a wonderful airplane into combat where you get the daylights scared out of you while engaged in a breathtaking theater. Then you are back in flight across beautiful country returning to home plate to debrief and brief the next morning and do it all over again.

It seemed that after a number of missions — some relatively uneventful — you become accustomed to the routine. Maybe even fairly comfortable. But it didn't always turn out that way. Once I was leading a ground attack mission that was diverted to a rescue mission when two pilots in my wing were shot down. In a situation like this, airplanes would be diverted from their primary mission to try to get the downed men out.

Divert missions left unanswered questions with little time to get answers before you arrive on the scene. The missions were rescue missions or ground battles that needed added air support because of unforeseen circumstances such as abnormal losses or impenetrable enemy forces, or just weather that created an adverse swing in the battle pendulum. A diverted fighter force is redirected from the programmed, briefed mission to a scenario you know nothing about. The fighter strike force leader is given a set of coordinates from the airborne command post and, if possible, a forward air controller to contact for some on-scene direction. The fighter flight has not been briefed on the geography of the diversion area or on the enemy forces it will be faced with. You arrive in the area and make the best assessments you can and attempt to attain favorable results for downed aviators or troops on the ground. The likelihood of incomplete appraisals and mistakes is extremely high. The possibility that tragedy could occur is even higher. You always know you will be held accountable for your actions, good or bad. In a divert situation I always agonized over the possibility that a tragic mistake would be made that I would have to live with the rest of my life.

On this day I had a flight of four F-4s, and we had just come off the tanker when Air Command diverted us into the zone where the two pilots had gone down. The pilots were on the ground and had been spotted. We moved in to hold the area until the helicopters, called the "Jolly Green Giants," could come in and pick them up. In a recovery mission, a transport C-130 with rescue facilities is brought in to provide medical supplies, food, and other provisions. The helicopters, which move slower, follow the C-130. Sometimes an A-1, a prop-driven airplane (call sign "Sandy"), would be called in for close air support to hold the ground area neutral until the helicopters arrive.

In this rescue attempt several A-1s came in near the downed flyers. My flight of four F-4s had a lot of ordnance aboard, and we were able to hold the area while waiting for the helicopter to pick the men up. We had been in the area for almost six hours and had refueled with the tanker twice since being diverted. When the helicopter arrived in the area to pick the downed crew up I believed we were going to get them out and everything was going to be okay. I could see their chutes on the ground. As the helicopter moved in to start its ground approach, the enemy moved the two pilots into the middle of a clearing. They shot both of them. I was in close proximity to the target—probably less than 5,000 feet—and could see the men on the ground when they were shot. I had been so certain that we were going to get them out.

When I got back to Ubon, I was emotionally depleted. I felt all the air had gone out of my tires. I was so weak, I couldn't get out of the airplane for a while. I just sat there. We had seven airplanes take hits that day. I was always concerned about pilots being shot down and killed or ending up as POWs. But this was a real eye opener for me. We had done our level best to rescue these men, and yet we had not been able to save them. The ironic part of the rescue mission was that the enemy could have staged the scenario to draw rescue aircraft in for added destruction—a common practice for the North Vietnamese. This was a devastating experience. I couldn't forget it, but I had a mission to lead the next day, the next day after that, and the next day following that.

In 1968 a prototype laser-guided bomb system known as Paveway was sent to Vietnam for combat use, although Paveway had not yet been sufficiently tested or evaluated. (The term *PAVE*, an acronym for Precision Avionics Vectoring Equipment, applied also to later iterations of laser-guided systems, including Pave Spike and Pave Knife.) Paveway put a laser-guidance system on the front of a 2,000-pound bomb that when launched would be directed to its target by guidance equipment in a second airplane. Because I was experienced in the combat arena and was a Fighter Weapons School graduate and test pilot, I was assigned to drop some of the initial Paveway weapons. It turned out to be a great system with extreme accuracy. We quickly realized that we could destroy difficult targets with two laser-equipped aircraft with far greater accuracy than could be expected from a 16-ship strike force equipped with conventional unguided weapons. The accuracy with conventional weapons is less than certain. You wind up having to drop a lot of bombs to get a target abolished. The lasers were nicknamed "Smart Bombs" for the obvious reason: they could find the target.

We were very successful with Paveway, although a drawback of the system was that it required good coordination between the aircraft that dropped the weapon and the aircraft that guided it, making the use of Paveway difficult and dangerous in the combat zone, especially for the guidance aircraft. The airplane that guided the weapon would have to remain in a constant circle until it guided the weapon to impact, a period of 15 to 20 seconds. Fifteen or twenty seconds in a combat zone when the shooting is going on is a long time. The way to minimize the amount of time the aircraft is exposed to danger could be compared to the movements of a quarterback and a wide receiver in a football game. The two must be well coordinated. Both must know the pattern and the target spot. The quarterback must time his throw of the ball in such a way that the ball and the receiver arrive at the target area at the same time. During this time, the team must minimize exposure to tacklers, or, in our case, to the enemy.

Paveway became my primary activity. We had only two airplanes with Paveway capability, so I wound up flying Paveway missions almost every day because they were so successful. Both Paveway aircraft are equipped to guide and launch the 2,000-pound weapons. Eventually, we got two more Paveway-ready aircraft. We now had four Paveway airplanes. We used Paveway on the most difficult, most important targets because the accuracy was better than 90 percent. The system was that good. I found I could put a Paveway weapon right on the enemy's front porch. My only recommendation for improvement was to get the system into one airplane; that is, to have the capability to drop and guide the weapon from one airplane rather than two, doubling our capacity to strike the enemy and with increased safety.

Along the borderline of North Vietnam, weapons storage areas were placed in mountainous areas, making them almost impossible to hit. Weaponry stored there was then moved by the North Vietnamese into South Vietnam for use of their ground soldiers. One large storage area had been a particular problem; a number of missions had tried to hit this ammo area with conventional weapons but had never been successful. I thought that if we did the job right, we could launch a 2,000-pound Paveway weapon and run it right into the front door of the weapons storage area. The idea was to fly a fairly flat approach at very high speed so the weapon could be launched with a lot of energy and guide it a long way. The coordination was very critical. I had to release at the precise point with enough energy for the weapon to get to the target but also minimize the vulnerability of the designator aircraft. On the mission, I accelerated over 600 knots and approached the face of the weapons storage area and released the weapon. My counterpart above guided the bomb right into the front door, and it totally demolished the entire weapons area. The secondary explosions were still going off when we streaked out of sight.

Another problem with conventional weapons occurred in the bombing of enemy roadways. By dropping enough bombs we could tear up a roadway, but the North Vietnamese would come back and quickly repair the damage. They had huge bulldozers, four or five times bigger than any bulldozer that you might see in the United States. These machines were just monsters, capable of clearing the roads again in a very short time. We could cut the road in the afternoon, and they would have it back open by the next morning. The next best idea was to eliminate the bulldozers. With Paveway, I thought, I could put a weapon right on the hood ornament. One of our forward air controllers, called "Raven," spotted the location where the big bulldozers were parked. We went in early one morning, and he put a mark on them. I dropped a Paveway on the target. After the explosion, the FAC said all he could see was a front blade off one. The rest of the bulldozers were totally demolished. The bulldozer mission turned out to be very effective. With the accuracy of the Paveway system, we were able to strike a small but very important target.

Terminal guided weapons are the backbone of tactical fighter air-to-ground weapons today. It began with the Paveway system, followed by the Pave Knife system, and then Pave Spike. I did the tests on Pave Knife when I was instructing in the Fighter Weapons School at Nellis after I returned from Southeast Asia. That weapons system was a significant factor in the success of Linebacker II, the final thrust against North Vietnam in 1972, which actually brought the North Vietnamese to their knees because they could not survive the continuous interdiction. Terminal guided weapons were yet another major step in the evolution of supersonic fighter capability.

I flew more than 70 Paveway missions, and all turned out to be successful. Because I was flight-test qualified, I was also required to do flight tests on airplanes that were in extensive maintenance or had combat damage. I would fly a combat mission almost every day and then, several days a week, after coming back from a combat mission, I would fly one or two test flights. I did the flight test profile as I had done on the Thunderbirds. I would exercise every system on the airplane during the test flights, out to Mach 2 and to the extremities of the aircraft's capabilities. I actually found flight tests relaxing. These were flights I could just sort of enjoy. Nobody was shooting at me.

On occasions I would take crew chiefs on test flights to let them see firsthand how critically important their mission was to the entire Air Force endeavor. Without the dedicated work of the ground crews, all is for naught in the air. I loved working close to the enlisted people. They have a unique code and integrity all their own. I found that the enlisted men would look forward to being able to participate in these test flights, to see how the airplane would fly, and to see what a combat area really looked like. For me, these flights were another way of letting them know how important they were to the mission and how valuable they were. I probably flew some 150 test flights during the year that I was in Vietnam, and I took crew chiefs with me whenever possible. This was a good initiative and became an almost daily activity.

During the first part of my combat missions, we lost a significant number of airplanes, some not in the combat arena. One reason was the weather: it rained a lot in Southeast Asia, and many times the fighters had to land on a wet runway. If combat damage had occurred, an airplane might be landing at a much faster speed than normal. Airplanes were skidding off the side of the runway or going off the end of the runway due to the combination of minor difficulties with the airplane and/or weather conditions. We needed to do something to stop the losses of airplanes after they have come back from a mission. Air crews could fly a successful mission, come back, and wind up getting hurt or tearing up the airplane because of poor conditions on the runway. We believed that if we had a capability to stop airplanes on the approach end of the runway — much as the Navy does aboard an aircraft carrier — we could avoid damage that occurred when airplanes touched down at speeds that could not be slowed under normal braking conditions.

We decided to try the approach-end method, which was a big cable stretched across the runway and equipped with decelerating cylinders. When the cable is hooked by the airplane the airplane will decelerate very rapidly, but smoothly. To test the system, I took a single F-4 up and accomplished multiple approach-end barrier engagements. I would approach at 175 to 200 miles per hour and hook the barrier as I touched down. The airplane would stop within about 200 feet. This is a pretty rapid stop. There is a significant jolt in the cockpit when you decelerate from possibly 200 miles an hour to zero in about two seconds. I did about ten approaches the first day. The second day I did about ten more. I would hook the barrier, pick the hook up, take off, come back around and do it again. The experiment was successful, although after the tests I had bruised burn marks across my shoulders for several days because of the sudden decelerations. We solved that problem by padding the parachute harness to reduce the amount of abrasion.

We implemented a procedure that if the weather was bad or the pilot returned with aircraft damage (or both), he would do an approach-end barrier engagement to stop the airplane rather than drive it down the runway under unfavorable conditions. I don't know how many airplanes we saved by using this procedure, but it certainly was a significant number. I believe this was the first time this procedure was applied by the Air Force. It is not used today because fighters are not equipped with a tail hook to facilitate an approach-end engagement. The F-4 had the tail hook because it was originally a Navy airplane and was designed with the capability to go aboard an aircraft carrier.

Later on, while I was instructing in the Fighter Weapons School, I used the procedure to land an airplane that had lost all flight controls. I would not have attempted the landing without the availability of the approach-end barrier system. In this case, the approach-end barrier saved the Pave Knife prototype, a very expensive and advanced combat weapon system. What I learned in Vietnam helped me throughout the rest of my fighter career.

Before I arrived to serve my tour, fighter pilots usually flew 100 missions, which would only take about six months. We ran out of fighter pilots quickly because training new guys took at least nine months. Even experienced combat pilots had to go through an upgrade process. We were having a shortage in 1967–1968 because pilots were going home faster than we could train new ones. The Air Force had to extend the tour of duty from 100 missions to one year, as it took nearly a year to train a pilot through all training, including upgrades and survival training. The purpose was to match the one-year training process with the one year of service in combat. In this way, the Air Force theoretically had one pilot trained to replace one pilot leaving. The extension to one year upped the mission requirement from 100 missions to somewhere around 150 missions.

Every day from dawn until dark and after, we were engaged in flying activities, briefing, debriefing, target study, and, for me, flight tests. I was busy all the time. Vietnam was the most active year of my life. With the extension of 100 missions to one year, the average pilot flew about 140 missions, which amounted to some 250 combat hours. That year I flew 214 combat missions and probably somewhere around 150 test flights: 505 total flight hours, 385 of these being combat hours. What upped the numbers for me were the Paveway missions, the approach-end barrier engagement tests, and the routine test flights that were assigned to me. My schedule was more than the average for other pilots. I remember someone once referred to me as "a one-man band." There could have been several reasons for this comment, but the fact was there were not always enough people around capable of doing what needed to be done, and I just happened to be the guy standing in the box at the time. Nonetheless, doing a combat mission in the morning and two test flights in a day was a heavy load, physically and emotionally.

I'm sure that was true for the crews who flew in World War II and other wars; pilots had to fly mission after mission, very long missions under very difficult conditions. There was combat fatigue, and some lost their lives because they were just too tired to be as effective as they could be. In the present day fighter world, combat scheduling has changed. There is more attention placed on a pilot's physical and mental condition before flying in combat. To reduce the fatigue factor, today's fighter pilots can fly only one training mission or one combat mission a day. Pilots do not normally do the double mission schedule that was permitted in my flying days. The Air Force is much more focused on pilot condition.

I was tired, and sometimes I didn't sleep very well. It took time for my emotions to settle down. I would think back on what had happened that day and think I've got to do this again tomorrow. I didn't want to engage in the same conditions I had on this day. I wanted to do better. It would be difficult to sleep through the night. I would sleep a little, wake up, go through the thought process again, and back to sleep (maybe). At other times I was so tired that I would lie down and instantly fall asleep. The next morning I would have to check my nametag to see who I was after shaking myself out of deep sleep. Although I sometimes worried that I might not be as effective as I should be, self-discipline came into play. I learned to do what I had to do as efficiently as possible regardless of the conditions.

A difficult time for me occurred about halfway through my tour. We were short of pilots, but the combat missions kept expanding. I had flown combat missions and one or two test flights almost every day for 60 days. These long, weary days were beginning to take a toll. I lived in the same quarters with Dr. Ramon, a flight surgeon. He was watching me on a daily basis and seemed to know I would collapse sooner or later. Early one morning, the doctor walked with me to the flight line, which was unusual, as he had never done that before. I got about halfway to the flight line and collapsed. I had lost a lot of weight and was just plain worn out. I simply could not go on. My body said "no more." Dr. Ramon took me to the hospital, where I stayed for 48 hours. The hospital staff intravenously fed me a high-nutritional formula. They woke me up to feed me every two to three hours, and then it was back to sleep. At the end of 48 hours, I felt fine and was back on the flight schedule. I walked to the flight line and started all over again. It was sort of like a lost weekend. I really don't have much memory of what happened. I just know that for two days I was out of the circuit and had to get pumped up to do it again.

I continued on just as before for the last six months of my tour, but the schedule didn't seem to have the same effect on me as it had during the first six-month period. I was able to accept the challenges of the day-to-day activities. It seemed that, like anything else, I had acclimated to the conditions and was able to adjust to different but equally grueling circumstances as those I had been exposed to during the first six months. Whatever situation transpired, I was able to carry on with basically the same heavy schedule and able to absorb whatever problems that surfaced. It seemed every day there was something new.

The complications of war are sometimes multiplied by "rules of engagement." These broad, catchall directives are established in an attempt to minimize unnecessary destruction and loss of life in a combat arena. Rules of engagement are an expansion of the normal rules learned in military training but are designed to be followed in real combat situations. There are a number of problems with this theory: If applied "by the book," specific rules of engagement may not be effective in meeting the mission requirement and may place others in danger. The enemy does not recognize our rules and will use them against us whenever possible. War activity changes dramatically and instantaneously, possibly leaving the prescribed rules of engagement well behind the action. The strategy of war is usually dismissed early in the battle, which then becomes a race to see which side can acclimate to change, absorb loss, and continue to fight. In this situation, the combatants may be stuck with a set of rules that actually hinder combat effectiveness. If one finds himself in a scenario where he must violate rules of engagement to survive, he may be held accountable for a violation, even if done to save life and accomplish the mission objective. I saw this happen from time to time. It seems unfair, but who ever said there was anything fair in war?

On one occasion I was briefed and assigned for a mission in Laos. After we came off the tanker in route to our target, I was diverted to a mission in South Vietnam. I normally didn't fly in South Vietnam, but sometimes airborne support was needed immediately. On this day when I arrived in the target area with a flight of F-4s the enemy was already overrunning the area. I could not distinguish or decipher the enemy troops from our own American soldiers. By the rules of engagement I was to drop weapons wherever I was told to drop. Our weapons were very lethal toward civilian or military populace on the ground. I did not want to take the chance of dropping lethal weapons into American soldiers. I elected not to drop the weapons. We took everything back home and dropped the unarmed weapons in a non-combat drop area. I had not forgotten the Battle of Dak-To, a heavily fortified mountain in South Vietnam. In late 1967 losses were high in a 24 hour firefight to take control of this stronghold. Some of the losses were incurred by a U.S. F-105 dropping a 500-pound bomb in a friendly area, killing wounded soldiers and command personnel including the chaplain. At all cost, I did not want to repeat such a tragedy.

I had not followed the rules of engagement as directed. In my judgment I had the authority to overrule when conditions in the target arena were unfavorable. To some, I had failed to meet the standards of the existing rules of engagement. I met with my wing commander. I explained why it was best not to bomb the area. In the course of our discussion, information came from the Marine ground commander stating he was glad I had not dropped the weapons because our American troops were infiltrated with the enemy. Clearly I should not have dropped. My decision may have prevented many casualties from friendly fire. Had the Marine commander not come forward, I probably would have received punishment for not complying with rules of engagement. What I am saying is that the rules of engagement are not always applicable where the conditions of the situation change rapidly from one minute to the next. Commanders must have flexibility to exercise appropriate judgment in any given circumstance. I respect rules of engagement, but they may not apply in every case. Later in the discussion of my actions I said, "I can live in jail for not following some predetermined rules, but I can't live with the memory of killing American soldiers. If I am faced with a similar scenario in the future, I will follow my moral instinct again."

There were other circumstances when rules of engagement were in contention. In some cases, the rules of engagement directed that we were not allowed to drop on certain enemy installations. The enemy would find out what targets were off limits and would move their firepower, antiaircraft batteries, to these installations. The enemy could fire at us, but we were not allowed to fire back. The off-limit areas could be a religious group, or temple, or some other facility that we would not want to damage. When these sites became enemy targets and were destructive to us, we should have been allowed to retaliate. For example, in North Vietnam we were not allowed to hit ships in the harbors because many of the ships belonged to other countries. Some of the ships were North Vietnamese and sometimes would fire on our aircraft. Yet, we were not allowed to retaliate against these ships. Sometimes in the heat of the battle we did retaliate, and those individuals who did were held accountable. As I said, "Who ever said there is anything fair in war?" Consider the many civilian people who are lost in a war they do not understand. This occurs in every war.

In any complex situation it may seem difficult to know what is right and what is wrong. When you face a basic issue, life or death, it is not hard to know right from wrong. Because a "rule" or authority has dictated what to do, does not mean it is always appropriate. If it's wrong for the situation, don't do it. If it's right you should engage. You must be able to justify your decision, and you must be willing to accept accountability for your actions. That is what command authority is all about: you have to have the courage to make decisions based on the best information that you have available, even knowing you may have to take heat for those decisions and you may get hurt. If you are entrusted with the responsibility of command over other people, you make the decision that is best for them, not what is best for your own career.

I was always concerned about making a mistake that would cost somebody's life. I agonized over it every day. I believed if I was at my best every day, all the time, we could survive. I never had trouble getting men to fly with me. They knew I was going to do the best I could. We had good rapport. I was happy I never lost anyone because of a bad decision.

I believe if you want to be a good military officer, or a good leader in any environment, you cannot think about your personal career. If you stand up for what is right, you are always going to face some opposition. Gen. Billy Mitchell, the famed World War I aviator, has been a hero to me. Mitchell stood up for this country and fought for what he knew was right. His career and ultimately his life were destroyed because he never wavered in his belief that superiority in air power was going to be essential if our country was to prevail in future conflicts. Years after being demoted and virtually forced out of the U.S. Army Air Corps on the grounds of insubordination, he was proved to have been exactly right: he predicted almost to the day when World War II would start, where it would start, and what would happen if the United States did not develop the air power that was needed to win that war. What Mitchell did was a remarkable thing. He died a broken man, but we know the truth today. Life is not always fair.

Mental conditioning is the hardest. I would sometimes come out of a target area and I would shake all over — the adrenaline shock, I suppose. I would have to collect myself because I must lead the flight to rendezvous with the air refueling tanker and home through whatever hidden hazards that prevail. My next thought would be, I will have to do this again tomorrow. To survive, you must remember, it is one day at a time. And it takes self-discipline. I stayed in good physical shape. I played handball whenever I could. I rode a high-speed Czechoslovakian racing bicycle every place I went on the ground. My son has the bicycle to this day.

My last mission was memorable. I was becoming anxious to go home. I hoped the Golden BB wouldn't get me on the last mission. I had flown over 200 combat missions; my nerves were a little edgy. I hoped the last mission would be easy. I flew my last mission with just two airplanes. The other pilot was Tex McVey, who arrived at Ubon the same day I did. We were both flight commanders, and we both were going home on the same day. We tried to schedule ourselves with a very easy mission to finalize our tour and go home safe and sound. We were scheduled to strike a bridge across the Mekong River. It was an area where there was no reported AAA in the target area. It was a target that had not been struck in some time. It looked like an easy target. We would go in, strike the bridge, come home, and live happily ever after.

It didn't work out like that. I had been doing it every day for a year and wasn't all that concerned. Tex and I went into the target area and decided to strike the target with three 500-pound bombs per pass. We had 15 500-pound bombs on each aircraft. We really didn't get the job done on the first pass, so we came back to make a second pass. I did not see any AAA or other firepower until we came off the second pass. I thought I saw some 37-millimeter coming off the ground. I turned around, and sure enough, firepower started coming up at a great rate. We both maneuvered as rapidly as possible and dropped the remaining 500-pound bombs. After delivering the last of the ordnance, we reached a high energy level to exit the area as quickly as possible. The 37-millimeters were going off right behind the airplanes.

The F-4 was a really rapid accelerator. We could stoke up the burners and move out at supersonic speeds very quickly; the 37-millimeter moves at a very rapid rate also, and the enemy had very good sighting devices. As we gained energy, increased our speed, and started to exit the area, it got very tense. All I could think about was, it's my last mission, I'm going to get shot down, and spend the rest of my life here. I don't mind admitting I had a lot of concern at that point. A flight of 4F-105s came in behind us, and they took a hit on the first pass from the AAA.

On a last mission some of the guys would pick you up in a classy painted-up rickshaw and haul you to the hooch area where the officers' club was located. Tex McVey and I landed at Ubon and took our ride back to the club for a last-mission champagne party. I left the next day or so, boarding a C-130 to Bangkok and from there to Saigon. I flew a C-141 all the way to San Francisco. I actually did fly the C-141 for 14 hours, as the real crew was worn out and slept all the way. It was a beautiful flight.

In total, the war was a totally unique experience with exposure from one end of the spectrum to the other — from the highest in courage and integrity to the lowest. I had been in the Air Force for 15 years, literally my entire adult life—years that coincided with the evolution of the supersonic fighter. In this historic evolution in fighter aviation, and in the war, the loss of fighter pilots was high. I lost many of my early associates from the Nellis Air Force Base Tiger Program in the early years of jet evolution in the 1950s and in the Vietnam War of the 1960s, in addition to losses on the Thunderbirds. There were not that many left among those I had begun my fighter career with. The emotional impact was heavy.

Major Haney returns from the Vietnam War with a mustache after a tour of duty, 1969.

Russ Goodman, who I was with on the Thunderbirds, was shot down. I thought the world of Russ. Bob Cameron, another close friend, was lost. Bob and I had gone through the F-86 school at Nellis Air Force Base and were together in the Far East on our first assignments out of the F-86 training. We later attended Squadron Officers School together. Bob was an All-American quarterback from the Naval Academy back in 1952. He was an unbelievable athlete, a 225-pound, six-foot-two mammoth of a man who could throw a football about as fast as a 37-millimeter shell. He was killed in a terrible accident.

Major Haney returns from combat mission #214 and is transported in a rickshaw to attend his final mission party.

He was on takeoff with a full combat load in an F-4. On the takeoff roll, the cockpit fogged up, impairing his vision. He veered off the runway, struck the arresting barrier, and the F-4 exploded. I came to understand that death is the nature of war; there are losses and tragedies. I saw a lot of them.

The worst impact for me was the loss of Colonel Iron Mike Meroney's son, Virgil Meroney, Jr., whom I had known as a boy in Japan. "Little Mike" completed flight training and came to Ubon about halfway through my tour of duty. Colonel Meroney was then the wing vice commander. He assigned young Mike to my flight, and I flew with him on all of his indoctrination missions. He was good. After my first 100 missions, I went home on leave. While I was gone young Mike was moved to another flight and was killed on a night combat mission. His death was a terrible blow to Iron Mike—and to me. I had learned in war nothing is fair or fun for anyone. The memory never goes away.

There has been unlimited dialogue concerning the validity and purpose of the Vietnam War. I have studied many wars in our history, and I can see flaws in all of them. They all create tragedy and loss for many people, many innocent of the political or irrational reason for the war. I have not been vocal about any of the dialogue I hear or my personal view of this war. I am a U.S. Air Force fighter pilot with a mission to fly and fight on behalf of duty, honor, and country, regardless. This is a significant job in itself, so I will attempt to do my best and leave the rest for others.

CHAPTER 10

Fighter Weapons School: Terminal Guided Weapons

"Top Gun."

Landing in San Francisco after my 14-hour flight from Saigon, I flew to McCarran Field, Las Vegas. I came in on a Wednesday and was to report for duty as an instructor in the USAF Fighter Weapons School at Nellis AFB the following Monday. My three boys saw me coming down the ramp before I saw them, and, for them, it must have been a bit of a surprise. I had been away for a year. I had lost 15 pounds, which for me was a lot. And, in the tradition of fighter pilots in combat, I had acquired a huge handlebar mustache. The boys did a double-take, but it didn't take long for them to realize that this skinny guy with the big mustache was really me. It was a very happy reunion all the way around.

I will never forget the look on Mike's face. He had ventured ahead and was the first to meet me, and then there were the expressions of Steve and Max. I hadn't realized that it was probably a more difficult year for them than it was for me. I was there and could see what was going on every day. All they could do was worry about me. On the block where we lived, there had been a couple of fathers shot down and who did not come back One had lived next door to us. I know that had been on their minds a lot, and they were very relieved this portion of our Air Force career was behind us.

I was relieved myself. It was a very happy reunion. After a few days we were back on the water skis again and back to normal life.

That first weekend after my return there was a party for the Thunderbird group. I had only been off the Thunderbirds a little more than a year, and many of the guys on the team were very close friends. The occasion was formal, and I went with my black tuxedo and my handlebar mustache. General R. G. "Zack" Taylor, the Weapons Center commander, was there. I admired him very much, and I knew he liked me and my kids, though he had previously been very direct with me concerning some of my colorful Thunderbird flight activities. (I had flown through that gate at the Palmdale aircraft factory once, and he got after me pretty heavily for that.) General Taylor walked up to me that night and looked me straight in the face and said, "Mr. Earl, that's such a beautiful mustache. It's such a shame it has to go." I knew exactly what he meant — on Monday morning I had better be at work at 0700, and the mustache had better be gone. That night I had a little persuasion in that respect. Dottie Goffstein, who owned the Four Queens Hotel and part of the Riviera in Las Vegas, was a great supporter of the Thunderbirds. She and a couple of Thunderbird friends shaved my mustache off. I went to work Monday morning, and it was not long before General Taylor showed up. He walked in, observed, and told me how nice I looked.

The Fighter Weapons School had been developed in the early days of the jet fighter to develop the newest and best tactics and performance capabilities of aircraft and the newest and best weapons systems and to disperse that information throughout the Air Force. Only the best pilots from each wing were selected for the school. On completion, the school graduates returned to their individual wings as the wing weapons officer, the fighter experts for their wing.

It was a very difficult school. To be at the Fighter Weapons School was to be at the top tier of the fighter environment. It was a reward to fly very high-performing airplanes in that environment with pilots who had arrived at the level of the best fighter ability in the world. The Weapons School required more flying and physical abilities than the Thunderbirds by a wide margin, and the missions, in terms of intensity of skill and energy required minute by minute, are sometimes more stringent than in combat. Flight activity is at maximum performance from the time you roll down the runway until you land.

Fighter pilots are a very competitive group with a lot of energy, and the competitive spirit in the Weapons School is almost out of sight. You can't drop your pencil without someone rolling right over you. Every day you get out of bed, you've got to be at your best. The competitive environment can be wearing, but in the fighter world it is this level of performance that is critical for survival. Every day in the air you must be on guard from attack by adversary fighter flights. You might be in an air-to-ground mission and a flight of four would attack out of nowhere. If you get caught not protecting yourself, you are fair game. It was an open field—a combat arena—all of the time.

Fighter Weapons School instructors teach in the classroom and also fly every phase of the school curriculum. I instructed both academics and airborne in terminal guided systems, plus air-to-air and air-to-ground, including nuclear weapons. Academic school was held in the morning, and air missions would be flown in the afternoon, meaning the instructor teaches from the podium in the morning and from the front seat of the airplane in the afternoon. The two phases were very closely related. Academic solutions taught in the morning were employed in the flight activity later that same day.

Before going to Southeast Asia I had attended the Weapons School, graduating in October 1968. Fighter Weapons School was now tasked with providing training in terminal guided weapons systems. I was assigned as a flight commander and charged with developing the new program. It was an obvious choice: I had dropped the first of the terminal guided weapons in the Vietnam War and would now be instructing pilots who would go to Southeast Asia to fight in the same environment. In addition to my duties establishing the terminal guided weapons program at the Fighter Weapons School, I was assigned to flight test the new Pave Knife system, the next iteration of laser-guided weapons.

Paveway, the first of the laser-guided weapons systems, was very effective in combat. It was deficient in requiring two airplanes to execute the mission: one to drop 2,000-pound bombs equipped with a laser-guidance system and another to circle the target to guide the weapon. These deployment tactics were exceptionally dangerous in combat because of the time interval from the drop of the weapons to contact with the target. When I returned from Southeast Asia, Pave Knife was in the design stages at the Philco–Ford Corporation. The Pave Knife laser system, once locked on the target, had the capability to hold the laser beam on the target, guiding the weapon even as the airplane exited the area. This combat capability was now contained in a single F-4 aircraft.

The Pave Knife tests were flown out of El Toro Marine Base near Long Beach, California. Because Pave Knife was highly classified, the test aircraft was hidden in a hanger. I would start the airplane in the hanger, taxi immediately to the end of the runway, and take off with no communication with anyone. The tests were flown at the Nellis–Edwards Air

Force base test ranges north of Las Vegas, Nevada, and Mojave, California. I would take off at a specific time and land at a specific time, planned to attract no attention to the unusual attached Pave Knife pod.

If an airplane was available I would fly from Nellis to El Toro for flight tests. Often I drove the 200 miles in my little red P-1800 Volvo sports car. One morning I got a very early morning summons to go to El Toro for a Pave Knife test flight. I would have to drive. Time to make the designated takeoff schedule was short. I was approaching Baker, California, at about 115 miles an hour when I looked in the mirror and saw a car overtaking me. The state police in those days drove specially built 150-mile-an-hour Ford interceptor cars. I pulled over, stopped, and got out. I greeted the officer and said, "You can't get me for speeding." He said, "Oh, really?" I said, "I wasn't speeding, just flying a little low." He said, "That is the best one I have heard in my 17 years of duty." I explained that I had to get to El Toro on time for a flight test mission. He looked at me, in my flying suit, and said, "You know, your story is so absurd, I believe it." He got back in his car and accompanied me at 100 miles per hour, red lights flashing. When we got to the county line just outside San Bernardino, he motioned me to go around him and saluted me as I went on to my mission. I got to El Toro and skidded up to my airplane with about five minutes to spare. I would have called the officer to thank him, and let him know I had made it, but I did not know his name.

Pave Knife was proving to be effective in flight tests, but the program had to be accelerated. The Air Force wanted it as soon as possible for the war in Southeast Asia. The Air Force and the company worked very well together. I went to El Toro often for several months to fly Pave Knife tests. After test flying a mission, we held de-briefings, analyzing data to be incorporated as quickly as possible for the next test mission.

The system had to work within the parameters of the F-4. The F-4 is a Mach-2 airplane with a 7.33 G radial acceleration capability. As we progressed, upgraded modifications were rapidly incorporated. The contract called for six Pave Knife pods. When the tests were completed the six pods were to be sent to Southeast Asia for combat. It was an earn-while-you-learn program. Pave Knife was a quantum improvement over Paveway.

Progress of Pave Knife was proceeding at a rapid pace. It seems there are always unforeseen obstacles. One setback was narrowly averted. I was on a high-G, high-speed parameter test of Pave Knife on the Edwards Air Force Base range. I was getting close to the end of the test when I lost the primary hydraulic flight control system. Pressure went to zero almost instantaneously. It is some distance from the Edwards range to El Toro, so my first thought was to start toward home. As I exited the area, I lost the second flight control system. Now I had no flight controls. I had a very limited amount of mechanical rudder control—about 15 degrees of rudder either side of center. The wheel brakes, an independent system, were available for landing but of little use under these conditions. At this point it did not appear I would get to the landing phase. This was very similar to the situation I faced back at Holloman six years earlier. I said at that time I would never again try to land with no flight controls. But this time I was faced with a very strange situation. I had the only operable Pave Knife pod in existence hanging on the airplane. It was critical to attempt to save this needed combat weapon system.

As the second hydraulic system failed, the airplane started to oscillate in pitch. The nose was going up and down, and I had no control over it. I tried to get control by accelerating and decelerating engine power at appropriate times. I finally got the aircraft to settle down to level flight, but it looked like we would have to bail out. In correcting the oscillations I realized that the extensive power of the F-4 allowed some control over the airplane. The left engine and right engine gave some capability in the yaw axis. If a wing did start to drop, use of the engine on that side and limited rudder would pick that wing up. Still, I thought, there is no way I can land this airplane. It is just not controllable enough.

I called the command post at George Air Force Base, east of Long Beach, and told them of the conditions. All the time I was working with it, I have the only Pave Knife system in the world hanging on this airplane, and I am about to dump it into a hole in the ground. As the minutes went by I realized I could control the airplane better than I first thought. The F-4 is an amazing airplane. I kept working with it and started to descend a little bit. It occurred to me that if the airfield had an approach-end arresting barrier so I would not have to control the airplane on the runway, I might be able to land it. I asked the command post if they had the approach-end barrier engagement system (which I had been involved in testing at Ubon). They said, yes, it was available.

I had a weapons operator in the back seat. He said, "I'm not going to sit through this landing." I told him, "Go ahead and get out. You're on your own. Just tell me when you're ready to go." As the minutes went by, the weapons operator began to realize we had control. So he sat it out.

I told the George Air Force Base command post, "I am going to land it." The response was, "No, you are in an eject-situation, unequivocally." I replied, "This is not an ordinary flight. I will attempt landing." Twenty miles out on the approach to George I had the airplane level and lined up with Runway 23 with about a 1,000-feet-a-minute rate of descent. The winds were pretty high, 30 to 35 knots. I was about 12,000 to 14,000 feet at this time. I was able to control the descent and control the airplane with the power. I thought, "I can do this." I called and said, "I'm going to land on the southwest runway. I'm about 15 miles out on final approach, I will land in about three or four minutes." I was about a mile out on final approach when a very aggressive voice came on the radio and said, "This is the wing commander at George Air Force Base. Take the aircraft out and eject." I said, "No, I am ready to land. It is of extreme importance." He said, "I'm ordering you." I just shut the radio off.

By this time I was over the end of the runway with a speed of 220 knots. The tail hook picked up the cable, and I screeched to a halt in about two seconds. As the dust started to settle, a blue car was coming down the middle of the runway. "This is going to be fun," I thought. He skidded up to a stop as I got out of the airplane, and he said, "I told you to go and jump out of that airplane!" It was the wing commander. I said, "No, I am in charge of this aircraft. I told you I would land." By this time he had realized there was a very strange-looking device, the Pave Knife pod, hanging underneath the airplane. He didn't know anything about Pave Knife. I just told him, "This is a high-security program, and it was of necessity to save it." Then he went through me like a dose of salts. I think he finally realized that strange-looking piece of equipment under the airplane probably came from a whole lot higher authority than he had. He softened up some.

On inspection of the airplane we found the left aileron actuator had split open, dumping both the primary and the secondary flight control system hydraulic fluid out into the world. I called El Toro and told them what had happened. They sent security people to guard the airplane, and the aileron actuator was changed that night. That evening the weapons operator who had been in the back seat declared, "I'll never do that again." I said, "I don't plan on doing it either." At six o'clock the next morning we took off from George Air Force Base to land at El Toro. As I rolled down the runway I thought, "I've finally learned to think like Iron Mike Meroney: it is just another day."

The Pave Knife system, with the accelerated flight test and development program, proved to be well worth the effort after the six pods reached

A photo of an F-4E Phantom flying over Hoover Dam. The Phantom was flown by Major Haney at the Fighter Weapons School, Nellis AFB, 1970.

Southeast Asia. Pave Knife was taken into combat for Linebacker II, which was the extensive air interdiction of North Vietnam in 1972 to stop the war. Previously we had lost a high number of airplanes in efforts to destroy the bridges in the Hanoi and Haiphong harbor industrial areas. It was of great strategic importance to hit these bridges and stop the North Vietnamese from transporting combat equipment to the south. Pave Knife was very successful in this interdiction mission. The laser-guided system proved it could hit almost any target with tremendous accuracy and effectiveness. We had lost a lot of airplanes trying to do a job the F-4 and Pave Knife did in one mission without a loss. Terminal guided weapons became the backbone of tactical fighter air-to-ground combat capability.

My time at Fighter Weapons School, with dual assignments instructing terminal guided weapons and flight testing Pave Knife, offered no relief from the long duty hours that I had become accustomed to. However, in the two-and-a-half years I was at the Weapons School I usually was able to be home at night and most weekends. With the family with me at Nellis, this period was one of the best of my career in terms of time I was able to spend with my three sons. We had a lot of fun together. As a family, we

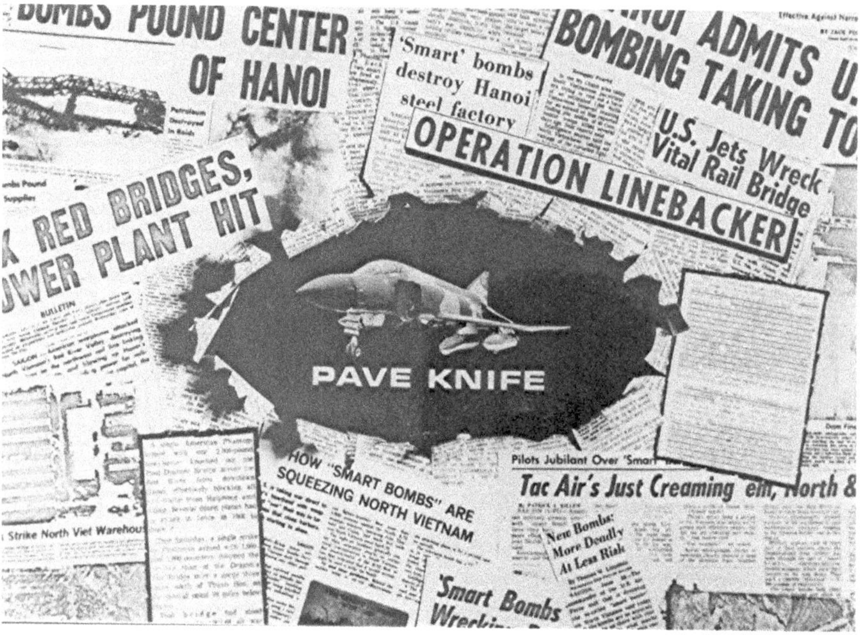

An F-4D carrying a Pave Knife pod. Pave Knife was a significant terminal guidance weapons system for tactical aviation. Major Haney accomplished important flight tests for this weapons system.

spent time almost year round water skiing on Lake Mead. During the winter we would go to Bryan Head, Utah, and ski all weekend. The sky was the limit when it came to activities with the kids. If it was there to do, we were going to do it. We even rode our bicycles to Boulder City, Nevada, 25 miles, for a Saturday excursion.

We enjoyed the community life at Nellis and the occasional parties in Las Vegas, where we had many friends. After a year in Vietnam I enjoyed participating in Thunderbird family activities again. Most of the guys were good friends, except one who became involved with my wife while I was in Southeast Asia. It wasn't the first time she had done this. For me, I was backed into a corner. Divorce meant I would probably lose my children. During this time I also found Betty had been abusive to the boys — locking them in the house at night while going out, leaving them alone in the car with 107-degree temperatures, and abusive language, among other things. I still believed in duty, honor, country, and in the future of my children. I chose to continue with what I believed in, and maybe solve the problem with Betty, intending at least to protect the children. To me, it appeared we were so fortunate, we had it all, and it was worth saving if possible. This scenario is very common in society, so I didn't feel like the "lone ranger." I decided I would do my best each day considering all factors, hope for the best, and try to handle the worst. Time would tell.

In 1970, while flying daily, instructing in the Fighter Weapons School, and flying Pave Knife tests, I was assigned an additional duty, which turned out to be one of the most rewarding experiences of my Air Force career. The Israeli government had purchased a number of F-4s from the United States, with pilot training included as part of the package. Five of Israel's best fighter pilots were to be trained in the high-performance terminal guided weapons delivery capability of the F-4. I was assigned to provide this training.

I was a little apprehensive at first because I did not know much about these pilots and their experience in fighters. The F-4 is a Mach-2-capable aircraft with outstanding performance up to 50,000 feet. It is not, however, forgiving of errors in judgment or lack of pilot competence. The training envelope included speed from 800 miles per hour at low altitudes and up to 7.33 Gs radial acceleration on any given flight. To say the least, this is a most dynamic and hazardous environment. I wouldn't mind this if I was alone, but with anyone else in control I knew I would be uncomfortable. I would have to ride in the rear seat of the Phantom during the early phases of training. I believe my concerns were obvious.

I soon realized these were not novice fighter pilots; all were outstanding. Among them was Avihu Ben-Nun, who was no doubt the best pilot I have ever seen in terms of mastery of the F-4. He could fly the airplane in the out-of-control environment better than most could fly inside the control envelope. Avihu also was a great intellect. He could have designed the aircraft if needed. I soon forgot any apprehension I may have had over the skills of these pilots and really began to enjoy this unusual assignment.

Later, while I was at the Air War College, I encouraged the government to give Avihu Ben-Nun an opportunity to attend the War College. He would be the first Israeli to attend the Air War College. He graduated two years after I did with the highest honors. I was not surprised. Avihu Ben-Nun and I had become friends and continued to communicate for many years.

We flew on a daily basis in this dynamic envelope of the F-4 performance, sometimes exhausting ourselves in our efforts to do the best possible. On a couple of occasions when I felt we needed a break, I led the F-4 formation on a sightseeing trip of the Southwest. We flew over

Boulder Dam, Lake Mead, the Colorado River, the Grand Canyon, Thunderbird Lake, and other magnificent Western landmarks. The site they liked most was Zion Canyon just northeast of Nellis Air Force Base. We had hours of discussions, not only about aviation but also about those sightseeing trips, which seemed ordinary to me but were so extraordinary to my Israeli friends. The extra training for the Israelis was very rewarding to them in their future war engagements.

In 1970 I was being considered to lead the Thunderbirds. The Thunderbirds were now in the F-4. I had 1,000 hours, a combat tour, and was instructing in the Fighter Weapons School. My credentials were unequalled. I wanted to lead the team. Maj. Gen. Homer Hanson, the new Fighter Weapons Center commander, did not believe one person should have more than one Thunderbird tour. I agree with this because there are so very few who get the opportunity to serve even one tour.

I was very surprised to learn my next assignment would be to the Air War College in Montgomery, Alabama. When the War College list for the Class of '72 came out, my name was on it. Again, I thought a mistake had been made. So far as I knew, I met none of the prerequisites for selection and certainly had not sought the appointment. The War College is the Air Force senior officers' development school, and most candidates are expected to have the rank of lieutenant colonel. A college degree, more often a master's degree, was a requirement, as was completion of the Command and Staff School. I was a young major. I had completed a significant number of college credits during earlier tours. I did not yet have my B.A., and I had not attended the Command and Staff School.

Maj. Gen. "Zack" Taylor, the Weapons Center boss when I was a Thunderbird, had made a recommendation that I should lead the team, along with several others of my commanders. When this did not happen I believe General Taylor may have intervened, recommending me for assignment to War College. I am not certain about this, but I have no other explanation for why I was selected at this point in my career.

While I was not looking forward to a year with the books, the assignment was an honor. As it turned out, the timing probably worked out well because shortly before leaving Nellis I had started having physical problems. Under high-G loads I found I was losing some control of my right eye and right arm, and the trouble was becoming more persistent. My right eye was really bothering me. I knew I should see the flight surgeon, but I kept putting it off. The first thing the flight surgeon will do in situations like this is ground a pilot, especially when it is not clear what's wrong. So the occurrence of this health problem in one sense came at the right time because the War College did not require me to do any active flying.

During my last flight at Nellis, the fighter pilots put me to a test. I wasn't off the ground before an attack came. As I was coming off the runway I saw an aircraft starting an approach from about 10,000 feet at four o'clock. I knew he was coming after me. I stroked up the burners and turned my flight over to the element flight leader. The attacking aircraft and I had a one-on-one right over the runway. I was taking off and was full of gas, and he was coming back from a mission and didn't have much fuel. He was a tough cat to handle, though. He was good. We were up and down over the runway for about 15 minutes. I knew sooner or later he was going to run out of gas and have to land. Out of gas, my adversary turned into the traffic pattern to land. As he pitched out I did a barrel roll around him. My opponent was also an instructor. He was junior to me, but a very experienced pilot. The fighter pilots at Nellis wanted to see if I would take on the fight over Nellis, in front of all, or would I go on to War College with "stars" in my future and avoid the fight. Sometime later my name was carved on the club bar with the designation "A Class Act." General Hanson was not all that happy with the engagement over Nellis. I soon left for War College.

I would have been glad to have remained at Fighter Weapons School forever. I was as happy as a guy could be, flying every day. As an instructor, I became close to my students. I worried about them going to war. Because we wanted to send the best, we had to give it our best. I had a very devout feeling about doing this job right because these students were going to do exactly what I did in Vietnam. I knew very well that war was a very hazardous environment. And I knew the secrets to their success in a combat mission were to have the very best airplane for the job, the best equipment and training available, the best possible support personnel — and doing their own absolute best as pilots.

The instructional program itself proved to have been very successful when taken into combat. We did not lose any pilots; not one of them was shot down. It was rewarding for me to see the results of a weapons system and instructional program with which I had been so deeply involved, in flight tests and combat in Southeast Asia and in the Fighter Weapons School. Throughout the remainder of my career I participated in evaluations of terminal guided weapons systems. Terminal guided weapons development was another major milestone in the supersonic evolution of fighter capability.

CHAPTER 11

Air War College and Test and Evaluation

"Just Do It."

I started the Air War College in Montgomery, Alabama, in mid–1971, following a memorable cross-country trip with the family. While we were at Nellis the boys were still youngsters but old enough to join in the restoration of a 1926 Model T Ford I had found. Together the boys and I put a big Ford engine, automatic transmission, and modern running gear into the frame of that old car. From the outside it looked like a '26 Model T, but inside it was a modern automobile. It didn't have any glass in the windows yet, but the boys and I drove that Model T to Wyoming, where we went through Yellowstone Park, and on to the Black Hills of South Dakota and Mount Rushmore. The boys' mother drove our Mercedes sedan. I actually taught the boys to drive when we were in Bon Durant, Wyoming, near Yellowstone. We toured all the way across the country in that car and had the time of our lives.

Air War College is basically a political science military war gaming program. It prepares senior officers to fully understand the international political environment and what possibilities an officer may face in the event war occurs. At the time I attended, we were still in the Southeast Asian War as well as involved in the Cold War with the Soviet Union and other communist countries. War College prepares officers to better understand the history and dynamics of international relations and geo-political factors that affect the conduct of the military in national defense as well as war time. This training is directed toward preparing officers to assume command positions in the Air Force and other services as well as developing relationships with civilian and military leaders in our own and other countries. To that end, enrollment in the War College includes officers from foreign countries; from the U.S. Army, Navy, and the Marine Corps; officials from government agencies from our country; and some foreign allies also. All are outstanding individuals, not only from an academic standpoint but also in terms of demonstrated leadership and career direction.

Academic studies at the Air War College are geared to master's level course work, and I was at that time still working on my bachelor's degree. I had accumulated about 80 hours of college credits—which included proficiencies in engineering, propulsion, and electronics plus credits earned from night school courses I took at UCLA while I was at Edwards Air Force Base. I completed another three semesters of college requirements, including 12 hours of language study, through the University of Maryland University College while I was stationed in Europe.

Nonetheless, I had work remaining to fulfill all the specific requirements of a four-year degree, so while attending the War College I also took courses at Troy University's Maxwell campus. Because I had too much to do and very little time to do it all, I enrolled in a speed-reading course that enabled me to increase my reading speed from about 350 words per minute to over a thousand words per minute. As my reading speed increased, so did my ability to retain what I had read. My retention went from 80 percent to 95 percent. That course, which I took twice, was a major asset for me in my year at the War College, allowing me to handle a lot of academic work in a short period of time.

I learned that my best study time was the early hours of the morning. I would get up around 2:30 or 3:00 A.M. and study for a few hours, then go to the hospital where I was being treated for the medical problem that had developed in my last year at Nellis, and from there go on to the speed-reading course. I would attend War College classes from 8:30 to 11:30 in the morning. From 2:00 to 5:00 in the afternoon, while others were studying, working on their theses, or were engaged in other activities, I would be taking courses at Troy University.

I never buried myself in the books at night. The Air War College was very family oriented, with all kinds of organized social activities involving the whole family. I was able to spend a lot of time with the boys, including working together rebuilding our old Model T Ford. My early-morning study habit did not disrupt my family life. The three boys all were in school the year we were in Montgomery, and all were good students and good athletes. They were in bed by 9:00 P.M., and I made that my bedtime, too. I found that six hours' sleep was more than enough. I continued to follow that schedule even after I completed school. For the next 20 or more years when I was writing or working on a program I would get up at 3:00 A.M. to work when my mind was most clear.

However, while I was at the War College, the medical problem I had experienced in my last flights at Nellis was reaching a serious state. The right side of my face became totally paralyzed. This affected my right eye, making it more difficult for me to study. The neurologists I consulted thought that the problem was in the spinal column, but they were not all that sure. There was some evidence of injury to the third vertebrae that may have occurred during a high-speed ejection while I was on the Thunderbirds. Eventually, the paralysis caused even more difficulty. I couldn't walk steadily. In the early mornings, before speed-reading class, I would go to therapy with the neurologist, attempting to overcome the problems. Surgery was a possibility, but the risks were so significant as to be unacceptable. I decided against the surgery. It was just too iffy, with no assurance that it would cure the problem.

The good thing was that during my year at the War College I didn't have to fly, giving me more time for the academics. However, it began to appear that the paralysis might be permanent, leaving me with a loss of normal movement for the rest of my life. In this event, I wouldn't be able to continue to fly. I would not stay in the Air Force: I would have been medically discharged. This was of great concern to me. I had been in the Air Force and fighter aviation all my adult life. If I couldn't fly, I didn't know what else I could do. The mental pressure on me was heavy, from the academic challenges and from my physical standpoint. However, I was about two-thirds of the way through school, going to therapy every day, when the feeling started to come back. I was recovering. I still had a little difficulty with my right eye, a little bit of slowness in movement. For all practical purposes, when I left the War College I was back to normal and back to flying.

In addition to the course work, the Air War College program required training in public speaking, research and writing skills, and completion of an academic thesis. My fifteen-thousand-word thesis was on the evolution of testing and evaluation of tactical weapons and tactical aircraft — a topic for which I was well-prepared by my engineering background combined with several years of actual experience and practice in supersonic flight test, as well as testing, delivery in combat conditions, and instructing in the use of the revolutionary laser-guided weapons systems. The theory and conclusion developed in my thesis was a product of my experience and vision of future requirements.

This was a busy, busy year. Although I completed the master's level program at the War College, and successfully defended my thesis, I was in the unusual position of not yet having a college degree. I had almost three years of my college work completed, but most schools require a degree candidate to be in residence for the last two semesters. If I had been able to stay in Montgomery through the 1972 summer session, I could have finished my bachelor's degree at Troy University and possibly left the War College with a master's degree. But there wasn't time. I graduated from the Air War College in May 1972 and left immediately for my new assignment at the Pentagon. (I eventually completed the degree requirements at the University of Albuquerque, New Mexico.)

I did not want to go to a staff position, but it became apparent while I was at the War College I would be headed for the Pentagon because of my activities and specialty in terminal guided weapons and, to some extent, air-to-air weapons. And that is precisely what happened. The development and use of the new fighter weapons systems was expanding at a rapid rate as the war in Southeast Asia continued. I was selected to work in Test and Evaluation of Tactical Fighters.

When I received my assignment to the Pentagon we decided to have a house built in a place called Saratoga, a housing development south of Springfield, Virginia. It was a beautiful place: rolling hills, trees, absolutely gorgeous. The house sat in the back of a cul-de-sac, on a big lot. The kids and I spent lots of time landscaping the yard, and my wife did all the work for the decoration of the house.

Up to this time, we had usually lived in base housing, which, as a family, was what we had always known. I'd never really thought much about living in town. Most bases are somewhat isolated from metropolitan areas. Nellis was ten miles from Las Vegas; Holloman was ten miles from Alamogordo. In Europe, we lived in Verdun, France, 20 kilometers from Etain Air Base, where I flew. The purchase of the house in Virginia was a new and different venture, and it turned out to be a very good one. Buying the house was one of the best decisions we ever made. In the two years we were there, the price of the house doubled.

My new job was branch chief, Test and Evaluation of Fighter Weapons. This assignment was the result of my work in the development of Paveway, Pave Knife, and the new system called Pave Spike, which was an upgraded version of the laser terminal guided system. I was also in charge of development of air-to-air weapons for the new F-15 and the F-16 fighter aircraft.

Having been in fighters for a long time, and spending a tour in combat, I realized that many of the published capabilities of the weaponry in reality did not meet the standards that the contractors claimed. For example, the published probability of kill-rate for an AIM 7, an air-to-air guided missile, was 0.75. That's very high. You figure if you fire ten missiles and get seven hits, that's pretty good. Similarly, the AIM 9, an infra-red, air-to-air, mid-range missile, was said to have about a 0.8 probability of kill. In combat, I found this wasn't true. The actual probability of kill for the AIM 7 and the AIM 9 was about 0.2, meaning if you fired everything you had aboard the airplane, you might get one hit.

I thought this was a terrible situation — to think you had such capability in the air when you really didn't. I did a study on the probability of kill, tracing the history and the background of the AIM 7 and the AIM 9. I found the biggest problem was that a thorough test on the systems had never been conducted. We never really knew what capability those weapons had because we failed to evaluate what happened in the last seconds of the missile's travel to the target. In testing missile capability, the Air Force never used an actual simulated combat target, employing instead small targets that had electronic augmentation that wasn't realistic in terms of the effect on the weapon of a real airplane: we failed to get realistic results because targets similar to real combat vehicles were never used.

I was charged with evaluating Pave Spike, the AIM 7, and the AIM 9 upgraded weapons. I now believed that the biggest problem in conducting these tests was the lack of a realistic target — that is, a target airplane with an afterburner that will go supersonic and do everything a real combat aircraft can do. I started looking. I found there were a lot of non-flyable airplanes in the Davis-Monthan Air Force Base bone yard in Arizona. I located serviceable J-57 engines from out-of-service aircraft resources. Because the Air Defense Command was beginning to be dissolved, with Tactical Air Command taking over the inner perimeter defense mission, I found that a number of serviceable F-102s were soon scheduled for the bone yard.

I suggested, "Why can't we develop the F-102s into an airborne target for the AIM 7 and the AIM 9 air-to-air tests?" The answer was, "We don't have any money to develop that type of target vehicle." I pointed out, "I have funds to do the AIM 7 and the AIM 9 tests." The reply was, "That's a different program funding." I said, "I need the targets to do my programs.

That tells me the money is available to do whatever I need to do these tests."

But I didn't have enough money to do the complete development and to fly the target airplanes from the ground. I learned that the Army had a very similar target problem in Test and Evaluation of some of their Nike and Polaris ground-to-air weapons. I worked with the Army to build a mechanical electronic control system that set in the cockpit of an F-102 so the airplane could be flown remotely from a ground position. This concept is very similar to radio-controlled aircraft models. We put our first PQM-102 test site at Tyndall Air Force Base, Florida. Because of test range capability available at Holloman Air Force Base in New Mexico, we later moved to Holloman to do the missile tests with the PQM-102 target as well as support the Army requirements.

The development of the F-102 for use as a target was appropriate because it was a high-performing aircraft with characteristics and capabilities such as those that would be engaged in an actual war. To shoot these aircraft down in testing weapons would seem to appear extreme, but such was not the case: the aircraft were no longer in military use, and the dividends reaped in evaluating new, more effective weapons were priceless. (Years later, F-100 and F-4 aircraft also were modified and used as targets.) The use of real fighter aircraft for targets improved the testing capability monumentally, adding another dimension to the supersonic fighter evolution.

We now had the targets required. The AIM 9 upgraded test missiles were being constructed. I believed this was going to be one of the best missile or weapons tests ever. Tactical Air Command then announced that the AIM 9-L wasn't needed anymore; they were going to go to a new air-to-air weapon called the "Claw."

When I looked at the design and capabilities, I saw that the Claw system was basically the same AIM 9 that we had 15 years before. TAC's idea was, "We're going to be able to build these weapons at less cost. We'll have six or eight missiles available on one airplane and therefore have a good kill probability." I argued, "I don't care how many you put on the airplane. If the weapons are not capable of hitting the target, the capability is zero. We've already gone through this exercise in the AIM 9 and the AIM 7." I said, "I think we have solved those problems in the AIM 9-L. I have a target that will prove whether the weapon is of any value or not. If you build a Claw, it's going to take two years to get where we now are with the AIM 9-L. We need an air-to-air weapon to go on the F-15 and the F-

16 immediately, not two years from now. We have 30 test missiles available. We have targets at Holloman. We have money for the test. When the test is complete, you do whatever you want, but we're going to do the test."

We did the AIM 9-L test. We fired those 30 missiles in many air-to-air scenarios, and it turned out to be the most successful missile test and fighter air-to-air weapon the services had ever possessed. Everything that could be done in combat, we could do with the PQM-102. We designed a test that was a complete tactical fighter envelope, similar to what F-15s and the F-16s would see in a tactical air war. (Coincidentally, when the Air Force established Operational Test and Evaluation at Kirtland Air Force Base in New Mexico I was assigned as the fighter test director and was able to complete the last phase of the AIM 9-L test.)

The tests were so successful the Air Force bought the AIM 9-L, and, some 35 years later, the system remained the backbone of the air-to-air capability in the F-15 and the F-16. The advances with air-to-air missiles, terminal guided weapons, and realistic targets for test and evaluation again were significant steps forward in the evaluation of the supersonic fighter. Years later, even after I left the Air Force, people would come up to me to discuss the AIM 9-L project. One, who went on to become a high-ranking official in the Air Force, recalled this story of the battle of the AIM 9-L: He said, "If Colonel Haney never did anything else for the rest if his life, they could pay him full pay and allowances and never pay him enough for what he did on that test." That story has come back to me several times. It was a struggle, but a successful one.

Although the PQM-102 was a Research and Development project, I managed the development and controlled the missions from my office in the Pentagon, which was an operational Test and Evaluation facility. As I was going through the iteration there were people who argued that I was spending money from the Test and Evaluation budget for Research and Development. A couple of guys even thought I would be strung up over this. My response was that my charter was to test and evaluate the weapons—which I could not do without adequate targets.

As it turned out, the way I managed funds on the PQM-102 was never questioned. The reason for this was simple: the program was a success. I did what had to be done to test those weapons. There really was not anything wrong. It was just that I did not do this in the accustomed way. But that's how changes are made. That's how progress is made. If you did everything the way it was done yesterday, you'd never progress a step. When something has to be done, you just do it.

Accomplishment is in numbers at the Pentagon. For me, personally, some of the things I worked with during my direct aviation years — in flight test, in combat, and in Fighter Weapons School — were much greater achievements, but they were small in numbers. When I went to the Pentagon I dealt with problems that were going to affect the entire Air Force and in some cases other services. The AIM 9-L, for example, turned out to be a very successful weapon, one that has proven its value over many, many years. But to me that accomplishment was not as great as landing an F-4 with total flight control failure under very unusual conditions. That was a very personal achievement.

It wasn't my choice to go the Pentagon. I would rather have been out there doing it. I liked being involved with the flying activity. The administrative part was much less satisfying for me because of the long hours spent fighting with people over funding and the design of a particular test or development of a weapons system. Long hours are spent in the administrative and budgetary work — the architecture involved in putting a large program together and assuring it will be effective. There are always disagreements, conflicts, turf battles, and other obstacles to overcome in the world of pencils and papers and people.

Looking back over my two years in the Pentagon, I realized that the success of some of my projects there were for the most part a result of my experience and beliefs about what needed to done — what absolutely had to be done — for a successful development into the next iteration of fighter aviation. It wasn't necessarily that my administrative activities were very good. It was that I couldn't see a successful outcome in any way other than my experience had taught me. And I believe my ideas turned out to be pretty close to correct.

Photograph of PQM-102 and AIM 9-L. The AIM-9-L missile is exploding above the PQM-102 target aircraft. These test projects were assigned to Col. Haney during his Pentagon tour of duty, 1972, and his Air Force Operational Test Center tour, 1974.

I remained flight

current during the time I was in the Pentagon. Years earlier, while at Edwards, I had gone through the instrument instructor flight school. I learned how to instruct instruments in all kinds of environments. While I was in the Pentagon I flew the T-39, which is an executive jet airplane I had flown during the instrument evaluation days back at Edwards. While I was at the Pentagon I flew the T-39 for proficiency and also did instrument checks for the training facility at Andrews Air Force Base. I flew about once a week, and, rather than take a civilian airline whenever I had to make a trip, when possible I would fly a T-39 to keep my flight proficiency up during the time I was in an administrative job.

I wasn't required to fly in order to continue to receive flying pay. But I wanted to fly. I was in the Air Force because of flying, which is what I loved to do. I believed I was going to return to flying when I got out of the Pentagon, moving on to an assignment that I hoped would be back in the aviation world. However, it wasn't all that common for career officers to keep logging in flight time as pilots. By the time they reached the rank of full colonel, most held administrative or command jobs requiring long hours. To stay proficient in an airplane and to fly all the instrument approaches and night time — the things you have to do to maintain a proficiency level — takes a lot of hours. It was difficult to find the time, but I wanted to remain an active aviator.

Flying fighters was my signature. That's what I was recognized for — being able to fly and, supposedly, able to do it very well. I did not want to lose that signature or lose that capability. To me that's what the Air Force is about. I believe that commanders must be good aviators in order to be good aviation commanders. A good leader can't be a second-class pilot and command a first-class organization. That was my opinion, and I stuck with it.

My hours in the Pentagon were long. I usually would leave very early in the morning and didn't get home until six o'clock or later. I used to say that I worked half a day — from six in the morning until six at night. I was close to the boys, and they were all athletic and always had a lot of energy. I worked with the kids in the evenings and on weekends. They went to an outstanding school in Springfield, Virginia, probably the best they attended during their school years. The high school was unbelievable. The administration, the teachers, and the athletic programs were the best I have ever seen.

On Saturdays we would usually go someplace, just the boys and me. There was a fine gymnasium system in the basement of the Pentagon, with every kind of athletic facility. I taught the boys to play racquetball and handball there. Racquetball was just becoming popular in those days. We would eat breakfast some place, and then go to the Pentagon facility to play racquetball, run a mile, and work out, whatever, until maybe two o'clock in the afternoon. Then we would go somewhere for lunch and maybe drive down to the waterfront and see the boats go by. On Sundays the whole family usually would go to some historic place, and there were hundreds of them along the East Coast, including Civil War battlegrounds that weren't far from where we lived in Virginia. Or we would go to one of the many museums in the Washington area.

The Smithsonian National Air and Space Museum was being developed at that time, and we went there several times. A T-38 had been hung from the museum ceiling that I recognized as the actual aircraft I flew at Edwards Air Force Base back in 1960. I recognized the aircraft immediately because of the number 194 on it. This T-38 was part of the original test program: it was the first prototype built and the first one we flew. That airplane was somewhat different from the eventual production model. The paint job was different, and there were several other idiosyncrasies. It was pretty crude, as most early airplanes or most prototype airplanes were. The first time we flew the T-38, it didn't even have afterburners. We had only seven T-38s during the whole program at Edwards, and I flew all of the seven airplanes.

I also spotted an F-104 that I flew at Edwards hanging at the Air and Space Museum. I wasn't involved with the early test of the F-104, but I later flew that airplane. I didn't have the attachment to the F-104 that I felt to the T-38. I sort of grew up with the T-38 and, in fact, I touched parts of the T-38 advancements and iterations of that over the rest of my career. Even when I was at Holloman, I flew the T-38. We used them as chase planes for chase of test vehicles. I flew the T-38 off and on from 1960 to 1982 and was always affiliated with it in some way.

One of the X-15s we had at Edwards also hangs at the Air and Space Museum. I never flew the X-15, but one of my closest friends, Pete Knight, flew it. He and I flew together on the T-38, and we did some things jointly, including the Apollo astronaut selection board, later in our Air Force careers. Pete's an extraordinary test pilot and one of my favorite guys. There are a lot of other things in the Air and Space Museum that are very close to my life and career, including a presentation in the panoramic theater featuring the Thunderbirds in the F-100, back when I was on the team.

In addition to our weekend outings, the boys also kept me busy with projects at home. My youngest son, Steve, is very ingenious, and was always thinking of something to do. At the time he was looking for some way to make some money to continue the development of our old 1926 Model T Ford. He had an idea. The property developers had cut trees and put them in a valley a couple of blocks from our home. Steve came home one day and said, "Dad, we're going to cut firewood and sell it to the neighbors." Most of the homes around us had fireplaces, more as a luxury item than for heating. "That's a good idea," I replied. Clearly, I wasn't really thinking when I said that.

It wasn't long before he had orders from ten households, with more to come. Guess who gets to help him cut the wood? Ten cords of wood to cut, and I am already busy as I can be. Sensibly, I bought a chain saw to assist this project. The boys and I spent a lot of Saturdays that fall of 1972 cutting wood to fill those orders. We made 30 or 40 dollars a cord, and eventually made several hundred dollars. We reupholstered our old Model T and put some new racy tires on it. By this time, we had windows in and a horn. We could go wherever we wanted to go. Our old Ford was slick. It would run down the highway at 75 miles an hour along with the best of them. We got plenty of attention in that old car. It was a lot of fun.

CHAPTER 12

Operational Testing

"On the hot seat."

Normally the Pentagon tour is four years. I had been at the Pentagon for two years when the U.S. Government implemented new test and evaluation processes. It was believed that Research and Development test and evaluation was not sufficient to take new equipment into the operational environment where it was to be used — that is, equipment that had not been tested under actual operational combat conditions. You can build a machine that does the things you want it to do, but if you can't train with it or can't maintain it properly when it is in the field, it will not win the war. It was a good concept, and the major services were charged with developing means of testing and evaluating in the intended environment.

Maj. Gen. J. J. Burns, who was in the Pentagon the same time I was, selected a few people, including me, to come to Kirtland Air Force Base in Albuquerque, New Mexico, to establish the new Air Force Test and Evaluation Center (AFTEC). I arrived at Kirtland in mid–1974. At first I was the branch chief responsible for fighter weapons, the same as my Pentagon job. In 1975 I was promoted to colonel and later was assigned division chief for operational evaluation of tactical fighter and weapons systems. At that time we had the newly developed F-15, the F-16, and, soon, a new attack airplane called the A-10 to be evaluated in an operational environment. (All of these airplanes were being evaluated in a research-and-development environment.) In addition to the fighters, there were bombers, helicopters, transports, and weapons to be evaluated. I remained in the fighter world commensurate with my background and experience.

The new procedures, although good in concept, encountered some difficulties in the implementation stages. Research and Development, with some justification, believed their responsibilities were being usurped. They claimed they could evaluate aircraft and equipment in an operational environment just as well as we could. The problem was this: operational testing was not being done. When the airplanes went to operational units they were used immediately for the mission requirement. That's what commanders are tasked to do. They don't have the time or the resources to do tests and evaluations after the airplane is assigned in the field if the test and evaluation has not already been accomplished.

The authority and responsibility to do the operational tests and evaluations of new airplanes was given to the Air Force Test and Evaluation Center. We began to put the processes together. It was a difficult situation not only because of disagreements with Research and Development but also because of disagreements with the commands, such as Strategic Air Command (SAC), Tactical Air Command (TAC), and Military Air Transport Service (MATS). There was resentment on all sides. AFTEC was stuck in the middle, but we were in full charge by charter. AFTEC, the Air Force Test and Evaluation Center, was later re-named AFOTEC, the Air Force Operational Test and Evaluation Center, to specify its area of responsibility.

There were real problems when the A-10 came along. The A-10 was designed to function in a European full-combat environment much like that of World War II. We did the evaluations, and the airplane did not even come close to its operational requirements. It was underpowered. It had virtually no radial acceleration capability — that is, the capability to maneuver under high-Gs. The airplane could not be flown with more than one added G force. Two Gs was about the best you could get out of it for any period of time. It was not adequate for multiple re-attacks in combat and not adequate to evade high-threat weaponry in the war world of the day. It was a twin-engine airplane, and it would not fly successfully on a single engine. If you've got two engines, and the aircraft won't fly on a single engine, you don't need two engines. You also multiply the factor of loss by two by having two engines. There were significant problems with this airplane. Tactical Air Command believed they could train and work around the problems. There is no way you can work around these problems. The airplane was not serviceable in its intended environment, although the A-10 had excellent armament in a rapid-fire 30-millimeter cannon, terminal guided, and conventional weapons. If the aircraft carrying the weapons can't survive in the combat areas, it is all for zero.

Let's put this in perspective: at this point in the supersonic evolution we are in an envelope of combat aircraft that operate at speeds of over 2,000 feet per second (1,500 miles per hour) and radial acceleration sustaining 10 Gs. The A-10's maximum speed is approximately 400 feet per second (300 miles per hour) and it has no capability to sustain acceptable G-loads to survive in an AAA ground-fire arena or a Mach 2 air-to-air arena. This degraded performance also severely limits the A-10's capability to perform its designed mission of close air support: the ability to perform multiple strikes in a combat arena with sophisticated ground-to-air defense weapons and survive to fight tomorrow.

I'm on the hot seat, and not for the first time in my career. The A-10 came to a serious contention at the Armament Systems Development (ASD) headquarters at Wright-Patterson Air Force Base, where Lt. Gen. James T. Stewart was the commander. The AFTEC team went there to brief. The research and development on the aircraft had been completed, and it was said to be serviceable. The AFTEC report on the operational capability of the airplane said it absolutely was not a serviceable airplane in a combat arena. Gen. Jay R. Brill, a one-star general, was in charge of the A-10 research-and-development program. He was very upset by the findings of the operational evaluation.

In the middle of this heated meeting General Stewart stood up and said, "Where is Colonel Haney? I want to ask you a question." I stood up, and he said, "Would you buy this airplane for Air Force utilization?"

I said, "Not in the configuration it is right now." That upset everybody.

He said, "Tell me why."

I said, "There are a lot of little reasons, but I'll give three basic reasons. This is not an AFTEC position or an Air Force position. It is my position from experience as a combat fighter pilot and from my experience with this test and evaluation.

"Our test data will support my position. First, it's underpowered for a fighter airplane in today's combat world. It really is not a fighter because it has no tactical capabilities in terms of high-performance fighter activity or fighter performance. It will not survive in a high-threat combat environment.

"Secondly," I said, "it is a twin-engine airplane, and it will not fly on a single engine, so if you lose an engine you're dead in the water because it won't sustain flight. If you lose an engine on takeoff, you will not be able to continue to take off.

"Third, there is nothing you can do with it unless you put bigger engines on it, or one great big engine on it, which would be my particular recommendation. Nearly every airplane we have bought in the past has a high-performance level because we know there are going to be added requirements and responsibilities for the airplane to meet as it travels through its life. The A-10 has no growth potential the way it is."

When I got back to Kirtland my boss, Gen. Robert Rushworth, met me at my airplane and said that I had really upset the applecart. I said, "I just told it like it is." He agreed with me because I had briefed him before going to ASD. We were now in a full-scale fight with Tactical Air Command and Research and Development Command over the A-10.

We then had to brief two four-star generals: Gen. Alton D. Slay, who was Research and Development commander, and Gen. Robert J. Dixon, Tactical Air Command commander. General Rushworth, as AFTEC commander, was responsible for doing the briefing. He gave the same ASD briefing and got into very serious difficulty with General Dixon, who intended to buy the airplane for Tactical Air Command for close air-support missions. The plan was to have a mission to support Army troops on the ground in a combat environment, as the Germans had attempted in World War II when the Stuka was armed with 105-millimeter cannon to provide support to troops on the ground and destroy tanks. This World War II effort was personified in the highly decorated German officer and Stuka pilot Hans Rudel.

The mission was sound, but the A-10 was not. General Dixon said they could work around the deficiencies, and they were going to proceed to develop and purchase the airplane for USAF combat utilization. General Rushworth was now in jeopardy because he had given a briefing that was not accepted. Both of us were on the hot seat. General Rushworth was reassigned and shortly afterward retired. General Howard Leaf assumed command of AFTEC, assigned from TAC under command of General Dixon.

We also had, in test process, the F-15 and the F-16. There were some problems with the F-15. A marvelous airplane, it just did everything a combat command could want. It was so versatile, powerful, and such an easy airplane to fly. It did have some discrepancies that needed to be corrected. If you went into a high-G turn at altitude, the inside engine sometimes would stagnate, and you couldn't control it. It would roll back to idle RPM, or sometimes it would flame out. This was a problem that had to be fixed. In a combat situation you can't be engaged with other airplanes and have one engine roll back to half power or no power. This was not a new problem. We'd had a similar problem in the J-57 engine in the F-100, the J-79, and in the F-4.

The other problem with the F-15 was in the fire control system. It did not function as designed in an electro-countermeasure environment, that is, in receiving and processing electronic countermeasure information to the fire control system. The system should be able to overtake incoming signals and blank them out and still function properly. It did not work right in this environment. There were other small things, but I consider these two problems as being pretty significant. The problems were curable, but the time for curing is in its test state, not waiting until it is operational. Then you have to go back and retrofit all the airplanes, which is extremely expensive. This was the whole idea on which AFTEC was organized, to catch and correct these problems before they get into the field and become so expensive you can't fix them.

There was contention in Tactical Air Command, believing they could use the F-15 as it was. I said, "You can use it like it is in the training environment but not in a combat environment. It has to be fixed." So I was on the carpet for surfacing things that the command believed they could solve. Col. Larry Welch, who was the first F-15 wing commander, and I had strong disagreements. The argument continued on throughout the operational test and evaluation of the F-15. The United States did buy the airplane with those deficiencies in it. Colonel Welch got his way. He said he could train and work around the deficiencies. I'm a young colonel, and I'm on the hot seat for what I believed was just doing my job.

The F-16 evaluation was extremely well designed. About a third of the way through the tests General Dixon decided the airplane had been tested enough and he would bring it into the operational environment as it was. I was strongly against this because the most difficult part of the test had not been completed. We knew the airplane would fly well — it had good performance — but it had a computer-controlled electronic fly-by-wire flight control system that had never been evaluated adequately in thunderstorms or electronic environments which may seriously affect flight control of the airplane. There also were weapons system evaluations that had not been done.

I was ordered by General Leaf to write a letter stating we would release the airplane to Tactical Air Command as it was. I said, "No, I won't write the letter because it is not ready to be released for operational use. It has a series of evaluations to be completed." General Leaf was somewhat unhappy with me. I believe he knew in his mind that it wasn't really ready for operational use, but I stood alone with this. I was in charge of the test and evaluation, but I was fighting a lot of high-ranking authority above me. I still had to do my job with responsibly and with integrity regardless of the adversaries, rank not withstanding. The F-16 was given to Tactical Air Command without the appropriate testing completed. The USAF has lost many F-16s with apparent uncontrollable flight conditions. The F-15 also was released for operational use without those two major discrepancies being corrected. The A-10 went on to be produced as an Air Force close air support airplane.

In all of these combat aircraft — A-10, F-15, F-16 — there are some simple but absolute axioms necessary to win and survive in a fighter aviation combat arena: you must have energy maneuverability and the weapons to destroy the enemy. The fighter aircraft must have the energy level to evade and strike the enemy. The fighter pilot must have the ability to use energy maneuverability to defeat the enemy defenses, deploy the weapons, destroy the targets, and return home to fight again. Without these axioms you will not win the war. I attempted to keep these simple but absolute axioms — these fundamental truths — in perspective in the evaluation of fighter weapon systems.

I was directed to finish my undergraduate degree. This was unusual. I was assigned to go to school under "boot-strap" authority, which ordinarily does not include full colonel or above rank. I enrolled in the University of Albuquerque. I carried 21 hours for two semesters, which was a heavy load. It was a much easier life style than I had as a division chief at AFTEC. I got to spend a lot more time with my kids. I would sometimes leave school on a Friday afternoon and go skiing up on Sandia Peak with my son Steve, who was then a senior in high school. I became associated with the ROTC cadets, who were going to be young second lieutenants when they graduated from school. When they did graduate, I did the graduation speech and commissioning for the ROTC group. It was a very memorable occasion. Over the years I have maintained contact with a number of those kids, including Lt. Col. Pete Robles and Col. Greg Neubeck. We all had a very good rapport. It was a unique situation — a 44-year-old colonel graduating with a bunch of 22-year-old kids.

It was my hope that after school I would go back to Tactical Air Command and be a wing commander. I went before the TAC evaluation board and was considered the number-one guy and was to be assigned the 388th Tactical Fighter Wing — the first F-16 operational unit — at Hill Air Force Base in Utah. My arguments with Larry Welch, now a major general and

TAC director of operations, and General Dixon, the TAC commander, surfaced when it appeared I would get the wing assignment. General Welch rejected my assignment to get the wing. I believed my Air Force career was over because I had gotten crossways with General Welch and General Dixon.

As it turned out, Col. Jerry Gentry, a close friend of mine and an experienced fighter pilot and test pilot, was assigned to command the 388th Tactical Fighter Wing. Shortly after his assignment a fatal F-16 crash occurred. It was difficult to investigate because the F-16 was at the bottom of Salt Lake, Utah. The result of the investigation was "pilot error." Colonel Gentry did not believe this was correct. He believed a flight control problem ultimately caused the crash. He went to TAC headquarters, Langley Air Force Base, Virginia, to discuss the situation with the new TAC commander, Gen. Wilbur Creech. They had disagreements, and Jerry was fired on the spot. His USAF career was destroyed.

There were other questionable F-16 accidents. One occurred in Korea with a "pilot error" conclusion. This was contested by the pilot's wife. After a long, difficult battle, it was proven there was a control malfunction. Other accidents followed. I believed when we released the aircraft prior to test completion it was a mistake. I still believe it was a mistake.

After my graduation General Leaf brought me back to AFTEC. I was assigned to Joint Test and Evaluation. This is the operational/evaluation of USAF, Navy, Army, and Marines equipment in a combat environment — a good operation in concept. I was first assigned as deputy to Col. Hervey Stockman, a very experienced fighter pilot and extraordinary person. I knew I would learn immeasurably from him — and I did.

Col. Stockman's fighter life began in World War II flying P-38s, the rare P-39, and the P-51. He also was among the first detachment of pilots to fly the famed U-2 high-altitude reconnaissance aircraft. Like me, he was privileged to fly with Virgil "Iron Mike" Meroney in the early days of the jet fighter evolution. Hervey had the same respect and admiration for Iron Mike as I do, so the two of us had something in common on the day we met. In the early days of the Vietnam War, Hervey was assigned to the 366th Tactical Fighter Wing in the Phantom F-4 aircraft. Hervey was forced to eject in a mission over North Vietnam. He was taken prisoner and was held in the "Hanoi Hilton" prisoner-of-war compound for nearly six years. A tough experience. He was repatriated in 1972 together with other POWs. Hervey and I came together in June 1978 to develop the Joint Service Operational Test concept. We worked together in harmony during the early days of the new Joint Test mission.

In November 1978 Hervey decided to retire from his distinguished Air Force career. I volunteered to prepare and execute the retirement of this dedicated American warrior. We presented this highly decorated fighter pilot with a colorful, full honor parade with an Air Force military band. As the parade began to pass in review, a flight of A-7 fighter aircraft flew close over the parade and then climbed out of sight in final salute to Col. Hervey Stockman — a day all who participated will not forget.

As director of Joint Test and Evaluation my first job was to do an evaluation called TASVAL (Tactical Aircraft Survivability Evaluation). It was the evaluation of the A-10 — bless its heart again — and the Army AX helicopter in a European war environment. I knew it was going to be a difficult test. I had trouble with the position I had taken on the A-10 before. I knew the A-10 was never going to survive in a high-threat environment that would be met in a European war.

I did a very stringent preparation to test and evaluate. The original idea for the unique, profound, and accurate test process came from a young female captain, Leslie Kenne, who worked with me in Joint Test and Evaluation. We used laser pods on all aircraft and a large computer to record every move the airplanes made and every shot that was fired in terms of antiaircraft artillery and missile attack in a high-threat simulated combat environment. We had the capability to record everything we were going to do. There would be no "opinions" when the test was over about how the airplanes performed and whether they performed within their required capability.

We commenced the test at Fort Hunter-Liggett. It did not take very long to see that the A-10 was never going to measure up to the requirements in the high-threat world. I am back on the hot seat again with the A-10. As before, I had loads of empirical data to prove my position. The airplane was not performing in the initial engagements in the European environment. Over 50 percent of the airplanes were lost on one mission. You cannot survive in a war if you sustain more than 0.2 to 0.3 loss percent per mission. You just cannot maintain your combat posture.

Back to the Hans Rudel Stuka-105 match-up in World War II: the Germans had generally the same problem with the Stuka. It was an underpowered airplane with huge cannon on it. The assumption was that the cannon would be able to knock out tanks and do the same thing the A-10 was intended to do. The Stuka was totally unsuccessful. The airplanes were shot down as quickly as they could be launched. A pilot assigned to the Stuka-105 in World War II would be lucky if he flew five missions before he was dead.

During that era the Germans decimated their tactical fighter pilots. The U.S. Army shot them down by the gross loads near the end of World War II. The Germans did not have adequate fighter capability because of the loss of pilots and loss of airplanes. Hans Rudel was shot down 29 times during that era and survived. He was an absolute superman. He lost one leg and still continued to fly. I have read articles and seen programs on the History Channel where it is claimed we designed the A-10 and mission after the very successful Stuka involvement in World War II. The design part may be true but the Stuka-105 most certainly was not successful. Hans Rudel has been cited as the model for German successes, noting that he survived all this. Yes, he survived, but he got shot down 29 times, and the Germans lost the war.

If you use the example of Hans Rudel's life in World War II you would have to have 30 airplanes and 30 parachutes per pilot. There is no possible way any military force can afford the level of losses the Germans experienced. The close air support plan executed in the war with Hans Rudel was a total failure. I talked personally with Hans Rudel about this whole issue during our A-10 evaluation. He told me face to face of the terrible destruction that was done to the German fighter pilots and the loss of that war. A major factor during the late part of the war was the fact that the Stuka did not perform or accomplish the mission: they lost so many pilots they could not field an adequate airborne attack. Rudel also signed and gave me a copy of his book *Stuka-As*.

When I returned from my meeting with Hans Rudel I wrote a lengthy report, after a lot of study myself on all of the activities in World War II. I concluded that we were buying an airplane, the A-10, that was not serviceable in a high-threat environment, a situation similar to that of the World War II Stuka. In a benign environment when there was no AAA firepower, the A-10 might be a successful airplane. But we don't buy combat airplanes to fly in a benign environment. Combat aircraft are required to fly in a severe antiaircraft artillery, and missile as well as air attack, environment. I wrote the report, and I gave that and the book to my boss, General Leaf. He concluded that it was the best report he had ever read. The report was classified, so I did not keep a copy. Again I am on the hot seat with General Leaf, General Dixon, and General Welch because of my written report and my conclusions concerning the serviceability of the A-10.

Because I knew the A-10 was not an adequate airplane, I prepared a proposal that some two thousand F-100s that were then in mothballs be fitted with J-79 engines, which would develop almost 20,000 pounds of thrust and allow increased internal fuel capacity for use in the air support mission. The F-100 had leading edge slats for low-speed performance. The F-100 also had very good loitering capability, tremendous acceleration, both radial acceleration and x-vector acceleration. The F-100 had a vast and versatile weapon capability. We could have done the F-100 upgrade for about $1 million per aircraft. The A-10s were some $15 million per aircraft. My proposal was looked at but rejected because the A-10 had to be the airplane.

The A-10 was never used in a high-threat environment. It was used for road reconnaissance and close air support in Desert Storm and in Afghanistan and Iraq. There were significant A-10 losses. An A-10 was destroyed by small arms flying over Baghdad. General Welch went on to become Air Force Chief of Staff. Robert Dixon retired and became president of Fairchild-Hiller, which produced the A-10. At first I was shocked but I now realize it doesn't matter how right you are if the facts are not part of the political equation. I had been in this assignment for almost four years, and once again I thought my career in the Air Force was over because I had continued to fight city hall. It wasn't that I wanted to fight with them. I just had to present the facts as I found them to be.

In retrospect, with the exception of my time with Col. Stockman, I can say this period was the most uncomfortable time I spent in the Air Force. It was like the one day I spent in Sondrestrom, Greenland—with the difference that this was a period of continual confrontation, every day, over two or three years. I personally did not want to deal with it anymore. This also was a time when I was having more trouble with my wife and was trying to raise three teenage boys. Between the trouble at home and the trouble with the A-10 there were days when I got out of bed and just wanted to run south. I was getting it 24 hours a day.

I went to work every morning knowing that in the end I was probably going to lose this battle over the A-10. But I also knew that when preparing for war we had to put into production the absolute best equipment we can develop and accept no degradation. I knew that there are some days you cannot survive even when the absolute best equipment is working perfectly. But I also knew that it is far less likely we will survive and prevail in a war without adequate machinery.

It would seem that I had choices. But I did not. I was assigned to direct the evaluation and report the findings. Although I was advised at one time to re-write the A-10 test report, I could not do that without compromising both my responsibility and my integrity, not to mention possibly jeopardizing the success of the intended mission. The information was solid. What I reported was fact, not opinion. Had I revised the report I probably would have gotten the F-16 wing. But who knows what would have happened then? I might not have survived that. Jerry Gentry, trying to do what was right, did not survive.

I remember sitting in my office, in the dark, by myself, wondering where I was going to go next. It must have been about five o'clock in the morning, and the phone rang. I picked up and answered. The caller asked, "Is this Mr. Earl?" That was my old combat, old Thunderbird, name. I said, "Yes, this is he." He said, "This is General Bond."

Maj. Gen. Robert (Bobby) Bond was then in command of the Weapons Development system under Research and Development Command at Eglin Air Force Base, Florida. I had met him years before when I was on the Thunderbirds and he was at Nellis doing work with John Boyd and some of the guys in the Weapons School. I had only known him briefly but had always admired his capability and his character. He said, "I want you to come to Eglin. I want to talk to you. Can you come?" I said, "Yes, with General Leaf's approval, as soon as I can get there." "I would like you here at seven o'clock in the morning." I said, "Okay." I got an airplane and flew to Eglin the next morning.

Chapter 13

Field Commander

"Fly the colonel every day."

The morning after receiving a call from General Bobby Bond I met him at his office in Weapons Development Command at Eglin Air Force Base. I was then director for Joint Tests and Evaluations at AFTEC in Albuquerque, but I was curious about the reason for General Bond's call, and I was surprised both by what he had to say and what he knew of my circumstances.

"I know you are in position and want a wing in Tactical Air Command," he said, "but there have been difficulties with that assignment." He continued, "I have a field organization, a test organization, at Holloman that I want you to command. I have some really difficult test projects for you: we have to develop the new AMRAM air-to-air missile, and we are working on the new Stealth program." I was aware of work on an advanced medium-range air-to-air missile, but I wasn't familiar with the Stealth project. He also mentioned the Pave Mover program, which was a tactical version of AWACS in the F-111 aircraft, similar to the airborne radar system in the Boeing 707 (the Air Force KC-135). These projects, plus 83 others, were to be evaluated by the 6585th Test Group at Holloman Air Force Base in south central New Mexico, the region where the White Sands Missile Range is located.

I said I would be glad to go, but added "As you well know, I have had difficult problems with high-rank officials over the A-10. I also have some difficult family problems with my wife. I don't know if you really want to take me for a field commander. I don't think my wife will go. She has a personal, not family, agenda now." He said, "I don't care. I know about the problems. I know about the A-10. You're the commander I want."

I wasn't sure the assignment would meet the approval of Gen. Alton Slay, who was then commander of Air Force Systems Command where I would be working with General Bond. I thought, we will never be able to convince General Slay because of his position previously on the A-10. But General Bond told him he wanted me as a commander, and there was no second choice.

General Bond told me he wanted me to report to work at Holloman on Monday morning. He asked, "Do you care about change of command and all that?" I said, "No, if you want me to go to work, I'll go to work." On Monday morning I drove to Holloman and assumed command of the 6585th Test Group. I started a new life. My wife had interests of her own in Albuquerque and refused to move. I was the first Air Force officer assigned as a field commander unaccompanied by his wife.

I told General Bond I wanted to continue to fly if I took the command. I had stayed current while I was at AFTEC and flew the T-38 and T-39 on a regular basis. My request presented no problem for him. He was a two-star general and remained current himself in the F-16 and was actively involved in the world of tactical fighters. I would be a line pilot and fly regularly as the commander of the unit.

The people at Holloman in 1980 were working on development of advanced systems with almost unlimited technical capabilities. These included global positioning systems (GPS), developed for use first in space vehicles, later incorporated into aircraft, and which now have come into everyday use in automobiles and other hand-held devices. We had a high-speed sled track that evaluated equipment up to speeds of Mach 9. Most people don't believe there is a vehicle on the ground that can go that fast, but we had that capability on a sled track. We put different vehicles on the sled track and ran them up to supersonic speeds — sometimes hypersonic speeds — to evaluate their capability in supersonic or hypersonic environments. Much of the equipment and biological evaluations made for space vehicles were developed at Holloman. We did seat ejections and escape systems for fighters in addition to the air-to-air missiles. The organization had immense capabilities.

I had not been in the experimental flight-test environment since Edwards Air Force Base in the 1960s, with the exception of my participation in the mid–1970s on the Apollo astronaut selection board where I served with my friends, astronaut Tom Stafford, X-15 pilot Pete Knight, and test pilot Bob Titus. I had a lot of work to become capable as commander of the 6585th Test Group. I found, however, the people were so dedicated to their mission and so skilled that I had very little trouble acclimating to my job. I had very few discipline or social problems to contend with as commander. The caliber of the people in this unit was remarkable.

Command is difficult when things don't go right, but in working with General Bond and the people of the 6585th' everything seemed to fall in place. I had only been there about six weeks when I said, "The only thing wrong with this organization is nobody knows you're here, nobody realizes what unbelievable things you're doing here." So I devised a meticulous detailed briefing that told the history of what had been accomplished at Holloman, all the amazing test projects and all the accomplishments of this unit. I gave this briefing when and where appropriate. The people in the 6585th, deservedly, were very proud. This exposure outside of Holloman also inspired other services and even civilian industry to use this unique test facility.

The buildings and environment within the organization had been allowed to run down. I believed the appearance of the buildings and grounds should be brought up to standard or better, reflecting, even in this way, the professionalism and capabilities of the organization. I asked for money to do restoration on buildings and grounds. I was told there was no money available to contract outside agencies to do the work; all that could be offered was materials for self-help programs. My first thought was that to rebuild this organization physically with self-help alone was an impossible task. People were working long hours and to ask them to paint and repair on top of their other duties probably was above and beyond the call.

I still felt we needed to do this. One Friday after flying, about one o'clock in the afternoon, I started painting the administration building, which was my command building. That got a lot of attention: a full colonel with a paint brush in his hand painting a huge building. It wasn't long until a couple of young airmen came by to finish their week and get their mail. One asked if I needed any help. I said, "I need a lot of help." The first two airmen picked up brushes. Within an hour there were perhaps 20 airman helping paint. We finished the building before the day was over. I ordered pizza and beer for everybody, and we had a spontaneous party that evening. At the staff meeting Monday morning I was told by division commanders they would like to do some of this, too. I said, "I can get you all the paint and brushes you want; we need to refurbish this whole organization." So they took on the task. I only gave two rules: keep it within military specifications, and make sure it is something you are proud of when you finish, no foolishness.

This beautification project became competitive among the divisions. It was amazing. In a few weeks our organization had become a model place. I was suddenly in the good graces of everybody. We had not only a proud mission but also a proud appearance. People came to see our accomplishments. High-ranking officials came by and would say it was the most improvement they had ever seen in an organization. It was beautiful. To match the building restorations, some members of the unit had taken on the task of adding well-designed landscaping, all in good taste and in keeping with military and mission responsibilities. Everyone was proud of our entire operation.

During this time, I went into one of the large administration buildings, a three-story building where administrative people worked, and found the building had a horrendous smell. "What in the world!" I asked somebody. "What is this smell?" The reply: "It's bats. They're up in the ceiling. They've been there for years." I don't have anything against the bats, but, beyond the smell, they could be a tremendous health problem. I said, "We must get rid of them." I was told, "They've been there for years, and we've never been able to get rid of them." I said, "You can't tell me in this day and age we can't move a bunch of bats!"

At the staff meeting the next morning I selected a young lieutenant and said, "You've got seven days to tell me how we can move the bats. I don't want to kill the bats. I want to move them out to where the rest of the critters in this area live." "Okay," he said. "But I've been told it's been tried before." I said, "I don't want to listen to that. You've got seven days to tell me how we're going to move the bats."

The following Monday morning as people gathered for the staff meeting, all the lights dimmed, a huge silhouette of Batman was projected on the wall, and the Batman theme began to play. When the meeting opened and the lights came on, the lieutenant briefed me. He had contacted, I believe, an expert at the University of Michigan who knew bat habitat and how we could move the bats. I was designated "Batman." My assistant, the young lieutenant, was "Robin."

We now knew how to do it. I wanted the bats moved out in the desert where they belonged by the end of the month. With the information provided by the expert at the university, we trapped and moved the bats. We then sealed all the openings under the eves in the attic with a foam material. Most of the bats followed their leaders out to the desert. A few tried to come back into the building, but our good sealing job prevented them from doing so. The desert became their new home. In a matter of 30 days we removed bats that had been infiltrating the building for some 15 years. People were very surprised by action taken to solve their problem. They had been working under those conditions for so long they had accepted the hardship. They had become trapped in their own habitat.

During this period we started to test the Stealth aircraft in a radar environment. We had a large facility, the Radar Target Scatter facility (RATSCAT), on the White Sands Missile Range to accomplish this test. We were also working with the Pave Mover project, as well at AMRAM, which was the follow-on to the AIM 7 air-to-air radar missile. The AIM 9-L that I started while in the Pentagon was finished. The PQM-102 airborne target project was now under my command. The PQM-102 has been very successful, not only for the Air Force but also for the Army, the Navy, and the Marines.

I loved working for General Bond. He would fly with me at Holloman on a regular basis. We would not discuss business at these times, just flying. He was very much like Iron Mike Meroney: character, strength, and ability personified. I became personally close to Bobby Bond, not as a commander when we were flying but as a friend. General Bond was just a great man to know. Working with him was a dream come true.

As the days rolled on, the organization worked on several programs simultaneously. People came alive and did the impossible. The pride of developing the facilities and programs all came together. Things moved along at a rate much greater than I thought possible. We had some difficulties with scheduling test range time. I moved my office for a while and did the scheduling with the rest of the White Sands Range activities. I felt we were losing time during the test programs. One test would prepare to launch over the test range and would not be able to fly or function, and the test mission would be cancelled. We would lose that whole period of time. I believed we should schedule two or three events. If one fails, another can step in and take the range time. We had been losing more than half our range test time by aborting projects. We accelerated the testing by having two or three programs standing by. We accomplished more test activity than previously because we had back-up missions.

I received a call from General Bond about two A.M. one morning telling me the Columbia space shuttle was going to have to land at Holloman Air Force Base. We had a contingency operation to handle the spacecraft in the event it couldn't land at Kennedy Space Center or at Edwards Air Force Base because of bad weather or other problems. Like Edwards Air Force Base with Rogers lake bed, we had White Sands lake bed, presenting a ten-mile landing strip. We also had all required facilities to meet the shuttle needs, similar to other missions within our capability and responsibility. This was the only time in the history of the space program the East Coast and West Coast had both been weathered in. I got out the contingency plan and started quick planning because, ready or not, in a few hours Columbia was going to land at White Sands. There were security difficulties that must be overcome. A significant number of NASA personnel would arrive for landing and the turn around of the Columbia. As usual, my organization came alive and put the plan together. We provided the facilities to feed and house the people and secure the Columbia. All fell into place, just like we knew what we were doing. For the space vehicle to land at Holloman was a monumental thing. We had to assure that it was successful. Being the AFSC Air Force Systems Command commander at Holloman, I was the on-scene commander for the space shuttle. The Columbia landed. It all went like clockwork.

I kept thinking General Bond was going to call any minute to ask how things were going. He didn't. He gave me the responsibilities. He had total confidence in me. I had the same kind of confidence in him. He didn't call until about two o'clock in the morning. I had a red secure phone in my quarters. I seldom got a call. I knew that if the red phone rang, it probably was him. He did not say a thing about the space vehicle. We just talked about flying and some personal matters. He never said a word about Columbia, though he surely knew the landing had been successful. He also knew if there was anything wrong or I needed anything, I would have asked him. We talked for a while and hung up.

The following day the 747 "mother ship" landed at Holloman to return the Columbia to Kennedy Space Center in Florida. One of my old friends from Edwards was the 747 pilot, Fitzhugh Fulton. The Columbia was loaded onto the 747 and launched for home. Again, people in the 6585th Test Group were very proud. We had met the space vehicle, turned it around, and launched it to its original base without incident: another major accomplishment.

I had installed one of the incentive measures I had used previously. I took individuals along on supersonic missions to let them see the final mission accomplishments. This approach had been very effective for me in the past. The flight and mission exposure left a profound impression on those who never had the opportunity to fly or view the final result and to see how important each and every participation was for mission success. I had said many times, "If everyone does not do their job right, the final

"Piggy Back" ride of the space shuttle aboard a 747 leaving Holloman AFB, New Mexico, 1981.

result in the air is zero." This approach created good communication throughout, sending the word to all: we are a team.

People were happy, and I was happy. I flew almost every day. They used to say, "You have to fly the colonel every day to keep him out of our hair. If you keep him in the air all the time he stays off of us." That got to be the standard joke. Fly the colonel every day, and we'll get the job done. This was exactly right. They did get the job done, and I did fly. I believed as a commander I should lead the mission, observe the results firsthand, and prepare for the accomplishments of the organization and the welfare of people, rather than directly supervise their professional responsibilities at close range. We worked well together. As time passed we completed all the projects as scheduled. We met all the initial responsibilities.

It was time for me to think about another assignment. I continued to have difficulty at home during my time at Holloman. My wife had remained in Albuquerque, and there had been an escalation of problems that had been developing over the years. These were now at a pretty serious level.

I was then being considered to be the commander at Edwards Air Force Base, where I had served back in the 1960s. General Bond wanted me to go to Edwards, mostly to bring research and development closer to

"Fly the colonel every day" become well known throughout the unit. The colonel was happy when he flew every day.

operational tests. I had been in fighter operations, combat, and operational test at the Pentagon, at AFTEC, and at Holloman, as well as in experimental flight test at Edwards. General Bond wanted to bring operational activity and test and evaluation closer together to be more effective and efficient in the total development of a new Air Force weapons system.

General Bond always looked way out in the future. He had visions 20, 30, years out of what needed to be done to further develop new combat requirements. Supersonic fighters during the Cold War period had developed by leaps and bounds and had become very significant in our force structure for war. Now we had the new F-15s and the new F-16s in service. There was also the A-10, which was not performing very well. The accident rate for that aircraft was fairly high, and there were a lot of complaints the airplane wasn't meeting acceptable performance requirements. We had already bought the airplane, and it was too expensive to re-engine it and put it in the performance category that would be required.

Although the decision that I would go to Edwards was not final, I assumed it was pretty close. General Bond had paved the way. He was now a three-star general and the deputy commander for Air Force Systems Command. He worked for a four-star general, General Robert T. Marsh, as General Slay had retired. It appeared that Edwards Air Force Base would be my next assignment. I really looked forward to that. It was the assignment in my Air Force career that I wanted most. I just had a great desire to go back to Edwards (where I was as a young captain) and meet those new mission demands and test requirements.

I had severe problems at home that had developed to a point where I felt I couldn't be both an effective commander and a father. One had to go. Edwards was about 600 miles from Albuquerque, whereas Holloman was only 200 miles from Albuquerque, where the family had been during this particular assignment. I came home to discuss the situation, and it exploded into a serious confrontation between my wife and me. I found out that she was involved with a man at the bank where she worked. The boys were aware, I am sure, of the circumstances. This was a serious problem.

I could either go on to Edwards and continue my Air Force career, or get out and devote my time to the family. In her usual rage, my wife hit me with a bookend, leaving a laceration on my head. I flew back to Holloman with a handkerchief under my helmet covering the injury. I called General Bond and told him I had difficulties. I believed I would have to leave the Air Force.

His first response was, "No, you're not going to get out. I have plans and things that we have to accomplish that are important, and I want these things done." He said, "Go home as often as you need to. You have an airplane available to you. Do whatever you need to do to try to solve that problem." Because of classified security programs at Holloman (I was in a top-secret, special access, special information category) I was watched on a daily basis, not because one is going to do anything wrong but for one's own safety as well as matters of national security. I think General Bond was even more aware of circumstances of my family life than I was. He said that I should go on in the Air Force, that I would not be able to solve my wife's problem. It is my belief she had been observed for security reasons and that General Bond knew details that even I did not know of the situation. I certainly considered his advice, and I wanted to continue on in USAF aviation.

It would be about six weeks before I would have to report to Edwards. I came home to Albuquerque on a regular basis during those six weeks. Things only got worse. I took off from Kirtland to return to Holloman on a Sunday evening. The weather was bad at Kirtland. It was very bad at Holloman. I climbed out to about 40,000 feet above the clouds where I had a clear sky and hopefully a clear mind. It was an easy decision to make: I have one career, and I have three children. Any dumbbell can figure out the priorities. I made the letdown into Holloman and called General Bond, telling him I would have to leave the Air Force. He was averse, but he said, "I want you to come and talk to me one on one." A couple of days later I flew to Andrews Air Force Base, outside Washington, D.C. I talked with General Bond personally. He conceded. I would retire.

CHAPTER 14

The Last Day

"May God always fly on your wing."

My formal retirement took place at Holloman Air Force Base on Friday, the 14th of May, 1982. My very close friend and commander Lt. Gen. Bobby Bond came to retire me and fly my last fighter mission with me. As all who knew him would attest, General Bond was "a fighter pilot's fighter pilot." To be able to fly with him on this day was a privilege, an honor, and an altogether unforgettable experience. We went out over the White Sands desert and just tore the place apart for about an hour, much as I had in my most memorable F-86 flight—except that was the beginning, and this was the end. We came back and landed at Holloman, ending my last flight as a fighter pilot in the United States Air Force. As the flight came to an end, I thought, "I have come full circle."

We had a small party after the flight, and General Bond doused me with a bottle of champagne. The champagne soon wore off, but the memory of that flight will be with me always. Many of the fighter aircraft I had flown in my career had been flown in and placed in a circle at Holloman. Later this final day General Bond retired me amidst the assembled fighter aircraft and many friends. The events included a parade of aircraft and all personnel. That night we had a social party at the officers club. Over four hundred people attended. Some of my commanders from previous assignments were there. Six or seven generals also came to attend the party. The evening for me was a happy event, seeing so many friends and colleagues and appreciating their recognition. But it was also bittersweet, realizing that my Air Force career was suddenly over. I had never thought about the day it would end.

There were many memorable moments. Most memorable were the

Col. Haney and son Mike ride a van to the aircraft for Col. Haney's last Air Force flight, 1982.

Champagne flight for Col. Haney with Lt. General "Bobby" Bond. Col Haney's last Air Force fight at Holloman AFB, May 14, 1982.

General "Bobby" Bond awarding Legion of Merit for outstanding service above and beyond the call of duty to Col. Haney at the retirement parade.

Parade for Col. Haney's retirement, Holloman AFB, May 14, 1982.

words my son Mike spoke about our lives together. He and my son Steve had taken great care to prepare their gifts: my portrait with an F-4 fighter in the background, done by Alan Polt, a well-known artist, and the restoration of my 20-year-old Volvo sports car. I was proud to see my sons stand up and share this evening with me. In the background, Frank Sinatra was singing, "I Did It My Way."

I received a number of mementos from organizations and individuals, including an encased model of my Thunderbird aircraft, hand-built by a young officer, Capt. Bill Schurer. The engraved message read, "To Colonel Haney — Your leadership has been an inspiration to us all. May God always fly on your wing." My long-time friend Gen. Chuck Horner gave me an encased American flag that he flew in an F-15 at my last military retreat, May 14, 1982.

General Bond was seated in front of me, and we joked and reminisced back and forth throughout the evening about our flying activities. As the party came to an end a young captain made his way through the crowd. He was easily distinguishable among all the people dressed in evening clothes. He was in a flying suit. He stopped close to Mike and me and saluted. He said, "Colonel Haney, you are a legend in jet fighters, one person we young people look up to for ability and integrity. We want you to know we won't forget you, and we will miss you." He looked briefly at all the mementos, and then filtered off through the crowd and left the room. To this day I do not know who he is. He was not in my organization. I often wondered if the things I tried to stand for and believed in so strongly really made a difference. The young captain's thoughts and my son's words about our lives were enough evidence and reward for me.

General Bond and I stayed in communication on a regular basis, as friends but also because he occasionally wanted my input on programs I had worked on. One evening about two years after my retirement, he stopped to visit me at my home in Albuquerque. We discussed many things that night, including the fact that two days later he was going to fly a MiG-23 out to Mach 2. He had flown mostly A-7s, F-100s and F-16s, but no MiGs at Mach 2. He was a highly qualified pilot. He left early the next morning to fly one flight, maybe two, in the F-4, followed by a flight in the single-seat MiG-23.

About noon on the day of the MiG flight I received a call telling me that General Bond had died in the MiG-23. He had flown out to Mach 2, and the airplane became unstable, tumbled, and broke apart. He did eject at about 1,600 to 1,700 miles an hour. The impact forces broke his

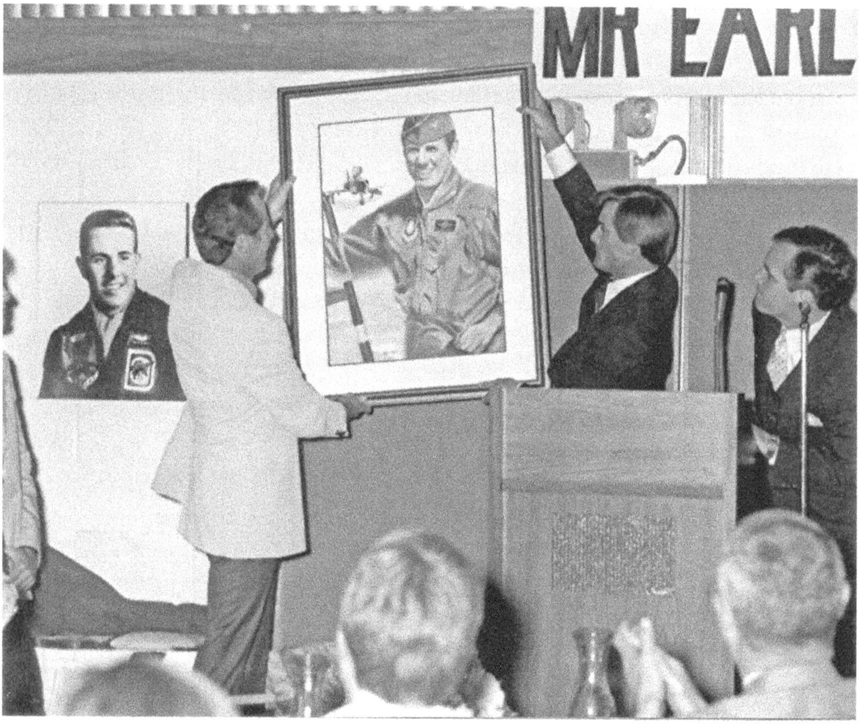

A gift from Mike and Steve at Col. Haney's retirement party, Holloman AFB, May 14, 1982.

neck, and he died in the ejection. This was another terrible loss for me, for the United States Air Force, and for the United States.

Later there was talk that a three-star general should not have been involved in this type of flight. Why not? He was a highly skilled fighter pilot, and he was a genuine leader. His death had a terrible impact on me personally because I had become so close to him. He was such a remarkable individual. I thought nothing would ever happen to him. I learned, finally and the hard way, that none of us are bulletproof. We'd like to be, but we're not. I struggled with his loss for a long time. I still do.

Only a few months after General Bond was killed, I got word that Colonel Virgil Meroney had died of cancer. He was in his 60s, healthy up to that point, and too young to die. During a test period in the South Pacific he had flown through atomic clouds to collect research samples in an F-84 that had specially designed tanks to pick up samples. It is believed this exposure to radiation may have brought on the cancer that eventually became terminal. Colonel Meroney was my first operational commander, and General Bond was my last. They died within months of each other. With the deaths of these two leaders, I had lost the alpha and the omega of my Air Force life.

I do not look back often on my life in Air Force fighter aviation. But I occasionally wonder what might have happened if I had not made the decision to retire when I did and instead had taken the assignment at Edwards, which was something that I really wanted to do. Command of the Edwards wing would have been a one-star job and I had about eight more years to go. Perhaps I could have helped the future development of fighter aviation, enhancing better performance and safety in Air Force fighters.

On the day I retired, General Bond and I were standing by our airplane preparing for my last flight, when he said, "Retirement now is a shame because your Air Force life is just beginning. You have done the hard part; the easy part is yet to come." Life is not exactly like you want it to be, or think it should be. Often it is what circumstances dictate for you. I'm not sorry that I got out. I wish, for myself, that I could have stayed in. But the end of my marriage was imminent. I could not give up my sons. That was the most important consideration.

Had I stayed in, I would have been a lot closer to General Bond and his flight activities. One always looks back and thinks one could have done better, and maybe should have done better. I do believe I could have done better for General Bond by staying in, and I could have done better in helping him understand the serious pitfalls of very high-performance flight. Whether that's true or not, I don't know, but that's what I believe. I guess that's what I want to believe. Beyond that, I have no regrets. But I will always wonder, "What if?"

Things moved along in my Air Force life at such a rate that I seldom thought about the significance of the period while it was happening. I knew every day how much I loved flying and the association with some very remarkable people, including Bob Hoover, Iron Mike Meroney, Bobby Bond, and many others. I stumbled into the Air Force as a youngster, and I stumbled into flying in an accidental way. I never fully realized how deeply involved I had become in a remarkable era in the history of aviation—the advent and evolution of supersonic flight.

I have thought a million times or more what life might have been for me if I had not been lying on the football field at Scott Air Force Base at the precise moment four of the first supersonic fighters in the world flew close overhead, changing my life forever.

Chapter 15

Epilogue

"Lucky again."

The transition to civilian life was not easy. I left a busy and wonderful Air Force career behind me. The first years of retirement were difficult because of all the problems I faced at home, the problems that made me decide to leave the Air Force in the hope of creating a more secure environment for my three sons. The situation, however, reached a critical stage.

I tried to engage with Betty to straighten things out, but she would leave on weekends, be gone all weekend, or sometimes a week at a time. She was now involved with one of my Edwards Air Force Base associates. As circumstances became even more intolerable, I wrote a letter to her stepfather and mother to ask for any help or counseling they might be able to offer. Betty at the time was on the East Coast, where they lived, and they confronted her with the information I had written. She returned to Albuquerque and, without any discussion with me, filed for divorce.

The divorce was not as bad as I anticipated. The situation created some loss in finances, but for a time I kept the home where we lived, and Mike and Steve stayed with me. Like all kids, they needed support, guidance, and understanding to develop into responsible adults. For me, when Betty left I felt like a 100-pound anvil had been lifted from my neck. Trying to deal with her had been an extreme burden: many infidelities, suicide attempts, and defiance creating a perpetually destructive environment. I was glad when it was over, but I also worried about how the divorce affected the boys. Max left with Betty, saying "She does her thing, and I do mine." This has been sad. The situation was difficult, but we had to move on.

Mike and Steve have grown and progressed in their adult lives by leaps and bounds. From the beginning I wanted Mike and Steve to have the opportunity to discover aviation. Mike was developing in the civilian commercial aviation world. One day while at Kirtland Air Force Base I saw a beautiful Super Decathlon in a hangar. It is a fully aerobatic aircraft that can perform all the three-dimensional maneuvers in the spectrum. The airplane was leased to the Kirtland Aero Club. I soon checked out in this marvelous aircraft and began training Mike and Steve. We trained in the aerobatic environment, learning how to control the aircraft in any attitude and flight condition. This was a very productive and memorable time in our lives.

Mike continued in commercial aviation and went to work for Don Ferrari, owner of Amador Financial Group in Albuquerque. He was flying a twin-engine executive aircraft, a Piper Aerostar. Mr. Ferrari allowed Mike and me to train in his aircraft to advance and hone Mike's skills as a pilot. This was a giant opportunity. The training period proved to be very beneficial in bad weather and emergency conditions. We also were allowed to take many memorable trips, while still enhancing Mike's training. In September 1984 Mike, Steve, and I took the Aerostar to the Reno, Nevada, air races. On this trip the boys were the pilots. I was just along as Joe Passenger. We saw Bob Hoover and some of my Thunderbird associates there and watched some very special aviation events. We won't forget this trip.

Toward the end of this period Mike was hired by America West Airlines in Phoenix, Arizona. I helped him move and stayed with him for his first year there. He became a 737 captain at the age of 32. I returned to New Mexico for Steve's birthday in April 1993. As usual, he was overworking, and I decided to stay a while and work with him.

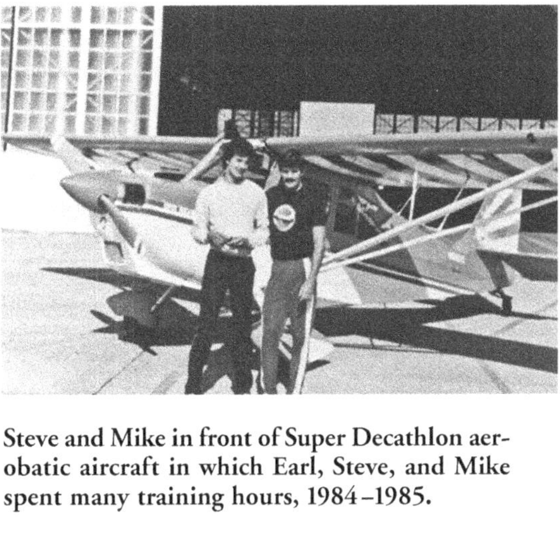

Steve and Mike in front of Super Decathlon aerobatic aircraft in which Earl, Steve, and Mike spent many training hours, 1984–1985.

At the time I retired, Steve restored my 1963 Volvo and did a beautiful job on it, drawing on skills he had developed many years earlier when we restored our old Model T Ford. He remained interested in the challenge

Steve's restoration of our 1963 P-1800S Volvo sport car, a retirement presentation, May 1982.

and went on to restore several other exotic sports cars. His expertise was recognized by many, and requests from potential customers began to mount. He began what has become a very successful self-built restoration business. Steve's latest creation is the total restoration of the 1941 Packard limousine that daily transported Dr. J. Robert Oppenheimer, the father of atomic energy research and the Manhattan Project during World War II. This masterpiece sits in the entrance of the National Atomic Museum at Kirtland Air Force Base, New Mexico.

In 1992 Steve located and purchased property in Cedar Crest, New Mexico, east of Albuquerque, and I helped him as much as possible as he began construction of what ultimately became two homes of significant value on this beautiful home site. Steve was married in 1995 and continues his successful business and develops his family and life with amazing skill and character. Mike eventually left aviation and entered Arizona State University for advanced education. He has a great interest in music, takes meticulous care of himself, and has grown with strength and maturity. A proud father I am. I always hope that Max will realize what he has missed and return.

Steve and Mike gave me a Harley Davidson "Fat Boy" for my birthday a while back. What a surprise! I never know what they will do next. It is always way off the anticipation scale. The Harley Davidson is my supersonic fighter now — it just doesn't get off the ground, hopefully.

A 1990 Harley Davidson Fat Boy. A 58th birthday gift presented by Mike and Steve on July 17, 1990.

My life changed in a totally unexpected way when Steve and his wife's little daughter Shelby Lynn came into the family. What a joy she has been! When Shelby was born, Steve was building his business, and his wife, Tammy, had a career. It appeared Shelby would have to stay in a daycare facility with many other kids. I didn't think that was a safe thing to do, so I volunteered to watch her — for a while. That was 14 years ago, and I have helped watch and grow with her ever since.

Shelby and I have experienced so many things together. When she was one, I began reading to her, everything from *Cat in the Hat* to Rudyard Kipling. When she was two, we started going to the zoo. We saw all the animals, including the koalas and pandas. We saw baby polar bears there for the first time, and each year for the next ten years and more we visited the "cubs" in their polar bear pool to see how they were growing. Like Shelby, they have grown to be beautiful and strong. At the zoo Shelby and I rode a camel many times. Every time we rode that huge camel was a far scarier experience for me than any Mach 2 fighter ride.

Shelby and I walked a lot in the years before she started school. Once when we stopped to rest, she picked a white rose and handed it to me saying, "I love you Gran'pa." — an occasion I have never forgotten. We visited parks almost every day and went down the slides together a thousand times or more. Just before Shelby was to start school, she said, "Gran'pa, I am

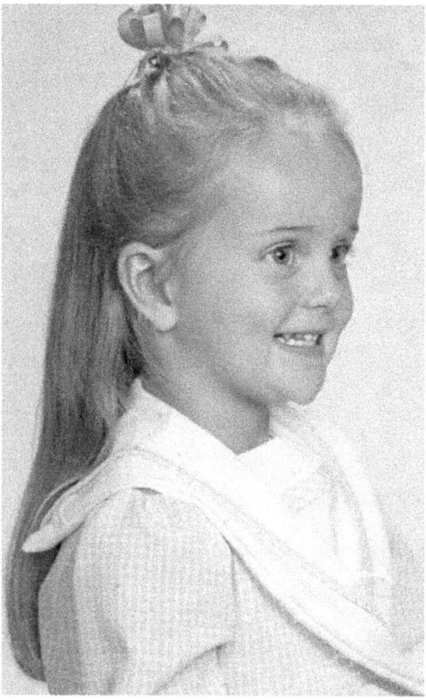

going to school soon." I said, "I know. What will Grandpa do when you go to school?" She replied, "Don't worry, Gran'pa, I will always take care of you."

I am very lucky to have grown up in my early adult life with my sons, Mike, Max, and Steve, and now that I am older I am lucky all over again to be able to grow up with my granddaughter, Shelby. I have learned more from them than they learned from me, though I always tried hard to keep just a step ahead.

Next to some of my experiences with my sons, my time with Shelby has been the most fun I have ever had. Who could have imagined that I would go from flying fast airplanes to caring for an infant granddaughter, seeing Shelby grow, and over time falling into such a close and rewarding relationship with her? It has been a wonderful thing. We have great fun together every day of our lives.

As a boy my mother wanted me to be involved in music. There was a store called The White Elephant down the alleyway from where Mother worked. It was just a little hole-in-the-wall where you could buy anything from a used toothbrush to a Picasso. She bought a Selma trumpet there for me when I

Top: **Haney's granddaughter Shelby at age 4.** ***Bottom:*** **Shelby and her grandfather, Earl.**

was about seven years old. She paid two dollars for it. The Selma trumpet is made in France and is probably the best-made trumpet in the world. She just stumbled across this beautiful gold instrument. It had pearl valves and a solid silver mouthpiece. In my school years I learned to play the trumpet. In high school I played in a dance band that was a part of the music school. This was about a ten-piece band—a couple of trumpets, a couple of saxophones, a drum, and a bass, among other instruments, depending on the year. We played at school dances and local events.

My mother didn't really understand football all that well. After I got my teeth knocked out in a game, she became more certain that football was not such a great thing for me to be doing. With the loss of two front teeth, it did become a little difficult to play the trumpet, but I continued to play football. She, nonetheless, was proud when in my senior year we won the state Big 12 Conference championship.

By that time I was close to graduating from high school. I went into the Air Force, and didn't play the trumpet any more. I started the piano when I was at Edwards Air Force Base. I wanted to get my boys interested in music, as my mother had done for me. I bought a piano and started lessons. It was something I always wanted to do, but there was not always enough time. When I retired I had an opportunity to take lessons from a very accomplished pianist. I have enjoyed every minute of it. I just wish I had done it earlier and wish I were more accomplished.

In these past years of retirement and my close association with my buddy Shelby, I am continuing the piano as Shelby begins the viola. My greatest goal in life today is to play "Rhapsody in Blue" with Shelby. She will lead, and I will follow.

* * *

My closing words must speak to the memory of Gen. Robin Olds and, in his name, recognize other extraordinary aviators and leaders in the era of the evolution of the supersonic fighter who, like General Olds, deeply influenced my life and shaped my career as an officer of the United States Air Force: Col. Virgil Meroney, Gen. Bobby Bond and others I have previously mentioned.

On June 30, 2007, I attended the memorial for Robin Olds, the Billy Mitchell of the supersonic fighter evolution. He was a friend, warrior, and leader by example. Robin had his work cut out for him from the day he was born. His father was a front-runner with Billy Mitchell as they paved the sky for fighter combat capability. Robin exceeded all expectations.

He was a West Point graduate, an All-American Hall of Fame football player, and a fighter pilot beyond compare. He became an aerial ace and up-front commander and leader of tactical fighter aviation before he was 25 years old. Like Col. Iron Mike Meroney, Robin Olds possessed strength and courage beyond ordinary human limits. Throughout his life he fought for duty, honor, and country without regard for personal safety or self-advancement.

On the final salute at the service for Gen. Robin Olds there were fly-bys of many of the fighter aircraft he had flown. As the service came to an end, the emotional "missing man" formation came in overhead—except at this one-of-a-kind memorial, the *flight leader*, not the wingman, accelerated up and away from the formation into the Wild Blue Yonder where Robin Olds was King. I know as his image soared out of sight he reached out and touched the face of God, as John Gillespie Magee's poem "High Flight" so gracefully expresses.

I express every measure of admiration, too, for the civilian pilots who also were pioneers in the evolution of supersonic aircraft, including Bob Hoover, who always will be counted as one of the greatest among them.

In June 2008 I was asked to present the eulogy for the memorial service of one of my close friends and fighter aviation associates of over 50 years, Lute Eldridge. Lute was a Lockheed test pilot in the F-104 days. He was a front-runner in the supersonic fighter industry, developing the best aviation equipment available. It is always difficult to say goodbye. But death is the nature of life.

In January 2009 I attended the funeral of Col. "Hoot" Gibson, my friend of 50 years. He was my close associate from the Thunderbirds and my squadron commander during the Southeastern Asian war period. He was another great fighter pilot and leader that I admired.

Major Russ Goodman, my close friend, from my USAF Thunderbird experience, was shot down over North Vietnam in February 1967, flying an F-4 Phantom off the aircraft carrier "Enterprise."

Russ was not recovered and was listed missing in action (MIA). After the Vietnam War terminated, the United States organized a process to find and return as many MIA as possible. Based on information provided by a North Vietnamese man, who was a boy in 1967, Russ Goodman's crash site was located. In 2010 Russ's final identification was verified, and his remains were returned.

I attended Russ's memorial at Nellis AFB, January 14, 2010. A "Missing Man Formation" was flown by the Thunderbirds in his memory. Welcome home Russ.

As the era of supersonic aviation becomes history and the old, bold pilots of this era fade into the Wild Blue Yonder, fighter aviation is transitioning to the future of combat capability. Hypersonic aircraft with scramjet engines (rocket-jet combinations) and hypersonic high-heat structures will skip in and out of the atmosphere and space at speeds of Mach 5 and above, carrying equally high-tech weaponry in a continuing effort to protect our freedom in a never-ending hostile world.

Index

Milton Keynes UK
Ingram Content Group UK Ltd.
UKHW041830121124
451104UK00012B/88